THE WAY
TO THE SEA

THE WAY
TO THE SEA

The Forgotten Histories
of the Thames Estuary

CAROLINE
CRAMPTON

GRANTA

Granta Publications, 12 Addison Avenue, London W11 4QR

First published in Great Britain by Granta Books, 2019

A CIP catalogue record for this book
is available from the British Library.

1 3 5 7 9 10 8 6 4 2

ISBN 978 1 78378 413 4
eISBN 978 1 78378 415 8

Typeset in Caslon by M Rules

Printed and bound by
CPI Group (UK) Ltd, Croydon, CR0 4YY

MIX
Paper from
responsible sources
FSC
www.fsc.org   FSC® C020471

*To my parents, who first showed
me the way to the sea*

CONTENTS

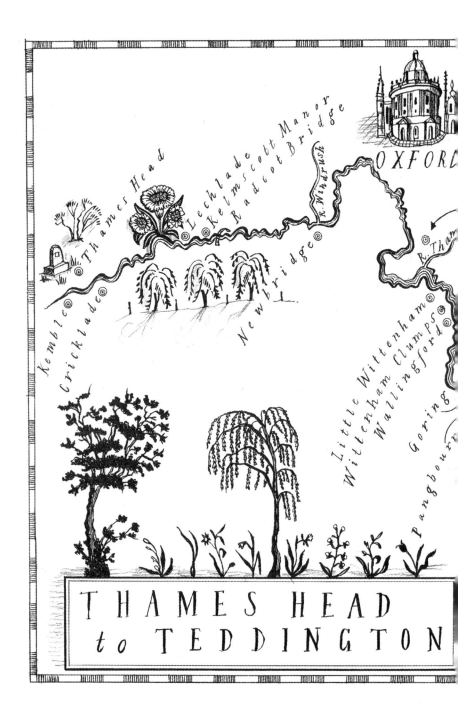

Kemble · Thames Head · Lechlade · Kelmscott Manor · Radcot Bridge · R. Windrush · OXFORD · R. Thame · Cricklade · Newbridge · Little Wittenham · Wittenham Clumps · Wallingford · Goring · Pangbourne

THAMES HEAD
to TEDDINGTON

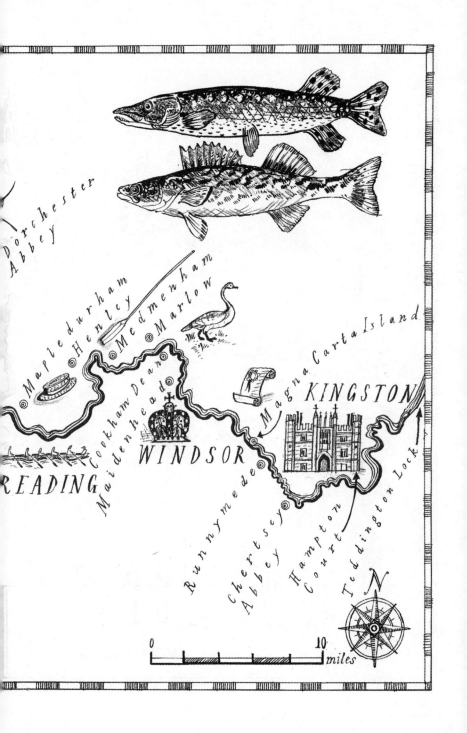

Dorchester Abbey

Mapledurham

Henley

Medmenham

Marlow

Cookham Dean

Maidenhead

Magna Carta Island

KINGSTON

WINDSOR

READING

Runnymede

Chertsey Abbey

Hampton Court

Teddington Lock

N

0   10 miles

TEDDINGTON *to the* THAMES BARRIER

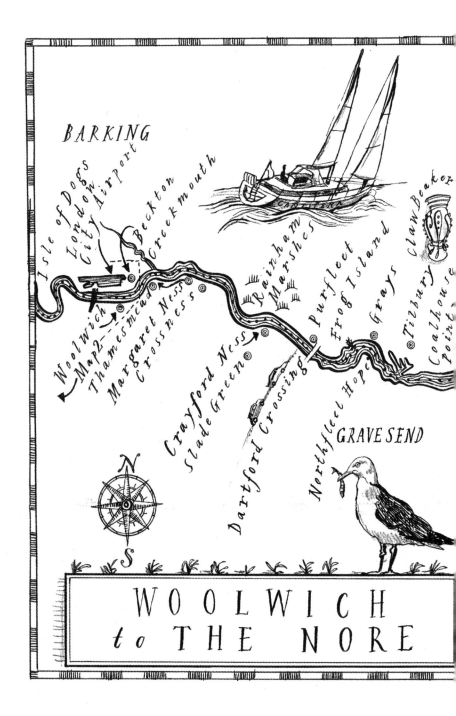

BARKING

Isle of Dogs
London
City Airport
Beckton
Creekmouth

Woolwich
Map 2
Thamesmead
Margaret Ness
Crossness

Rainham
Marshes

Purfleet
Frog Island

Grays

Tilbury
Claw Beaker
Coalhouse
point

Crayford Ness
Slade Green

Dartford Crossing

Northfleet Hope

GRAVESEND

N
S

WOOLWICH
to THE NORE

London Gateway

Lower Hope Point

CANVEY ISLAND

Southend-on-Sea

Shoebury-Ness

THE THAMES

The Nore

Wreck of the Montgomery

Sheerness

Cliffe

Cooling

St. Mary Hoo

The London Stone

All Hallows

ISLE of GRAIN

Queen-borough

Minster

ISLE of SHEPPEY

THE HOO PENINSULA

R. Medway

Chatham

Gillingham

ROCHESTER

Stangate Creek

Bedlams Bottom

Deadman's Island

0   5 miles

Illustrations

THE WAY
TO THE SEA

Introduction

Night is darker at sea than it is on the land. The water absorbs the gloom and is reluctant to relinquish it, even when dawn arrives. That particular night, no wakeful observer on the Essex shore could have seen the boat. Alone in the silent dark, she traversed the mouth of the estuary in mile-long sweeps, making a little more progress up the river each time she turned. Wind and tide were pushing her away, back towards the sea.

It was 3 a.m. on 17 September 1984, and in the outer Thames the wind had picked up and was causing choppy waves to slap haphazardly against the hull. On board my mother was scanning the darkness for the flashes and glimmers that could mean navigation marks to guide them safely through the channel or ships that might run their small boat down. My father bobbed up and down the cabin stairs, checking the chart. That paper map was their only way of knowing where they were.

My parents had been at sea for almost five months, covering over 8,000 miles. They had sailed here from Cape Town, in a boat they had built themselves during weekends and evenings snatched from their full-time jobs. This trip into the estuary was the conclusion of a voyage that had been ages in the planning. Building the boat alone had taken three years.

Since their departure from South Africa in April, they had sailed up the Atlantic, stopping at St Helena, Ascension Island and the Azores. After arriving safely in the English Channel, they spent the summer familiarizing themselves with some of these islands' most dramatic coastlines, in the sea lochs of western Scotland, Ireland and the Irish Sea. They spent a memorable fortnight stormbound on the Isle of Man, sitting in pubs with the tax exiles and the motorcycle-racing enthusiasts waiting for the winds to quieten, and made contact with the few British cousins who make up the pre-colonial emigration branch of our family.

It was only when the days started to shorten, signalling autumn's gusty arrival in the northern hemisphere, that they began to realize they would not be sailing south again that winter. Like many other nomads before them, they settled on London as their next destination, reasoning that they were unlikely to freeze living on a boat if it was moored in a large city, and that there might be a chance of earning some money there. They made their way along the south coast, stopping to buy charts and almanacs in Eastbourne. At 9 p.m. on the previous evening, they left the harbour at Brighton and headed north, towards the estuary.

By the time they rounded the corner of Kent at North Foreland, passing Ramsgate and then Margate just after midnight, the wind had gone into the west. It strengthened considerably and the tide turned against them. The boat's log entry for 0315 contains all the obligatory navigational data in its neatly ruled columns, and then just four words in my mother's firm, loopy handwriting: 'Tacking in lumpy sea.'

The process of tacking – that is, sailing at an angle so as to zigzag in the direction that the wind is coming from – is arduous, tedious and often unpleasant. With both wind and tide against the boat, the water beneath the hull becomes turbulent and unpredictable. Combined with the natural difficulties of navigating this stretch of water even in calm weather, it makes sense that the Thames estuary contains more shipwrecks per square metre than anywhere else on Britain's coast.

Their charts and almanacs told them that they were in constant danger, with obstructions under the water on either side of narrow, twisting channels between treacherous sandbanks. Yet from the deck all they could see was emptiness, a great watery flatness stretching off into the dark. After the azure seas of Cape Town, this was another world, of rocks and slime and currents so changeable they appeared to be flowing in every direction at once.

At first light, they passed the Isle of Sheppey – the marshy, muddy island off the north coast of Kent where the River Medway, the final Thames tributary, flows into the estuary. Using the binoculars, my father picked out the landmarks of this low-lying, tidal island: a prison, a port and a steelworks. There was little else for him to see, as the dawn gradually slid over the water and touched the land.

When I am asked where I'm from, I find it difficult to reply with a place name. I have South African parents, grandparents and great-grandparents, but have never lived there. I had lived in six different houses by the time I was six years old, so it's difficult even to point to one of those as a convenient place of origin. In fact, the idea of our family, a tiny immigrant outpost in a new country, began in a small boat moored for the winter in St Katharine Docks on the Thames, just by Tower Bridge, because it was there that my parents realized that they were never going home.

St Katharine Docks opened for business in 1828. Two deep basins were dug out of the north bank of the Thames, right next to where the Tower of London's moat now stands empty. Boats enter from the river via a gated lock and a short canal, before tying up at one of the quays around the edge, upon which stand the warehouses that used to house goods from all over the world. Although for over a hundred years it did a thriving trade in everything from wool to ostrich feathers, by 1968 the docks' business had moved downriver to bigger ports and St Katharine's was closed.

When my parents turned up in the early 1980s, it was home to a motley collection of houseboats, Thames barges and sailing vessels. The warehouses were mostly derelict, since nothing had yet arrived to replace the shipping business and the area was poor. At that time, St Katharine's was on the edge of the area that was just becoming known as the 'Docklands', thanks to the Thatcherite programme of regeneration aimed at turning formerly industrial areas into expensive apartments and City offices. This was the battlefield of east London's capitalist gentrification and the fight was just beginning. My parents, with all their worldly possessions aboard a small boat that they had built themselves half a world away, fitted right in.

Despite the fact that an old London by-law prohibited permanent residence in the docks, a friendly lock-keeper arranged a way for them to stay there for the winter. He allowed them to lock out into the river and then come back in again immediately once a month so he could record them as departing and returning, thus proving that they weren't long-term residents. They settled quickly into this strange, transitory life on the river, although they did have to turn the boat around in her berth so that the tourists who occasionally wandered along the old wharves couldn't see straight into their living quarters below, where laundry was hung in the cabin and meals were prepared on the small gas stove tucked in by the companionway.

That winter, in an echo of the great Thames frosts of centuries past, the water in the docks froze around their boat. Ducks walked on the ice and my mother was kept awake by the knocking of the frozen chunks against the hull. It was an extraordinary sight for two young people from the southern hemisphere, used to the powerful waves and warm waters at the southern tip of Africa. In an attempt to feel some connection to their erstwhile homeland, they bought a tiny black-and-white television and rigged it up on board so they could watch the news reports from South Africa. Inside the condensation-filled cabin, they saw the footage of lynchings, disappearances and police brutality. Such was the censorship and media blackout at home that they were learning about much of this for the first time. The place they thought they were from dissolved before their eyes and was replaced by the sharp reality of riots, oppression and endemic, institutional racism. This boat on the Thames was now the only place left they felt they belonged.

In his maritime autobiography, *The Mirror of the Sea*, first published in 1906, Joseph Conrad wrote that 'amongst the great commercial streams of these islands, the Thames is the only one, I think, open to romantic feeling'. This river, unlike most other British waterways, has a peculiarly timeless sensibility; a particular way of sliding memories and stories together, so that they overlay each other in a palimpsest of experiences within the landscape. It has a historical and literary character all of its own, distinct from the country through which it flows. The Thames can be at once T. S. Eliot's strong brown god, William Blake's visionary waters of Sion, the sweetly medieval stream of Hilaire Belloc's imagination – and also the watery backdrop to a thousand tourists' selfies.

Spanning 215 miles, the Thames is full of contradictions: at one end, it exists as a gentle, rural stream at its source in the Cotswolds and, at the other, as a vast estuary that merges seamlessly with the sea. Day by day, it is a changeable creature. Perhaps it is because its mud is so readily reshaped by each tide that it has accreted such a layered identity. Every twelve hours, it presents a blank canvas upon which a new age can leave its mark. At low tide in central London mudlarks flock to the foreshore, tenderly sifting through the debris of ages past for treasures. As the tide flows back in, I can stand and watch the mud disappear under the water and reappear a few hours later in a new guise. And yet I know that someone standing in the same spot a hundred or a thousand years ago could have observed the same process of reincarnation. The Thames's mutability is its permanence.

At high tide on a calm day, the river can be so wide and flat that it looks as if the sea has entered the city. Stood on London Bridge at high tide, I have observed the silver surface at my feet and gloried in the way it slices through London, a strand of contemplation in a busy metropolis. It flows past the key points of the city, as if posing for the postcards: the Palace of Westminster, the London Eye, City Hall. This is an extremely well-documented landscape. For centuries, writers and artists have been producing work around a seemingly endless array of Thames topics: its secret underground tributaries, its literary connections, the afterlives of its ships, docks, bridges and wharves. However, the vast majority of these explorations end long before the river does. The picture that the collective consciousness of the Thames provides looks a lot like the one from the *EastEnders* titles. Seen from above, it shows the great loop of the river's meander around the Isle of Dogs and then a thin blue squiggle coming in from the top where Barking Creek joins the main channel. But then the right-hand edge of the screen slices through and awareness leaks away. The estuary is off-screen, unseen.

There are many reasons for this. The myriad stories that London holds draw focus from the rest of the Thames, crowding out the elsewhere. Then there is the problem of access: the estuary, with its marshy shores and wide expanses of water, is not particularly easy to visit, especially without a boat. A bigger obstacle, though, is its unlovely reputation. Over centuries, London has acquired the habit of displacing everything from sewage to silt to the working poor downstream. If the archetypal picturesque English landscape is like something that Capability Brown might have devised, or that

E. M. Forster immortalized in his 1910 condition of England novel *Howards End* – a politely reticent vista of rolling green hills, interspersed with charmingly crooked farmhouses and the occasional copse – then the Thames estuary could not be more different.

As a result, it is not a landscape that has ever accrued cultural value, nor is it an obviously pleasant place to visit or walk, describe or paint. Even now that much of the pollution that used to choke the river has been removed, the estuary mud has a brackish, rotting odour. The land barely shows above the horizon, and in the murky grey light that prevails for much of the year, it is difficult to distinguish between sea, shore and sky. The remains of cooling towers, cranes and pylons dot the banks, but there are few ancient ruins that might lend historical resonance to the region. It possesses an overwhelmingly pervasive atmosphere of vacancy and purposelessness.

For Conrad, though, it is this 'mysterious vastness' of the outer estuary that provides the true romance of the Thames. To him, an exile from the shifting geopolitics and fluctuating national identities of eastern Europe in the late nineteenth century, its featureless expanses and lonely shores are to be revered, not reviled. It is a place of potential, where journeys begin with the promise of 'every possible fruition to adventurous hopes'. His estuary is both a modern, industrial space and a ghostly wasteland peopled by the shades of those who sailed here in years past: the Vikings, the Romans and the early Britons. His imagination delighted in populating this bare landscape with possible pasts and futures. With the eyes of an immigrant and a sailor, unencumbered by English preconceptions of landscape, he saw beauty. Joseph Conrad had inhabited many roles: as the son of a noted Polish political revolutionary; as a trainee teenage sailor in France; as a despairing debtor; as a master mariner in the British merchant service; and as an émigré novelist. 'It is an extraordinary sequence of lives, made doubly remarkable because none of its lines appear to flow into each other,' his biographer Frederick R. Karl wrote. 'His life becomes like a plotted novel, full of seeming inexplicables.'

When illness ended his twenty-year career at sea, Conrad's final passage brought him through the estuary one last time, before he disembarked in the London docks to make his permanent home in Britain. The estuary is an in-between space, neither one thing nor the other. For this reason, it holds great attraction for the rootless. To my family, it rapidly came to feel like home.

Spring had come and the ice in St Katharine Docks had melted by the time my parents decided to remain in Britain. My father, an engineer, travelled all over the country, looking for work in the steelworks of Cardiff, Sheffield and Teesside. But finally, it was the plant at Sheerness he had seen through the binoculars on that first trip into the estuary that offered him a position. My mother, a computer scientist, found a job at the Shell headquarters on the south bank of the Thames in central London, just about within commuting distance from the estuary. Once spring had truly arrived, six months after their arrival at St Katharine Docks, they locked out for the last time, waved farewell to the friendly lockkeeper and sailed downstream to the Isle of Sheppey.

Moving from a boat into a house proved challenging – they had no furniture – but the people of Sheppey were welcoming. By the time I was born, in 1988, my parents had migrated again to the mainland, just across the Swale, a tiny Thames tributary, to Sittingbourne in north Kent, but the boat and the estuary remained a central part of their lives. My mother sailed throughout the time she was pregnant with me and my first time on the boat was at six weeks old. The moniker 'water baby' attached itself to me from an early age. Unlike my parents, who even after three decades of living in the northern hemisphere still can't bear to swim in Britain's chilly seas, I have always loved being in the cool, salty water.

Before long, their beloved boat *Scherzo* was customized to accommodate an adventurous toddler and our weekends and holidays were spent on the water. The entrance to the triangular berth at the bow of the boat was covered with netting my father made from some green string so I could bounce around in there without falling out. I learned to swing in the hammock-like straps my mother had created so she could stand safely at the gas stove and cook at sea when the swell was strong. Soon, I could sleep easily while the sails creaked overhead, rocked by the motion of the boat. I would wake in the dark, look up through the open cockpit hatch and see my parents silhouetted against the starry sky, still as the night. In the morning, we would be somewhere new – anchored in a hidden creek on the other side of the estuary, say, or rafted up with a Thames barge by the Royal Arsenal, Woolwich. On some mornings, I climbed up the steps to the deck and saw only the sea.

We lived a partitioned kind of life, divided between the land and the water. Our garden was a little bit overgrown and shaggy round the edges, because we weren't always there to mow and prune at weekends like our neighbours. Instead, we would slip away late at night to catch the tide in the Medway and see where it would take us. Holidays meant we could make longer passages, across the Channel to France or Holland. When school friends told stories in the playground of summer trips to Disneyland or beaches in Cornwall, I would join in with tales of diving off the deck into the silty water of the Veerse Meer and of how one day we had eaten syrupy peaches straight from the tin for both lunch and dinner because the sea was too rough to cook anything.

It is difficult to say exactly when I realized that the Thames estuary was the place I loved best. Perhaps it was when I was four years old and used my first disposable camera to take blurry pictures of the wooden posts in its waters instead of my family's sailing holiday. Or when I first read *Great Expectations*, curled in a bunk with the creek lapping at the hull beneath me, and understood that these were the very waters from which the convict Magwitch had emerged. It wasn't until I was in my teens that I began to understand that the estuary landscape – which for me, like Conrad, represented opportunity and a chance to belong – was not generally perceived so positively. When I was older still and on a press boat trip to see some historic military installations in the outer Thames, I was surprised to find myself bristling as if I had been personally insulted every time one of my fellow journalists looked out at the estuary and said, with a disbelieving inflection in their voice, 'Where the hell *are* we?'

Over the centuries, the estuary has played a vital role in Britain's industrial, military and commercial development, yet today it is valued so little that half-rotten boats are left to sink into its mud and wharves are abandoned to collapse slowly into the marshes. Its shores and islands have long been the preferred site of structures that the authorities in London would rather keep out of sight: prisons, factories, sewage works and power stations. Unlike in a more conventionally attractive landscape, where views must be preserved and space to build is at a premium, the estuary has never been considered desirable. As technology advanced, new structures were built beside the old, tumbledown ones. Often, there has been no need to bother with demolition when wind and salt will do the job. Just a few dozen miles upriver, central London's former power stations are now redeveloped into museums and luxury apartments. By the estuary, they stand empty, shadows against the sky.

The years I spent following my parents across the sea taught me how to sail close to the wind and tie swift, strong knots in pieces of rope. But it was more of an education than I knew: I also learned to see beyond the featureless monotony the world considers the estuary to be and discover the concealed beauty behind all that grey. I have never seen a painting or a photograph that can fully capture the way light slides between mud and water, smudging sea and sand and sky together at the horizon. The way to find it is to sit in the stillness, louring clouds above and water lapping nearby, breathing in the scent of the mud. It will creep upon you, this strange beauty, as silently as the shadows writhe amid the reeds on the shore.

The case for readmitting the estuary to our idea of landscape is only growing stronger. In the past decade, its vast open spaces and inclement weather have begun to be seen as an asset, not an obstacle. Its shallow waters, numerous sandbanks and easy connections to the shore provide excellent sites for offshore wind farms. With the UK government keen to meet its target of generating 15 per cent of the nation's energy from renewable sources by 2020, places where turbines can be sited and residents won't complain of ruined vistas are increasingly in demand. The London Array farm, which comprises 175 turbines and is situated in the estuary twelve miles off North Foreland, was formally inaugurated in July 2013. It is the largest offshore wind farm in the world, covering an area of nearly forty square miles – equivalent to 7,245 football pitches. At its peak, it can generate 630 megawatts of electricity, enough to power half a million homes. The turbines themselves are over 350 feet tall. They spin in the corner of the eye as you look at the horizon, a peculiarly elegant addition to the landscape. It's possible to hear the buzz and whirr of them at work if you sail just outside the security perimeter of the farm. Over the noise of the waves, it can sound like they are breathing.

It's not just the estuary's winds that have attracted new infrastructure developments in recent years. In 2008, the then mayor of London, Boris Johnson, revived a long-posited plan for a new airport in the Thames. Immediately dubbed 'Boris Island' by the press, it would have seen four runways built on new artificial land created by the Shivering Sands in the outer estuary. Although opposed by everyone from ornithologists to air traffic controllers, the scheme accrued a fair amount of political capital owing to its sheer expediency – why not solve the thorny problem of airport expansion by building a new one in an apparently empty area nobody cares about? – but it was eventually rejected in 2014 by the UK Airports Commission. The proposals raised the profile of the estuary, however, and helped to draw attention to its wildlife. It was partly owing to warnings from the RSPB about the airport's impact on unique habitats nearby that the scheme was abandoned. Several nature reserves and special protection areas have been designated in recent years in recognition of the precious habitats the estuary contains. Avocets, redshanks, lapwings, water voles, emerald dragonflies and plovers are just some of the many species that thrive there.

Turbulent political conditions have drawn greater attention to the area in recent years too. Over the centuries, London has displaced a whole segment of its population from the East End downstream into the estuary. The working poor moved in waves: in the nineteenth century to the rapidly expanding dock suburbs of West and East Ham; in the 1920s and 1930s to 'cottage estates' in Becontree, Barking and Dagenham; and then out of London entirely after the devastation of the Blitz and the Second World War, to the Essex 'New Towns' of Basildon and Harlow. This movement continued throughout the twentieth century, as east London gentrified and the Docklands were redeveloped into glass-fronted flats and high-rise office blocks. There was no longer space for the working communities that had once crowded into these areas. As these former East Enders departed, they took their language with them. The sounds of the city moved downriver, as working-class cockney blended with the lower-middle-class speech of Essex and Kent to form a new way of speaking: estuary English.

The economic anxieties of this primarily white working-class demographic has become a flashpoint in contemporary political debate. Estuary-adjacent areas like Thurrock on the Essex coast, where the decline of industry has increased unemployment and rapid rates of immigration have fostered social tensions, swung first towards the British National Party (BNP) in the early 2000s and then to UKIP and Brexit after 2010. In 2016, Thurrock registered the fourth-highest vote in the UK to leave the European Union, with 72.7 per cent choosing Leave. Post-referendum, commentators spoke of a divided Britain and those who felt 'left behind' by visions of a metropolitan, multicultural future for the nation. It became increasingly clear that overlooking the estuary, and the people who inhabit it, had social and electoral consequences.

Following decades of stagnation, the estuary's fortunes are finally beginning to shift. As property prices have spiralled out of control in London, more and more people are moving east by choice. New garden cities like Ebbsfleet are being built on the lower Thames, to accommodate these refugees from the capital's inequality catastrophe. The HS1 rail link follows the south bank of the river out into Kent, connecting the often-deprived and run-down towns along the way with London. In April 2017, an extra river crossing was announced for the lower Thames – a £6 billion tunnel between Tilbury and Gravesend that the government claims will create 6,000 jobs in the region and stop traffic funnelling inland to Dartford. Recognition is growing that the estuary is a place worth investing in, but there is still a perception that it is an empty, meaningless wasteland in need of development. Nothing could be further from the truth: this is a rich, varied and historic landscape. It's just waiting to be appreciated.

After years of living in London, I became accustomed to the
ache I felt every time I crossed Waterloo Bridge or wandered
along the river path at Putney. It was always there in the back
of my mind, this pull towards the invisible place downriver
where the mud smudged into the river and the sea was close
enough to taste on the wind. For a long time, I dismissed this
feeling as mere nostalgia – who doesn't miss the place where
they grew up and the person they used to be once they have
moved on? Then one winter I moved into a concrete high-
rise block just south of the river at Lambeth, in a flat level
with the tops of the trees. On stormy nights, when the wind
screamed in the open stairwells and mysterious pools of rusty
water appeared on every landing, it felt like I was sleeping in
the crow's nest of a great ship, battling through the waves out
in the North Sea.

The water was near: when the weather eased, I could climb
down from the flat and be at the Thames with just a few minutes' brisk walk. And so every Saturday evening, I would make
my way east along the river's south embankment, a little further
each time. At first I was only walking as far as the well-lit tourist-
filled paths at the South Bank, where the London Eye spins
and there are buskers in every underpass. But then I began to
push on further, threading through the tiny, ancient streets by
Southwark Cathedral, passing London Bridge, the egg-shaped
glass bulge of City Hall and finally on to the warehouses and
wharves of Rotherhithe, now converted into private flats, often
with electronic gates blocking off access to the river, requiring
me to dodge behind buildings and then slide back between
them to return to the bank. The streets I passed had names
which recalled an earlier, more exotic past when the Thames

was the route to the rest of the world: Elephant Lane, Cathay Street, Norway Gate.

On these walks, I discovered that London has lost sight of the night. There is so much artificial light from street lamps, billboards and floodlighting that it is no longer ever truly dark in the city. Once the sun has set, the orange glow from a million lighted windows reaches up towards the clouds, pushing the stars away. This is the brightest region of the UK, showing up on maps of light intensity as a dense red blotch. Research shows that the nights are getting lighter here at a rate of 2 per cent a year, and that the shrinking dark is responsible for everything from poor sleep patterns in humans to plants and trees opening their buds too early. But on my way east along the Thames's south bank, I found small pockets of secret darkness. There are no lights on the river itself and no council can afford to waste money erecting lamps on the foreshore where few choose to wander. If I crept down to the water towards midnight, with the buildings in darkness behind me and just a few lighted windows on the north bank reflected in the river's smooth surface, I could pretend that I was seeing the stars as clearly as I did when we sailed west through the estuary towards London with only the twinkling lights of Southend in the distance to distract from the brilliance overhead. At the eastern-most extent of my explorations, I would find something to perch on – an abandoned hunk of wood that might once have been a boat or the jutting edge of a forgotten concrete jetty – and I would watch as the mud, exposed by a receding tide, gleamed silvery-white in the moonlight. I could be alone with the river here, imagining myself spinning downstream and away from the city, towards the sea.

On New Year's Eve that year, after my friends had danced to charity shop soul records in the treetop flat in celebration of another year's passing, I took them down to the river. It was 3 a.m. and tempers were fraying a little as we muffled up in coats and scarves to walk past the scantily clad revellers queuing to get into the clubs under the railway arches. Next to the headquarters of MI6, where the Albert Embankment arrives at Vauxhall, there is a slipway guarded only by an empty security post and a single flimsy parking barrier. A few straggly stalks of ground elder had broken through where the tarmac was cracked, bent over by the wind coming off the river but still growing determinedly sideways, a small act of wild rebellion. We ducked under the arm and walked out onto the stony, silty foreshore. Like the old year, the water had receded, and this was a moment of slack before a fresh tide flooded in again. Bursts of merriment, brightly explosive as fireworks, came occasionally from Vauxhall Bridge or the road we had left behind. My companions soon forgot their irritation at being dragged out of the warm and began picking through the debris left at the waterline by the tide, turning over shards of pottery and pieces of metal, exclaiming and speculating as to the objects' previous lives.

It was a particularly low tide that night, one of the twice-monthly spring tides that accompany the new and full moons, when the earth, sun and moon are aligned and their pull is strongest, increasing the distance between high and low water. In the shadow of the dark building, with light spilling down in wavering gulps from the lamps up on the bridge, I picked my way as far as I dared into the water. The opposite bank looked very near, as if the water had drained away far enough that I could make a big stride and be across. I stood alone on a spur of silty earth and felt the silence all around me, the river lapping gently at my feet. There, in that quiet moment, I finally found the salve for that ache that beset me every time I caught sight of the river. I had to face up to my yearning for the place I used to know and follow the Thames to the sea, to discover the estuary all over again. After months of pacing the river's edge where it flowed through the city, obsessing over the gaps where its previous incarnations could still be glimpsed, I knew that what I had been feeling all this time went beyond sentimental childhood reminiscence. I wanted to see the estuary as it is now and explore what it could be in the future. When I grew up there, it shaped me into an observer, forever choosing to watch from the periphery. Finally, I understood how I would repay this extraordinary place for all that it had taught me: I would see it clearly, in all its strange beauty, and show others how to do the same.

To do this, I would need to make a journey, on foot and by water. We are prone to thinking of the Thames in fractured sections: the sweet simplicity of the stream in Gloucestershire; the majestic waves under Westminster Bridge; the deep course through the mud at Shoeburyness. But if the abandoned landscape of the estuary is to be recovered, then the Thames must be viewed as one being, from source to sea. No one part could exist without the other; the stories are layered thickly together, overlapping and coexisting. There can be no ending without a beginning. I would need to trace the Thames right back to its origins – a trek to the source, a place I had never been before. I wanted to understand the river at every stage, to feel how it shifts and changes before reaching its final form as it flows into the sea. It's not always a wild or abstract place, and even in its furthest reaches, it is entwined with our history. Generations of people have lived, worked and wandered everywhere along its banks, even in its remotest and least appetizing quarters. Some have recorded their impressions – the writers, the artists, the legislators, the photographers – but many, many days on the banks of the Thames have gone undocumented. If I was to restore the estuary to its rightful place as part of the English landscape, and perhaps to reveal the vital role it plays in the life and mythology of the Thames as a whole, I would have to build a picture of the many lives this river has witnessed.

A shout from one of my friends shook me out of my silent contemplation on the silty spit. The tide was turning and they had found what was possibly part of a Roman pot lodged in the gritty foreshore. As I turned my back on the water and shuffled carefully over the mud and stones back to solid ground, a couplet from Rudyard Kipling's 'The River's Tale' floated across my mind:

> For they were young, and the Thames was old,
> And this is the tale that the River told.

He wrote the poem for a 1911 children's textbook called *A School History of England*, and in it the river narrates its own life story from 'the Age of Ice' to when 'the Roman left and the Danes blew in'. It's a sing-song bit of doggerel, designed mostly, I think, for chanting in the classroom, but I've always had great affection for it because of the spiky, sardonic voice that Kipling gives to the Thames. It's also a rare work that addresses the river's full scope: at one point in the poem, the River says:

> Down I come with the mud in my hands
> And plaster it over the Maplin Sands.

The same mud I was squelching through now, which was sucking at my boots and threatening to trickle down my ankles, would one day top a sandbank out in the estuary. I staggered back inland with a different feeling settling in my chest. There is rich history buried out there in the mud. I would bring it back into the light.

The next weekend, I took the train to my parents' house in Kent. When I told my mother what I was planning, she was instantly practical. She crawled underneath their bed and from the huge stack of charts they keep there she produced the original ones they had purchased in 1984 for their first journey into the estuary. From the bookcase in the study she pulled out the original logbook, which begins with their voyage from Cape Town to the English Channel. Opening it, I felt a little daunted. This is the written record of every sailing trip they have ever taken, beginning on 9 February 1984. Although the black canvas cover and tan suede spine is as familiar to me as the front door of my parents' house, I had never actually turned back the pages to this first expedition into the estuary. I wasn't allowed to write in it as a child, much as its hefty weight and green marbled endpapers attracted me – the log is a serious document, full of technical information that must be entered during and immediately after a passage, before all the inconstant figures denoting wind speeds and positions can be erased from your mind by the thrill of arriving at your destination. It's not for children to doodle in. As I began to turn the pages, I was instantly absorbed, tracking the way my parents' familiarity with their new home grows from that first, formal passage. I kept reading, hoping for some evidence of my own existence, some note of my birth or first journey aboard, but there is nothing. Just long strings of weather and navigational data in my father's smooth, even hand.

The charts, however, are still covered in marks which have been partially erased and remade over the years. I remember well how in the time before instant GPS technology, every hour or so while we were sailing – if luck was with us and the few satellites were within range – my father would read a long string of coordinates out from a black box called a Decca, and I would use the scale around the edge to line up a ruler with the figures he was calling out. The two numbers, one longitude and one latitude, would then come together in a little pencil cross on the chart, which – under my father's vigilant supervision – I would draw a circle around and annotate with the date and time. Eventually, a trail of these little symbols would build across the chart, the pencil-scratched waypoints of our course. There are hundreds of them, rubbed out once each passage was completed, but still faintly visible. Peering down at them feels like discovering an old photograph or a family tree. We are here, among the crowded type giving depth figures and the names of sandbanks. You can trace us.

That evening, I sat with my father for hours as he talked about the estuary. As well as decades of sailing on it, it was also his place of work for a long time – after a stint at the steelworks on the Isle of Sheppey, he worked for decades at the port at Sheerness, where the Medway flows into the Thames, eventually rising to be its chief executive. Every ship that loaded or unloaded there and every worker who made it happen was his responsibility. In addition, he had duties towards the landscape itself, to ensure that the channels were dredged, the lights were maintained and the pilot ships worked efficiently, guiding the enormous tankers and container ships safely through the sandbanks to their berths. Even the wrecks, mostly out of sight other than during the lowest tides, were in his charge. I knew this, of course. I had grown up used to the fact that everybody on the Medway, where my parents kept their boat through much of my childhood, knew us and would wave across the water when they passed us going in or out of the estuary. It's one of the reasons that I was able to roam as freely as I did, rowing our little blow-up dinghy all over the place, safe in the knowledge that if I had a problem, someone who worked with my father would probably fish me out of trouble. But until I sat down and asked him what this place meant to him, I had not understood the depth of his affection for and knowledge of it.

As he spoke, I became more convinced than ever that this journey to the estuary was also a way of accessing our own story. I had so often been asked, 'Where are you from?' when my ignorance of some British cultural touchstone or a stray flattened vowel slipped out that my answer – about my parents' journey here – had become mundane. It's barely spoken of; my sister and I used to roll our eyes as teenagers when it came up in conversation. It's only now that I'm thinking of their migration in the context of the estuary that I can appreciate how unusual it is. With a sudden grandiose flight of fancy, it reminds me of a foundational myth, a bit like the story popularized by the twelfth-century chronicler Geoffrey of Monmouth in which Brutus, a descendant of the Trojan hero Aeneas, makes his way to ancient Britain and founds Troia Nova, or New Troy, on the banks of the Thames. It's a common classical trope: to settle peacefully and have a family in safety, the hero must first survive an extraordinary voyage across turbulent seas.

When it came time for me to return to London, my father released the logbook and charts into my charge somewhat reluctantly, with many gentle reminders to keep them safe. We don't have many family photographs or papers; these are our only records. I laid the charts out on the wall of my bedroom, pinning them so that the river flows from one to another until it expands out into the estuary. My mother spread the word of what I was doing among sailing friends and acquaintances.

Soon, bundles of papers and parcels of out-of-print books about obscure creeks and long-forgotten estuary voyages started arriving in the post. One night, I stayed up until the early hours, standing on a chair with a torch to squint at the charts on the wall so that I could make a list of every extraordinary place name I could find. Everywhere from Bugsby's Reach to Middle Deep seemed to hold the promise of a story. I sketched lines between all these marks, a great web of linguistic connections skittering around the curves of the river, getting wider with every turn towards the estuary. Eventually, I pieced together a course. After many hours debating it with my father, on the phone and in emails, we settled on it and a date was chosen for the journey.

One grey morning, as I walked to work, I found myself idling towards the centre of London Bridge, unwilling to carry on and reach the other side. I looked down at the river, listening to the tide rushing past the pillars below, swishing its way inland, defying logic for how the water in a river should behave. If I were to look at it too long, it would make me giddy, as though the water was stationary while the bridge was rushing out to sea underfoot. It seemed that the Thames could take me anywhere, even while my feet remained rooted to the spot. But it no longer made me ache with frustration that I could not follow it. Instead, I felt only anticipation – soon, very soon, I would be shadowing the tide out of the city, towards the sea, to a place where wrecks lie under the water, exposed by every tide, containing extraordinary, explosive stories. There are massive ships there too, transporting the fruits of entire industries, and delicate, rare birds leaving exquisite patterns on the sand as they trace their way across it. The spoils of centuries of exploitation – from the Napoleonic-era military forts to the landfill heaps transformed into wildlife reserves to the rusting half-drowned remains of industry – take on a fresh kind of dignity there. The estuary is a tingle on the back of your neck; a moment of reciting the catechism of landmarks still to come – Mid Swatch, Blacktail Spit, Shivering Sands, Whis, Knob, Knock John – and looking up to realize that all you can see is sky.

I

Thames Head to Tower Bridge

There is a stone at a place called Thames Head, just outside the village of Kemble in Gloucestershire. It has a level slab as a plinth and a dimpled vertical surface dappled with lichens. Inset near the top, there is a smooth grey piece of marble with words carved into it. They read: 'This stone was placed here to mark the source of the River Thames.' It sounds so definite. Yet standing in that spot, shaded by ash trees, looking out at an achingly English landscape of rolling green fields with hedgerows silhouetted against the horizon, I realized that something was missing. There was no water.

I had risen early that morning. At Paddington Station, I cut a curiously conspicuous figure among the besuited commuters in my waterproof gear and heavy boots, a sheaf of maps under my arm. The empty train raced west, leaving London behind. I stared out of the window as the low-slung warehouses and tyre depots of the Thames Valley flashed past. The grey sky pushed down towards the horizon and a dark, almost mauve fog swirled across the land. The air was heavy with stormy potential, the carriage airless and dull. Pinpricks of rain spattered across the glass.

After stopping at Reading the train crossed the river for the first time and I snatched a glimpse of it under the bridge, narrow and navy blue. The fog lifted briefly and I saw wheat undulating in the breeze, looking improbably yellow against the grey sky, before the fields disappeared as the train plunged through a series of new housing developments. A few minutes later, after pulling out of Swindon, it traversed a landscape that seemed to belong several centuries ago – wild hedgerows tangled at the edges of fields, the trees spreading thick branches towards the clouds, with the occasional worn red of tumble-down brick barns amid the green and grey. The river flitted into view several more times, encroached always by reeds, and then the train slowed down for Kemble and I disembarked.

I picked a pocket's worth of sour blackberries from the brambles in the lane outside the station before following the pencilled line on my map through the outskirts of this tiny Gloucestershire village and into the fields. The long grass had been curved over by recent rain and was still silvered with drops as distinct as tiny glass beads. To my right, a ditch full of weeds buzzed with insects. I climbed over a stile and found a wooden bridge across an empty grassy gully. Turning north towards the source into the field known as Trewsbury Mead, I walked along the bank of this empty stream. The gentle curve of the land and the protective way the trees overhung the depression in the turf suggested that there should be a river here, but there were only dock leaves and nettles growing from the bed. Cows stood their ground ahead, forcing me to pick my way around them as I followed an avenue of lime and ash trees towards the plinth, which stands on a knoll just in front of a barbed-wire fence. The boggy ground churned up by their hooves was the only sign of moisture at all.

Here, the Thames is always elusive. There is no dramatic

rising up or consistent point of origin. The spring that will eventually roar into a river runs underground, only emerging on the surface when the water table is high enough to enable it to filter through the earth. Where exactly this transition from submerged water to discernible stream occurs depends on the weather and the time of year – a wet winter can mean visible water almost as far up as the stone, whereas during a dry summer it is possible to walk for miles before stepping in anything you can imagine becoming a river. I had put this journey off, over and over again, confused by the conflicting accounts of the river's origins, and now it was summer – the most difficult time of year to find the source.

On that morning, the river flowed only in my head. I was fixated on the water, haunted by it. Alone in the ditch where the Thames should be, every noise – the movement of the grass and leaves in the wind, the swishing friction of my own jacket and trousers – made me feel sure it was near. My feet were wet from the dew, but the bed of the river was dry. Determined not to be cheated out of this moment of beginning, I walked for a couple of miles, tracking the invisible Thames. The further I walked, the deeper and broader the riverbed became. Rounded pebbles, which had clearly been well tumbled by a swift stream, lay eerily still amid knotted weeds, beached on the dusty earth. Its strands were still green and sappy, as if the water had only just drained away moments before I arrived.

Still following the space where the river should be, I walked through a cool silent wood, where the river had gouged a great ditch and then vanished. Although I met no one, there were occasional signs of previous Thames-seekers – a crumpled crisp packet, a rope swing hung from a bough. My path was shaded by a great thicket of hawthorn and lime trees, the latter dropping their sticky residue onto the stony bed. I emerged from the trees and – at last – saw a glimmer of water ahead. In a curve that had been eroded by the past flow, a pool of water had collected. Leaves floated motionless on its surface and the riverbed was dry again ahead, but I could see other pools further on. Finally, the change from one element to another was tangible. I took off my boots and tentatively paddled my blistered feet in the water.

This place might not provide the grand origin promised by the carved marble at Thames Head, but it's a beginning, of sorts. It all starts here.

For millennia, the sources of rivers have fascinated people. There is something potent about a definite point of origin, as if certainty can serve as a talisman and protect us against chaos and disorder. A river is a narrative and in order to control the story it is necessary to know how it begins. Nowhere is this more true than the Nile, a river and a story over which generations of conquerors and explorers have fought. Rulers of the ancient world, such as Alexander the Great and Julius Caesar, made attempts to discover its source and so demonstrate their mastery over the earth. The impenetrable Sudd Marshes in modern-day Sudan repelled all European incursions, however, and the mystery of the Nile's origin only fuelled the passion with which it was sought. That is, until the nineteenth century, when explorers broke through the marshes. On 30 July 1858, John Hanning Speke was the first European to reach the shores of the vast water he named Lake Victoria, from which the longer of the river's two branches, the White Nile, flows.

After a second trip in the early 1860s to gather further evidence of the Nile's source at Lake Victoria (rival explorers Richard Burton and David Livingstone disputed the location), Speke sent a now-famous telegram back to the Royal Geographical Society in London. 'The Nile is settled,' it read, as if there was nothing further to say on the subject. As with the Thames, his certainty was marked on the landscape, carved into stone. On the northern bank of Lake Victoria, where the water roars over the Ripon Falls down into the White Nile, there is a small monument. It reads, 'This spot marks the place from where the Nile starts its long journey to the Mediterranean Sea through central and northern Uganda, Sudan and Egypt.' Subsequent exploration in the 150 years since Speke's arrival has shown that Lake Victoria is merely a reservoir for waters that flow from much further south. Its main tributary is the Kagera river, which is in turn fed by the Ruvubu and Nyabarongo rivers. There is evidence to suggest that Speke knew Lake Victoria wasn't really the ultimate source of the Nile, but that he suppressed his doubts for the sake of keeping his discovery intact. It is still his name that history records in the river's origin story. The precise source is unknown: it could be where the springs that feed these rivers rise in Burundi or Rwanda, or it could be even further south. The beginning of the Nile eludes us.

The symbolism of the source, the moment when a story flows into being, haunts our thinking about rivers. Near the start of *Kubla Khan*, Coleridge declares:

> Where Alph, the sacred river, ran
> Through caverns measureless to man
> Down to a sunless sea.

The heavily accented beats and rhythmic, measured lines tumble his river across this landscape just as it surges through the stanzas of the poem, gravity and rhyme pulling the reader along with the water to its inevitable conclusion, when the river 'sank in tumult to a lifeless ocean'. The source is the place of drama and sensation, a moment of action. After that, the mystery is over – the river flows on, miraculous no more. This poem has been echoing in my head ever since I had to learn it off by heart for a recitation competition when I was a child. But the more that I have involuntarily chanted it over the years, the more I have come to realize that I see rivers differently. As I stopped for a rest beside one of the puddles at Kemble, I felt a little like Mole in *The Wind in the Willows*, who sits on the bank of the Thames 'while the river still chattered on to him, a babbling procession of the best stories in the world, sent from the heart of the earth to be told at last to the insatiable sea'. The image of moving water, an entity that shapes its surroundings but is not of a piece with them, that travels from a point of beginning to a climactic end, is irresistible. The source is just the beginning of the story. Look beyond and there is more to discover.

Having paddled in the beginnings of the Thames at Kemble, the temptation to keep walking in the stream was strong. At this point, the river is a charming, rural thing – all dappled shade and weeping-willow boughs reaching down to the water. The urban centres of Reading, Oxford and London seem a world away. This is a dreaming, pastoral landscape that feels, in places, like it stands outside of time.

William Morris experienced this sensation too when he first came to the village of Kelmscott, which lies just downriver from Kemble. He saw the seventeenth-century manor house that dominates the small hamlet for the first time in 1871 and declared it the 'loveliest haunt of ancient peace', which looked like it had just 'grown up out of the soil'. Soon after, he signed a joint lease for it with his friend the Pre-Raphaelite painter Dante Gabriel Rossetti. Morris was to spend much of the remaining twenty-five years of his life there. As a poet and designer, he was part of an artistic movement that revered the natural world and harked back to the preindustrial past of the countryside. At Kelmscott, the medieval era he venerated felt very close, as if he might duck under the water of the river one day and come up in 1600, when his house was newly built and there were no ugly iron railway bridges crossing the Thames or steam tugs (which he deplored as 'mercantile tin kettles') chugging upstream.

Unlike many of those who have romanticized this stretch of the upper Thames as an idyll unconnected to the rest of the world, Morris was keenly aware of the river's onward path through London and beyond – indeed, it was the river's movement from the pastoral, through the suburban and on to the urban that shaped his ideas about it. The river meant home to him: in 1878, he acquired a new property in the west London district of Hammersmith and named it Kelmscott House as a way of carrying the qualities of his beloved country manor with him into the city. The fact that he could travel up the river from one to the other deepened the connection between his residences. The Morris family first made this journey in 1880, in a boat they christened *The Ark* – it would be his family's salvation from the flood of modernity. Morris himself called her a 'biggish company boat', but his daughter May described her, perhaps more accurately if less romantically, as 'a large punt with the body of a small omnibus on top of her, a sort of insane gondola'. This craft was towed slowly upriver by 'a man and a boy and a pony' over the course of a week, and Morris later wrote of his delight at going to sleep every night 'with the stream rushing two inches past one's ear'. The further upstream they were towed, the closer they came to his ideal landscape.

This was a journey from city to country, smoke to clean air, sin to purity. These were ideas that had preoccupied Morris for a long time. The prologue to his epic poem *The Earthly Paradise*, begun in 1868, sets up this dichotomy:

> Forget six counties overhung with smoke,
> Forget the snorting steam and piston stroke,
> Forget the spreading of the hideous town;
> Think rather of the pack-horse on the down,
> And dream of London, small, and white, and clean,
> The clear Thames bordered by its gardens green.

For Morris, the Thames was a watery thread of history running through England which contained elements of the classical and the sacred. It was as if the Thames held some properties of the underworld's River Lethe, from which – according to Greek mythology – the shades of the dead must drink in order to forget their earthly sins before reincarnation. If only the world could imbibe the 'clear Thames', the wrongs that the industrial age had done to the landscape (in the form of ugly houses, ruined woodlands, dirty factories and rapidly expanding cities) could be righted.

In *News from Nowhere*, his 1890 work of proto-socialist science fiction, Morris further developed his thinking on the Thames as a vestige of an antique age. It is full of adoring descriptions of the beauties of the river – a 'slender stream' winding past islets 'begrown with graceful trees', bordered by meadows and meads of lush vegetation and overhung by willow and elm. Its protagonist, William Guest, falls asleep after attending a meeting of the Socialist League and awakens in the future. He gradually learns that a revolution has taken place and society now functions on a communist basis, with art, nature and the pleasures of work prized above all else. Money, divorce, prison and all the other evils of the nineteenth century have been abolished, and the Palace of Westminster is no longer the seat of Parliament but merely a store for the dung produced by Morris's new agrarian economy.

Yet for all that it is a speculative and utopian political treatise, *News from Nowhere* is chiefly a romance of the river. In company with several new friends from the future, Guest shadows Morris's own journey up the Thames, rowing from Hammersmith to Kelmscott and observing the countryside. The further they travel, the fewer differences there are for Guest to find – as if the upper Thames in 1890 was already very close to the ideal future form of the river the book imagines. 'Even this beginning of the country Thames was always beautiful; and as we slipped between the lovely summer greenery, I almost felt my youth come back to me,' Guest observes as they enter the river's upper reaches. Elsewhere, he notes with delight how 'de-cockneyised' the Thames has become, with the villas of the stockbrokers and well-to-do, 'which in older time marred the beauty of the bough-hung banks', swept away. Every hint of the urban, man-made or commercial must be obliterated for the Thames to attain its true state.

Morris's Thames is a blissful rural idyll, the antithesis of the pollution-choked commercial waters in London and beyond. It is an imaginary landscape, though – such a place has never existed. Even before the appearance of the 'Gothic' cast-iron bridges that Guest despised so much, there had been weirs, mills and locks on the Thames for centuries, as people sought to harness its power and make their livings on its banks. England's is a working landscape, but the utopian fantasy of picturesque leisure that Morris laid over it is a beguiling one. It is also there in Blake's 'green and pleasant land' and Wordsworth's 'pleasant

lea', and countless other nineteenth-century works responding
to the changes the industrial revolution had brought to Britain.
And yet still today, as I wander by Morris's 'sweet stream
that knows not of the sea' and hear the rustling breeze gently
moving the willow boughs that overhang the banks, it is all too
easy to imagine yourself slipping into another time.

Until the river reaches Oxford, versions of the past flicker
around every curve in the bank. In places, the water table
is just two feet below the ground and the banks are prone
to flooding. In a sense, all of this land – the meadows and
the scrubby fields and all the places in between – belongs
to the Thames. Ancient structures still stand here. The oldest
bridge on the Thames is at Radcot and was built in 1200. The
one at Newbridge was erected just half a century later. Each
village has a church spire showing through the trees as the
river flows towards it, which would have appeared in the same
way to a water traveller from five centuries ago as it does to us
now. Inns and tollhouses from several hundred years ago are
still common – although often transformed into gastropubs
with large car parks and pastel paint on the window frames.

Yet modernity has always nibbled around the edges of this
landscape and many structures have vanished altogether from
the river's banks. In his 1907 book *The Historic Thames*, Hilaire
Belloc mourns the loss of the great Thames-side monasteries
that once dominated the river around Oxford. He repeats
their names like the lines of the rosary, full of regret: Osney,
Abingdon, Chertsey, Cookham, Sheen, Reading. Belloc imagines how the landscape would have appeared to a 'traveller or
bargeman' in the late fifteenth century and the glories he would
have seen – huge, graceful buildings on the banks 'such as

today we never see save in our rare and half-deserted cathedral country towns', furnished with wonders we no longer know how to create. The walls and towers of these institutions would have seemed permanent and immovable, yet within the traveller's lifetime they would all be turned to rubble and fade from the horizon with Henry VIII's dissolution of the monasteries. It would no longer be possible to navigate the twists and turns of the river using their spires; it was as if they had never been.

At Oxford, the character of the river alters and the shadows of the past give way to the swirling fantasies that the city of dreaming spires gathers around itself. It is the river's first urban encounter, the first time since that thwarted moment of beginning at Trewsbury Mead that a city stands on the banks rather than the jungle of undergrowth and leafy canopy of trees. The city itself is all stone – golden sandstone that dampens to grey in the rain. The architects of the great university and college buildings favoured sharp corners and smooth planes for their quadrangles. Everything is geometric, ordered, unchanging. Down by the river, though, is rebellion. Lying unseen in the bottom of a boat tethered to the roots of a tree growing out of the bank, I have watched the quiet chaos that hums around the water. Mayflies and butterflies dance across the surface, tracing invisible patterns with their feet and wings. The trees continually drop leaves and pollen and seeds, so much so that with eyes half closed on the brightest of days it can look like rain. In some places, the river is choked with this abundance of vegetation, its emerald-dark surface turned a soggy gold or brick-red or luminous green by it all. A misplaced oar can get stuck and you can briefly think that the river is fighting for its possession.

Oxford is a point of pivot on the Thames, where, Janus-like, we can look both ways. As Peter Ackroyd puts it, 'From [Oxford] you can look upward and consider the quiet source;

or you can look downstream and contemplate the coming immensity of London.' In the late nineteenth century, walking to London was a fairly common pastime among Oxford students (in the 1890s, Belloc set a record by walking the fifty-six miles from Carfax to Marble Arch in eleven hours and thirty minutes), but for the less energetic, it can feel completely divorced from what happens downstream. Oxford is also the river's first encounter with a tangled knot of mythologies. The 'home of lost causes, and forsaken beliefs', as Matthew Arnold called the city, has always played host to the kinds of minds that are attracted to the river and the escapism – both physical and intellectual – that it offers. Even visiting for an afternoon, wandering in the sunshine, I am seduced by the layers of fictions that the city contains. Here is Narnia, Brideshead, Alice's Wonderland, Duns Scotus's Oxford, Morse's case history, Lyra's college playground, the site of Zuleika Dobson's conquests. The river runs through it all.

When I arrived in Oxford for university at the age of eighteen, I knew very little of this. For a book-obsessed teenager studying English literature, I was poorly read in the canon of the place I now lived. I was blissfully unaware of the Oxbridge experience I had signed up for, although after a week of the sort of student life so memorably summarized by Philip Larkin as 'vomiting blindly through small Tudor windows', I started to get the idea. Eventually, I borrowed Evelyn Waugh's *Brideshead Revisited* from the library to comprehend why all these brittle, clever people worked so hard to pretend their lives revolved around punting and port, rather than anxious cramming and late-night kebabs. Here, everyone is playing a part.

I also felt like I was pretending to be someone else, a role I could never set aside for a second, albeit of a very different kind. Shortly after learning that I had gained a place to study at the university, I had been diagnosed with Hodgkin's disease, a rare form of cancer in the white blood cells. Aged seventeen, I divided my last year at school between A-level coursework and chemotherapy sessions. Everyone around me struggled with what my illness might mean. I took to crying in the shower so that my family could believe I was handling it well. Through it all – the wig fittings, the vomiting, the weakness – I fixated on Oxford as my place of escape. When doctors and teachers told me I should delay university and make sure I was completely well before I left home, I politely disagreed. I was going, and the cancer would have to come with me. After a brief period of remission, I was released to start my degree – only for the disease to return just weeks into my first term. In the official portrait taken after the matriculation ceremony that certified me as a member of the university, I look like a different person altogether. I'm wearing a wig and a big smile, but my eyes are weary, as if even pretending to be healthy for the camera is too much of an effort.

Oxford is low-lying and surrounded by hills, so is prone to fogs that settle in the streets and muffle the spirits. The fog settles on the river too, especially in the early mornings, a filmy grey breath above the polished darkness of the surface. It might look very different from the Thames I knew from my childhood in the estuary, but it was still the same river, and that continuity was a great comfort. I walked hundreds of miles up and down its banks, shivering in icy frosts and sweating in muggy dampness. When I struggled with the limitations my health placed on me, or felt weighed down by the need to pretend to those around me that everything was fine, the vitality of the river could cure me. Quietly making its way through the locks and past the meadows, it connected me to home.

At the end of my degree, I jumped into the river. I believed it would be a kind of baptism – that I would hang there in the current, while it filtered out the unpleasantness and petty jealousies of student life. I planned this ostentatious gesture meticulously, agonizing over what to wear and how to leap in order to create a suitably dramatic ending for this chapter of my life. Although I had persevered with my studies, I did not really like the person that illness and Oxford had produced, full of glib arguments and insincere laughter. I would leave my worst self in the water and the river would take her away. She would become nothing more than a shadow to catch in the reeds and startle the ducks downstream, and I would climb out as somebody else.

It was the kind of limpid, golden afternoon that C. S. Lewis must have been recalling when he wrote – an undergraduate himself at the time – that Oxford was 'a clean, sweet city lulled by ancient streams'. The Isis, the godly name by which the section of the Thames between Folly Bridge and Iffley Lock is known, is restricted in width by the firm banks that shore against the river on one side and the flood-prone water mead-ows on the other side. It flows fast and full, seeming to burst with foliage as it thrusts the images of trees and reeds back up towards their originals.

It was the Saturday of Eights Week, the last day of my final university rowing regatta, and the grasses were glowing green in the smooth water, their reflections pierced by the skiffs slicing through as each race concluded. This day is a festival of the river, yet the river itself felt apart from the events that were happening upon it, as if it had flowed from a bygone age and merely tolerated this negligible intrusion. The water moved sleekly and silently through the din of chatter and megaphones and children's squeals. Sunburned students drinking straight from brimming jugs of Pimm's crowed from the roofs of the college boathouses, while their counterparts of decades earlier strolled more sedately along the towpaths, remembering their own river and wondering how a place could look the same yet be so different.

Triumphant crews of young men lifted their boats from the water and held them aloft over their heads while I cheered for the women's race from the bank. My best friend was out there, hidden from me by the river's gentle curve, sweating and skimming in perfect time with seven others. Earlier in the day she had told me she would be leaving as soon as term was finished – rejecting the pressure of work and progress and ambition laid on all of us, she would instead travel around Europe. She had not asked me to go with her and I was cheering loudly for her now because I didn't want anyone to know that I was seething with rejection and resentment, my jealousy of her courage in stepping off the path life expected us to take as green as the waving weeds.

By the time her boat arrived back at the boathouse, its crew flushed with their victory, evening had crept up on the day. The crowds were dispersing back across the meadows to the city and the river's silence had filtered up onto the banks. I waited for her by the water's edge, the river lapping inches beneath my feet. When she joined me, we said nothing. She took my unwilling hand in her warm, eager one and in the fast-falling gloom we jumped away from the bank. Hands still clasped, our eyes closed against the grit in the water churned up by the rowers, we both hoped we were marking an ending, and a beginning. The impact of the cold water rendered me briefly speechless, but soon we were laughing and splashing each other as we tried to climb back out onto the bank. The evening's spell was broken by our silliness; the self-consciously poetic sorrow

I had gathered around me had been washed away. I squelched home across the meadow in good spirits once more, leaving small damp imprints of the Thames behind on the path with every step.

A thousand years before, the residents of Oxford received a stark reminder that there is more than one way a river can flow. In 1010, a Danish chieftain known as Thorkell the Tall landed an army in the Thames estuary and marched up the river to burn London and Oxford. The invaders came 'on both sides of the Thames', the *Anglo-Saxon Chronicle* tells us. By establishing his base in the estuary (the Isle of Sheppey is a probable site), Thorkell lighted on a tactical masterstroke. The English fleet at Sandwich was too far away to intercept him and the Thames itself was so little defended that he could march into the heart of England just by keeping to its banks. Oxford was the target of this surgical strike – both as revenge for the English massacre of Danish settlers there on St Brice's Day a decade before and because control of this religious and legal centre was crucial in the pre-1066 struggle for power in England.

The river at Oxford has long possessed a symbolic dimension. The name for this stretch of the Thames, Isis, comes with its own mass of folklore. The Egyptians believed that it was the tears of the goddess Isis for her murdered husband, Osiris, that caused the Nile to flood each year and the land to become fertile once more. Her personal cult, worshipped by adherents from the ancient Egyptian era right through to the emergence of organized Christianity, brought to the rhythms of the river and its waters ideas of death, rebirth and fertility. As early as the fourteenth century, written records were drawing parallels between Isis's Nile and the Thames. The latter's great tidal range and central place in the English landscape, combined with the fact that the Latin name for the Thames, Tamesis, was mistakenly recorded by chroniclers as being partly derived from the name of the goddess herself, solidified this notion. British Pagans (of whom, according to the most recent census in 2011, there are over 50,000) still celebrate an English conception of Isis as a fertility symbol and the mother of the Thames.

In retaining the name Isis for its upper reaches, the Thames takes on the pure and sacred connotations. The name is everywhere in Oxford and its environs – there is even a cheese called after it. The Isis is the pastoral ideal of a river, as yet untainted by exposure to commerce and the ungodly sins of London. In Philip Pullman's 2017 novel *La Belle Sauvage*, a huge flood causes the Isis to break its banks and turn Oxford briefly into a Venice-like floating city, with the novel's protagonists, Malcolm and Alice, washed helplessly past the colleges and houses, all the way down the Thames to London, by the force of the freak tide. It's a deliberate echo of the divine inundations of the Nile in Egypt and also a reference to the biblical flood of Noah: the children's world is submerged as they try to evade the evil unleashed by adults. Pullman is far from the only writer to envisage an engorged Thames drowning the land. Richard Jefferies's 1885 novel, *After London*, sees the capital turned into a lake and a noxious swamp after the fall of civilization, while in J. G. Ballard's *The Drowned World* from 1962 climate change transforms London into a tropical lagoon. The power of the water is divine and unknowable; when it rises, it can bring fertility and destruction in equal measure.

The dark, dappled waters around Oxford, encroached by lush growth in the summer months, represent the ideal of what an English river should be. In 1806, J. M. W. Turner – who in his thirties developed a passion for sketching and painting on the upper Thames – named his watercolour of the river at Weybridge *Isis*, and included an imagined classical temple on the riverbank, its precise perpendicular columns contrasting with the tangle of tree branches weeping down to the smooth water in the foreground. Turner scholar Andrew Wilton has suggested that this was the artist's attempt to 'imply, if not actually create, an antique landscape' for the river. In Turner's vision, the temple belonged by the river – its sacred purity demanded veneration.

Rivers are often intertwined with ideas of divinity. Throughout history – from the living god of the Ganges and the vengeful droughts of the Nile to Coleridge's 'sacred' Alph and the tokens of the early Christian pilgrims that still surface in English riverbeds today – people have venerated the flow of water from source to sea. It is a metaphor for every stage of life: for birth through baptism, for the confluence of a newly solemnized marriage, for a funeral pyre floating away beyond sight and knowledge. Rivers are central to the ways in which we make sense of ourselves.

Dorothy L. Sayers, author of perhaps the greatest of the so-called Oxford novels, understood precisely how important the river could be in offering a bigger perspective. Her heroine in *Gaudy Night*, crime writer Harriet Vane, returns to her old Oxford college reluctantly to attend a reunion, but is then drawn into staying to help solve a spate of crimes. Whenever Harriet hits a sticky point in her investigations, or when the ghosts of Oxford Past gather too thickly about her, she takes to the river, as if to float or row or bathe is to slip between the shadows of the evening and vanish temporarily into another way of being.

It is to the river that Peter Wimsey, Harriet's sparring partner and detective ally, invites her once the case is solved. By exhorting her to 'send her love to London River' from a bridge in Oxford, he is reminding her that she has places to go beyond the stuffy confines of academia. The balance has tipped; she must continue downriver, to whatever London and the rest of life might hold. As Harriet says herself, 'No one can bathe in the same river twice, not even in the Isis.' Sayers is paraphrasing from the Greek philosopher Heraclitus, and the original continues, 'for other waters are always flowing upon you'. Past versions of ourselves feel very close in Oxford, but it is impossible to go back.

In the same way, the river I plunged into that balmy afternoon is not the same sombre river I watch dwindle and swell with the tides from London Bridge every morning on the way to my office, nor is it the river of my childhood, of wide expanses and secret swatchways at the coast where the sea rushes in. I could jump from the same bank as over a decade ago and still end up just as wet, but I will never hold my friend's hand like that again, both of us gasping at the daring of what we were about to do. Though the Isis carries the particles of memory suspended within its stream, the river of that day is no longer there to be found.

After Oxford, the river makes wide loops through the fields, heading south-east on its way to the ever-growing conurbations of the Thames Valley: Reading, Maidenhead and then, just after the M25 motorway roars overhead, Staines. But before that, it meanders around the Sinodun Hills at Dorchester, where the tributary Thame flows into the Isis, and the joined rivers together are called 'Thames' once more. Rising above the south bank here are two chalk hills known as the Wittenham Clumps. The trees that crowd the southern bank soon give way to a smooth grassy incline up to the two wooded peaks, known as Round Hill and Castle Hill. The beech trees at the summits date back to the 1740s, and they stand up against the horizon in two circular clusters, a clear 200 feet higher than their surroundings.

On a drizzly day in early June, during the heady period between finishing my final exams and leaving Oxford altogether, I took the bus to Dorchester. It dropped me at a stop on the bypass near to where the Thame, which has been dammed and split and cut into different streams over the centuries to power mills and fertilize the gardens of Dorchester Abbey, goes under the road. I walked down the deserted village high street in the early afternoon with the hood of my anorak pulled up, past modern houses and the occasional white-and-black thatched cottage with roses growing at the door. On my left, the timbered lychgate marked where a path forked off towards the abbey, but I kept going south, heading for the river. Eventually the tarmac road gave way to the gravel of Wittenham Lane, a narrow thoroughfare between cottage gardens where I saw just one determined gardener turning over the soggy soil of a vegetable patch in the rain. The lane ended at the water meadows, where a sign told me it was half a mile further to the official Thames Path, along the slightly boggy footpath that skirted the field boundary. I could see the final meanders of the River Thame to my left, just a few hundred yards away at times, the banks dotted with overhanging trees. The rain was coming down harder now, and when I reached the point where the Thame flows into the Thames, the rattling of the drops in the trees on the opposite bank was loud. The dusty scent of summer rain rose in the air and the river looked motionless, pocked with the circular splashes. I walked quickly upriver, following the curve of the Thames until I reached Little Wittenham Bridge, which spans the stream just below Day's Lock, where it divides around Lock House Island. Once across, I took the gentle grassy path up the slope towards the Clumps.

In his youth, the artist Paul Nash made regular visits to this area to see his uncle, who lived in nearby Wallingford. During his stays, he spent time exploring the surrounding countryside, and the Wittenham Clumps made a deep and lasting impression on him. He later described this place as 'a beautiful legendary country haunted by old gods long forgotten' where the Clumps represented 'the pyramids of my small world'. In September 1912 – when he was in his early twenties and fresh from a year of study at the Slade School of Art in London – he captured them for the first time in *The Wood on the Hill*, an inked drawing in which he elongated the trees as they rose from the smooth, cross-hatched hill, a flock of birds taking flight above. He would return to this landscape again and again throughout his life, and among the work he produced as an official war artist in both the First and Second World Wars there are quite a number of Wittenham paintings. As his style developed, he moved away from the neat, accurate drawings of his youth towards something that seems more in line with his feeling that this was a land of legend, rather than of reality. For instance, in a 1935 watercolour entitled *Wittenham*, the grass seems to bulge and undulate, as if the land is in shifting motion before the eyes and there are ancient burials hidden beneath. On the day that I visited, I felt as if I was walking inside this picture. The muted grey-greens and browns of Nash's landscape were all around me and the poor visibility in the rain made it hard to determine the exact curve of the hills. The river was behind me, out of sight, but at times it felt as if the land was flowing too.

Part of what drew Nash to the Clumps was the view from

the summit. Having followed the path up to the famous trees on the skyline, I could see all the way across south Oxfordshire. The Thames Valley was laid out before me, the river glinting despite the dull grey light of the afternoon. The squat chimneys of Didcot Power Station were visible, as was the far-off urban sprawl to the south-east. This is the point of transition, where the ancient, dreaming quality of the Thames in its upper reaches begins to slide out of view. From here on, we enter the area that William Morris lamented as 'cockneyised', in which the division between the country and the city blurs. 'Beyond the Wild Wood comes the wide world,' says Ratty in Kenneth Grahame's *The Wind in the Willows*. Both endanger the sunlit pleasures of life on the river – the wood because of the vulgar stoats and weasels it contains (creatures who in the story's vision of the late nineteenth century represent the rising working classes) and the world because of the existential threat that its expanding cities pose to the countryside. The city feels close here, with London just downstream, yet the rural character of the river is so venerated that newcomers go out of their way to replicate and imitate what they see as the 'true' style of the landscape. In 1865, a builder working on a country house in Medmenham in Buckinghamshire (a picturesque village on the river just downstream of Henley) was asked what he was doing. 'We're renovating the old place, sir,' he replied. 'Making it look more ancient-like.'

Grahame grew up on this stretch of river, at Cookham Dean just above Maidenhead. When he was five, he and his siblings were sent here from Scotland to live with their grandmother after their mother died. To distract the children from their grief, their uncle David introduced them to the pleasures of 'messing about in boats' and Grahame's fixation on the contradictory joys of this part of the Thames was born. Years later, when he lived in London and had his own son, Alastair, it was to the river at Cookham that Grahame's mind returned when inventing bedtime stories. Later, he worked up his tales of Ratty and Mole on the river into a book that I, like so many others, devoured as a child. Rereading it now it is tinged with wistful memories of childhood holidays spent on the water. *The Wind in the Willows* is itself a deeply nostalgic book, harking back to an idealized Victorian version of the river that had vanished by the time Grahame published it in 1908, and perhaps was already receding during his own childhood boating trips in the 1860s. Grahame's fiction was so closely tied to the actual landscape that when E. H. Shepard was commissioned to do new illustrations for a reissue of *The Wind in the Willows* in 1931 he visited the Thames at Pangbourne and drew from life. The author, who had been dissatisfied with previous drawings of Ratty, Mole and co., was delighted by Shepard's playful, exuberant representations of local landmarks.

The 'wide world' is present in Grahame's riverside landscape, whether Ratty likes it or not. The crass Mr Toad is its most obvious manifestation, with his love of new gadgets, fast cars and natty suits. The creek that leads to Toad Hall is marked off with a sign that reads 'Private. No landing allowed' – an indication that the moneyed classes are already restricting access to the river and its landscape. Toad's obsession with 'the open road' is another threat to Grahame's pastoral idyll. The lure of the new hovers at the edge of the story, with all the temptations of 'the whole world before you, and a horizon that's always changing'. The lives of the riverbankers aren't quite so permanent and unchanging as they may seem.

The crowning irony of *The Wind in the Willows* is that Grahame was himself a product of the city he purported to shun. He worked at the Bank of England in London for twenty-nine years, enjoying a successful career that culminated in his tenure as the bank's secretary – at thirty-nine, he was the youngest person yet to attain that senior position. When he and his wife moved back to Cookham in 1908, they were exactly the kind of urban interloper he deplored.

Part of Grahame's – and Morris's – frustration was the river's growing popularity. Their vision of the landscape was a depopulated one; it did not include hordes of day trippers in striped blazers having a rowdy time on the riverbanks. The rapid expansion of the railways out from London in the 1840s and 1850s had taken commercial shipping traffic off the upper reaches of the Thames, and also made it easy for Londoners to make affordable excursions from the city. After 1875, when Joseph Bazalgette's great sewerage system was completed in London, much of the noxious waste that had flowed straight into the river was diverted elsewhere, allowing for a much pleasanter boating environment in the upper Thames. Many Londoners now had more disposable income to spend on trips out of the city too.

The 1880s were a golden age for leisure on the river. On 5 July 1888, the second day of the Henley rowing regatta, the Great Western Railway company recorded that 6,768 people travelled by train from London to attend the event – for the time, an extraordinary movement of people on a single route in just a few hours. As well as the trains, other facilities expanded to accommodate the mania for Thames boating. Inns and hotels grew to meet the demand, and even indulged in a little rebranding exercise to suit the urban clientele who wanted the authentic rural experience. In the Thames-side town of Marlow, five miles upriver from Maidenhead, the old Anglers

Inn adopted the name the Complete Angler to chime with the title of Izaak Walton's popular 1653 fishing treatise, later adopting the book's spelling of 'Compleat' to really make the most of the tourist trade. It's still there, over a hundred years later, because the romance of the upper Thames is just as strong – it's now part of the Macdonald Hotels chain, with four stars and a conference room.

Hiring a boat and spending a day picnicking and punting became the principal activity for most of the visitors to the upper Thames in these years. Boatbuilders were quick to capitalize on the interest, turning out skiffs, punts, houseboats and all manner of recreational craft to meet the demand. Salter's of Oxford was one of the most influential, quickly pivoting away from creating racing craft for the Oxford versus Cambridge university boat race into equipping steamers and 'tent boats' aimed at the leisure market. By the late 1880s, this one company had a fleet of 900 boats for hire and was running regular passenger steamers between Oxford and London for those who would rather take their day trip by water than by rail.

In his autobiography *English Hours*, Henry James recalled the mania of Londoners for the upper Thames. 'If the river is the busiest suburb of London it is also by far the prettiest,' he wrote in 1888. There is a sense during this period, from the early 1880s until the outbreak of the First World War, that the city was colonizing the country, as more and more Londoners moved upstream. Before long, an entire publication industry sprang up to cater for this new river-dwelling suburb. It had its own newspapers, like *The Lock to Lock Times* and *The Thames*, which documented life on the river and carried advertisements for Thames-related services. An array of new maps was produced for day trippers too, specifically designed for oarsmen, anglers and punters.

Jerome K. Jerome's comic travelogue *Three Men in a Boat*, which first appeared in 1889, captured the spirit of this age. It relates a fictionalized trip that the author took with two 'overworked' London friends up the Thames from Kingston to Oxford. Critics deplored it as vulgar, but it was an instant best-seller among a reading public who no doubt recognized many of the incidents the book described – from the party's mishaps with campfire cooking and laundering clothes in the Thames to the dubious pleasures of nature for these city-dwelling fellows. Such was its runaway popularity that Jerome's publisher once commented, 'I cannot imagine what becomes of all the copies of that book I issue. I often think the public must eat them.' For all the book's absurd comic flourishes, Jerome captures the moods of the Thames better than almost any other writer of the period: it is both the 'golden fairy stream' that goes 'glinting through the dark, cool wood paths, chasing shadows o'er the shallows, flinging diamonds from the mill-wheels, throwing kisses to the lilies' and also, in adverse weather, 'a spirit-haunted water through the land of vain regrets'.

As with Grahame's Ratty, the likes of Jerome and his friends were drawn to the upper Thames as a form of escapism, a chance to leave behind the smog and smut and toil of life in London and splash around the willow-shaded banks of the river. As Henry James observed, 'There is something almost droll and at the same time touching in the way that on the smallest pretext of holiday or fine weather the mighty population takes to the boats,' he wrote. The fact that thousands of others had the same idea barely seemed to deter them. 'They bump each other in the narrow, charming channel; between Oxford and Richmond they make an uninterrupted procession.'

Whereas London was a hierarchical city, with unwritten rules about who belonged where – the wealthy in the West

End, the poor in the East End and so forth – the new popularity of boating on the upper Thames had a levelling effect. Nowhere is this more apparent than in Edward John Gregory's painting *Boulter's Lock, Sunday Afternoon*, which the artist began work on in 1882 and eventually exhibited at the Royal Academy in 1897. It depicts a hectic moment on the river above Maidenhead (just around the corner from Gregory's own residence at Great Marlow), with a dozen different boating parties trying to enter the lock at the same time. Although Gregory put himself in the picture in a punt over to the far right of the composition, the viewer sees the scene from a different perspective, looking straight upriver from high above the water.

We look down upon a complete cross-section of society on the water: a 'new woman' to the left asserting her independence by paddling her canoe alone; a lady in the foreground dressed in the high fashion of the 1880s tending to a lapdog while an unseen partner rows a luxuriously upholstered boat; a rowing boat crammed with a large, mixed party in light summer frocks and shirtsleeves; a steam launch with a rather more staid group on board; and plenty of others. Chaos reigns, sails billowing and oars everywhere. Standing in front of the painting, I can almost hear the splashing and shouting as everyone tries to keep their boats afloat and their clothes dry. Yet more spectators are gathered on the bridge over the lock itself – coming here by land just to watch the boats go past was a popular activity, with the promise that a celebrity like the Prince of Wales or the singer Nellie Melba would be glimpsed on the water, heading to a party at one of the grand houses on the banks of the upper Thames. In the far background of Gregory's painting is a sunlit rural vista, the trees of the Cliveden escarpment hinting at the fields and meadows beyond. So true to life was this kind of scene that when it was exhibited in 1897, *The Art Journal* wrote that 'it is in fact the three-volume novel in art, the guidebook and encyclopaedia of the manners and customs of the English people'. Gregory captured a moment in the life of the river, where the city floated temporarily upstream and took possession of the landscape.

As the river leaves the last of its water meadows behind, London begins to make its presence felt, even though it is still miles away. It wasn't until I moved to the city myself that I began to understand this. I knew places on this part of the river, such as Windsor or Eton, for what they represented, for their symbolic heft at the heart of the British Establishment. But I had not appreciated how close they were to the capital and how tied to its power. Then one afternoon about a year after I graduated, travelling back to London after a weekend with friends in Oxford, I experienced the kind of public transport disaster that can only occur in Britain on a Sunday. Multiple train and track failures had me criss-crossing the Thames Valley on rail-replacement buses and slow stopping-train services. I finally boarded a crowded train at Reading that was bound for Waterloo, only for it to inch along the line, crossing the Thames and looping south, and then rejoining the river to enter the city alongside it, via Twickenham, Richmond, Sheen and Putney.

In the early twentieth century, Skindles Hotel in Maidenhead became infamous as a place for dirty weekends and adulterous assignations. The reason for this was almost entirely logistical: it could be reached in just a few hours' drive up the Thames Valley from London, yet the town's riverside Edwardian charms made it seem remote enough from the capital for powerful people to feel safe from observation or discovery. As my train chugged slowly along the river, I grasped how long this combination of physical proximity and mental distance had been influencing this part of the Thames landscape. Take Windsor Castle, a strategic and political location chosen by the Normans after the 1066 invasion. They already had a fortress in the city, the Tower of London, but to entrench and extend their influence over the whole of the Thames Valley, they needed a second position of strength from which to resupply a military force in the event that they had to defend their territory against an uprising. A castle at Windsor gave them command of the river upstream of London, while the Tower guarded the area downstream. If necessary, they could blockade the river in both directions, yet by positioning the second fortress out of sight of the city, they avoided the appearance of a heavy military presence in what was meant to be a time of peace.

This near-and-far aspect of the Thames to the west of London has developed and deepened the associations between the river and ideas of political power and identity. One of the most significant products of it is the Magna Carta, the peace accord between the unpopular King John and his rebellious nobles agreed at Runnymede on the Thames on 15 June 1215, which subsequently became a potent symbol of British democracy and nationhood. The faction of discontented barons and landowners, unhappy with the king's authoritarian rule and frequent tax levies to pay for unsuccessful wars in France, raised their own military force and took control of the city of London at the start of 1215. King John's own forces were garrisoned at Windsor Castle. When the time came to negotiate an end to the stand-off, the water meadows by the Thames at Runnymede were chosen as a neutral, safe meeting place. The king could approach from Windsor in the west, the rebel barons from the Tower of London in the east. The area by the river was flat, giving neither side an advantage should the talks turn into a military skirmish. The surrounding marshy ground and water would prevent other forces from intervening to interrupt the discussions. There is some doubt about the precise spot upon which the king stood when he affixed his seal to the charter – some argue for the riverbank, others for the small island in the Thames at this point now known as Magna Carta Island – but there is no doubt that Runnymede was the location.

Nobody present that day could have known how consequential the meeting would prove to be. The provisions of the accord signed were wide-ranging and often unenforceable, and historians have disputed for centuries whether it had much immediate impact on the practical governance of the realm. However, the symbolic resonance of what happened was profound: the image of a monarch brought to heel by his subjects in the interests of justice and liberty echoed down the generations, influencing political thinkers from Oliver Cromwell through to Thomas Paine and George Washington. The Magna Carta resurfaced in the seventeenth century during the so-called Glorious Revolution of 1688, when the Stuarts and their notion of the 'divine right of kings' needed limiting. And again in the nineteenth century, when there were anti-monarchist revolutions across Europe, it was the Magna Carta that framed the debate in England. Such was its popularity that in 1834 a stone was placed inside the small Gothic cottage erected on Magna Carta Island to commemorate the great events of 1215. The imagined spectacle of the medieval barons and the king meeting on the banks of the River Thames had become more widely known and influential than the actual contents of the document signed that day. To think of Magna Carta is to think of the river, where 'the great cornerstone in England's temple of liberty was firmly laid', as Jerome K. Jerome put it.

Although the location has shifted a few miles downriver, from Runnymede to Westminster, the relationship between the Thames and the seat of political power is just as strong today. The riverside view of the Palace of Westminster has become associated with fundamental ideas about Britishness and democracy. The buildings themselves sit on land that was reclaimed from the Thames in the 1830s, after the fire that devastated the medieval palace in 1834 allowed for a great rebuilding project. Architects Charles Barry and Augustus Pugin worked in the resurgent neo-Gothic style of the time, its roots in the medievalist reaction against industrialization typified by the work of those like William Morris. And just as Morris would later use the river to travel between his residences, Pugin used to arrive to inspect the work at the Westminster building site by boat from his house on the coast at Ramsgate – until the railway reached the Kentish coast in 1846, he felt it to be the most efficient way to travel into central London. In its design, the new Palace of Westminster harks upstream, to Runnymede and beyond, to the simple purity of the upper Thames, while the river flows past and out to the rest of the world. The building as we know it today, the iconic image used in countless postcards and news reports, is inseparable from the river. It has long been synonymous with British victory and triumphs too. The week that the First World War ended in 1918, *The Tablet* published a report that stated, 'It is confidently anticipated that specimens of the U-boats will soon be towed up the Thames and moored opposite the Houses of Parliament, and then exhibited to make a London holiday.' It never happened, but its emergence as an idea just after Armistice Day is suggestive of the associations between the river and political might. Had the U-boats really been brought into London, it would have been a modern twist on an old image: the vanquished brought in chains to the victor's seat of power.

This stretch of the Thames is home to other power bases

too, from the great state institutions like the Ministry of
Defence and the intelligence centres at MI5 and MI6 to the
most expensive luxury apartments. Even when the views
aren't up to much (as in the case of the ongoing conversion of
Battersea Power Station into accommodation and offices) the
river conveys prestige. The Thames is the embodiment of
London as a city: powerful, historic, outward-looking.

At Hammersmith, the Thames experiences another moment
of transition. As the river makes its final approach to London,
it doesn't lose its rural aspect all at once, but rather sheds it by
degrees. After the last pastoral vistas offered by the riverside
stretches of the Royal Botanic Gardens at Kew, warehouses
begin to appear on both banks. There are still willow trees
here and there, and the river still seems calm and clean compared to its muddy, commercial character downstream, but the
'cockneyised' influence that William Morris so despised is well
in evidence. The industrial might of London arrived here in
the nineteenth century, with factory owners and speculators
buying up the market gardens and farmland that had previously
covered the banks. From the river, the most recognizable of
these is the strawberry-red brick edifice of what used to be
the Harrods Furniture Depository. It was originally built as a
soap factory upon what used to be 'one huge smiling garden
of flowers and fruit and grass and corn' and was converted into
a sugar refinery before reopening as the department store's
furniture warehouse in 1894. Four thousand people attended
the reopening.

Today, all of these buildings have been repurposed. In the
age of out-of-town distribution centres and global manufacture,
this prime riverside property has long since been redeveloped

into townhouses and penthouse suites – the Harrods Furniture Depository is now a luxury apartment complex called Harrods Village. In some places, though, there has been an attempt to return the riverbank to something like its former existence, as in the case of the former Barn Elms Waterworks, which is now the London Wetland Centre. The four reservoirs built alongside the Thames in the nineteenth century have been converted into habitats for a huge variety of wildlife, including over 180 species of birds, water voles, butterflies, moths and bats. Even so close to the crowded confines of London, it's a reminder of the space that used to exist here – the lakes, reed beds and water meadows occupy 100 acres of land, just inside the loop of the Thames as it flows past Hammersmith and Barnes.

For a long time, these inner western parts of the Thames were completely alien to me. I had only experienced Putney as a tourist would, getting off the train with hundreds of others to crowd onto the teeming towpath for the Oxford versus Cambridge boat race. My perception of the place was as the stomping ground for pink-trousered Hoorays, and I dismissed it as barely worthy of exploration. I found nothing of the Thames I knew elsewhere here. But then, looking through a book of late-nineteenth-century photographs of the Thames, I found the most extraordinary picture. Taken by Henry Taunt in 1875 from the south bank of the river at Putney, it shows the old wooden bridge, which a decade later was rebuilt in granite. In the foreground, there are a few of the typical narrow, pointed rowing boats of the period drawn up to the gently sloping, muddy bank, and on the north bank opposite it's just possible to make out a few of the buildings in Fulham. The part of the picture that I found so arresting, though, was the water. Taunt supposedly took the photograph at dawn on an extremely still day, using a very long exposure. The river's surface is absolutely

clear, as perfect as a polished silver mirror, but because of the slight blurring caused by the gentle motion of the boats and their reflections, it also feels as if the water is moving before your eyes.

In Taunt's photograph, the Thames at Putney has something of the countrified charm of Kemble and Cricklade – the rickety-looking wooden bridge, despite its length, could easily be in a tiny village rather than on the outskirts of a vast city. Yet the silvery water reminded me strongly of the estuary and of the flat calms I've experienced there when the wind drops to nothing and everything seems to hold its breath. In this picture, the different characters of the river come together, and I began to understand a little of why the river in west London is such a popular place for walking, rowing and dawdling.

The discovery of this picture also led me to a greater appreciation of the role that the Thames played in the beginnings of landscape photography. Henry Taunt, in particular, was a pioneer in the field, and some of his best work helped to shape how the river above London was perceived in the late nineteenth century. Born in Oxford in 1842, the son of a plumber, he was sent out to work at the age of ten. At fourteen, the young Henry got a job as an assistant to a photographer on the High Street, working long days in the cramped premises, helping to pose and then develop stern Victorian portraits. In his free time, the teenager liked to go down to the river and hone his skills by taking pictures out of doors. Over the Christmas holiday in 1859, he took a solo trip on an outrigged dinghy from Oxford to Cricklade and back, the first of many water-based photography tours. Taunt proved to be remarkably skilled at the difficult art of outdoor photography and some of his best pictures were taken on the Thames in the early 1860s.

Henry Taunt loved the river. Capturing it with his camera was very difficult, though – especially given how new and clunky photographic technology was when he was working. He used the wet collodion process, which required him to carry bottles of chemicals to sensitize his glass plate and also a dark tent to develop and fix his photographs immediately after taking them. He would row his skiff to the spot from which he wanted to shoot, take his picture, head back to the tent he had already set up on the bank to develop it, wash the prints in river water, and then move to his next location. In later years, he had his own houseboat with a tripod mounted on the roof to give him greater stability when taking photographs and assistants to do the developing, but in his early twenties, when many of his most atmospheric pictures were taken, he worked alone and perched in a small punt. The balance in his compositions is always superb – whether his subject is a Thames barge or a haystack, it's always in the right part of the picture to give the best effect – but what I find so compelling about his photographs is the sense of arrested motion. It always looks as if something has just happened, like a barge taking down her great expanse of sail, or is about to happen, like a woman caught on the point of stepping into a punt or a man just about to jump off a stile by the riverbank.

Taunt was photographing the upper Thames at a crucial moment, when many of its ancient working features, such as the weirs, the ferries and the mills, were being swept away in favour of amenities for pleasure boats and day trippers. In 1872, he published the first edition of his *New Map of the River Thames*, which included thirty-three hand-coloured maps and was illustrated with dozens of his own photographs. It was hugely popular, and it has been argued that Taunt's book was instrumental in popularizing the river's landscape with visitors and had a great influence over the likes of Jerome K. Jerome. Without Taunt's tranquil, attractive pictures, the idea of the Thames landscape as a worthy subject for the difficult and expensive art of photography would probably not have existed.

The free-flowing, easy atmosphere in Putney and Barnes that Taunt's pictures taught me to appreciate disappears once the Thames reaches central London. As the river flows past the famous landmarks, there is a solemn solidity about it, making it easy to think that it's always looked this way, the Palace of Westminster rising austerely from the north bank in a great mass of crenellations and turrets. In fact, London's river as we know it today is a mid-nineteenth-century creation, transformed by the two great embankments that run along both banks in the city centre. They feel solid and permanent, as if they have always been there – Londoners walk, cycle and drive along them every day – but they are relatively recent additions to the river's environs. The embankments were designed by the civil engineer Joseph Bazalgette as a key part of his sewer improvement scheme, long-needed but finally constructed after the so-called 'Great Stink' of 1858, when the sheer amount of debris and sewage in the river became a crisis that politicians could no longer ignore. The building of the embankments required huge amounts of land reclamation and vast quantities of cement and granite – it was estimated that an additional thirty-seven acres of land were created by narrowing the river and backfilling along its banks. By the time the embankment on the northern side was formally opened in 1870, complete with intercepting sewer beneath and road on top, this new hard edge to the river stretched from Battersea Bridge all the way to Blackfriars.

Where Northumberland Avenue meets the Victoria Embankment there is a memorial to Bazalgette, erected after his death in 1891. The Latin inscription on it, '*Flumini vincula posuit*', means 'He put the river in chains.' Whenever I see the swift motion of the river in the city – the rapid flood as the tide leaves, creating murky whirlpools and eddies around the bridge supports – I think about the way the embankments hem the water in, forcing it to flow faster through a narrower space. The rising tide can no longer filter up the gradual incline of the foreshore over many hours; it now appears to move only vertically, up and down the green-weeded granite walls. There were many advantages to building the embankments, including improvements to sanitation thanks to the new sewers they contained and the creation of green spaces like Embankment Gardens at the very heart of the built-up city. To the Victorian innovators behind this great infrastructure project, it was a triumph of progress and modernity.

Yet by reinforcing and expanding the bank, a part of the
river's changeable, impermanent sensibility was lost. The soft
mud was replaced with hard stone, and a distance was created between the people on the shore and the water beneath.
A whole world had existed in the few yards of land that lay
between high and low tide, a strand of existence that was obliterated when the embankments were built. I've long tried to piece
together the remnants of this life. Again, it was a photograph
that first got me interested – a view of the foreshore in Lambeth
taken by William Strudwick in 1865, shortly before the Albert
Embankment was constructed. It shows the houses in Fore
Street where they backed on to the river and it is apparent from
the picture that the river played a vital role in the lives of those
who lived there. The back walls of many of the buildings have
ladders down to the foreshore, and some have actually been
extended outwards with wooden platforms so that residents can
step straight out onto a jetty. Small wooden boats are drawn up
on the muddy beach and a group of men are resting, seated on a
wherry, talking up to someone leaning over a low wooden fence
at the back of a house. Many of the others in the row don't even
have fences – their yards just end at the river. Conrad wrote that
seeing ships lying moored in the older docks of London made
him think of 'a flock of swans kept in the flooded backyard of
grim tenement houses'; looking at Strudwick's photographs, I
could see what he meant.

Strudwick was one of a handful of photographers who
sought to capture the banks of the Thames before they
disappeared under the embankments. He was particularly
interested in the small businesses that relied on the easy transition between land and water, especially boatbuilders. One
of his best-known surviving photographs, now in a collection
held by the Borough of Lambeth, shows a group of craftsmen

on a wooden platform built out the back of a Thames-side shop. They're leaning on a pile of planks and the partially completed frames of several boats are visible below them, pulled up on the foreshore. Above, a painted sign reads 'R. Bain, Mast, Oar, Scull and Pump Maker'. Bain's premises were demolished to make way for the Albert Embankment, and a sense of this easy, symbiotic relationship between the river and the people who lived and worked alongside it vanished. The American artist James Whistler was similarly fascinated by this 'wharfinger' life, publishing a series of etchings in 1869 known as the 'Thames set'. In one, *The Lime Burner*, the titular figure leans against a stack of barrels, framed by a number of rickety wooden structures created from dense cross-hatching. At the very back, there is a glimpse of the river and the opposite bank. The first time I saw this picture hung in a gallery, I instinctively stooped as I looked at it, as if I was about to duck under the outer lintel and wander down the foreshore. Whistler painted extraordinary, almost abstract seascapes on the Thames too, working the low-lying fogs into billows of lavender-tinged magnificence. But his etchings have a similar sensibility to Strudwick's photographs, born out of a desire to capture the essence of the river in as much detail as possible.

Before the embankments, central London was full of ways to access the river. The grand houses and palaces on the banks had their own water gates to allow residents to quickly and privately board their water taxis and barges. Only one of these survives – the water gate for York House, built in 1625 and now stranded 1,500 yards away from the river in the Embankment Gardens. For the general public, there were the watermen's stairs, which allowed easy embarkation into water taxis from the many roads and alleyways which ended at the riverbank. Samuel Pepys's diaries from the 1660s are full of references to him 'taking water' at the stairs in the vicinity of the City, from where he would travel by barge or water taxi to Greenwich, Deptford or Chatham, where his work as a navy administrator required him to inspect the ships and dockyards. The embankments put a distance between people and the river – they blocked off the roads that used to run down to the water and drastically reduced the number of access points for boats. That easy transition, where someone could step out of their house, onto the foreshore and then into a wherry, was gone.

There are still ways down to the water, some in plain sight and others hidden. About a dozen of the old stairs survive, and there are new ladders and concrete blocks, largely unguarded or regulated. When I arrived in London from Oxford, a clueless graduate struggling to start a career in journalism just months after the 2008 financial crisis, I once again turned to the river to help with my homesickness. I soon discovered that there is no greater joy to be had in the city than pacing the strand at dawn, watching the light and the tide filter towards you in harness. Once down near the water, my eyes would adjust to a whole new colour palette: the greys of the water – pearly, metallic, silvery, slate – and the browns of the mud – dun, tawny, umber, coppery. At every low tide, a vast expanse of sand, mud and pebble is exposed on the riverbanks and on it lie the lives of Londoners past, waiting to be picked over. How could you not spend the dawn and twilight hours sliding down slimy steps to the mud, a time traveller armed with a plastic carrier bag and a flask of tea? This was the river I had lived beside my whole life, but in a new and magisterial guise. It was only right that I should devote my free time to wiping the ooze off its mysteries.

It took me a long time to align my sense of the river's geography – gathered from the many times we had sailed in from the estuary and moored in my parents' old home of St Katharine Docks – with the life of a land-based Londoner. The city's dwellers can be prone to think of the river as a barrier, a dividing line between the north and south crossed with difficulty – hence the black cab driver's immortal refrain, 'I don't go south of the river this time of night, love.' In a 1974 study by the architectural psychologist David Canter designed to test Londoners' internal sense of place, researchers asked subjects to estimate the distance between two points as the crow flies, some across the Thames and some on the same side. The ones spanning the river were by far the most overestimated. The curve of the extreme meanders in central London confused matters (another experiment that asked strangers to the city to draw sketch maps at intervals during an extended stay in London shows the fascinating evolution of the Thames from a straight line to a wavy one, to an approximation of its actual shape), but the river was also a significant psychological barrier.

Tower Bridge had always been my centre of gravity, because it represented both the last navigable point on the Thames for a boat with a mast as high as ours and where you turned right to enter the lock for St Katharine's – a place I have always considered a home away from home. And it had long been an important family landmark. At the end of my parents' first journey into London from the estuary, my mother took a wonky photograph of the bridge from the foredeck, the tops of the two towers faded out by fog. It hangs at the bottom of the stairs in their house still, the final frame in a sequence that tells the story of their sea voyage to Britain. Further up is a photograph of the parts for their first boat being delivered in South Africa before they built her, another of my mother proudly holding up a plate of hot-cross buns she had baked from scratch while at sea, the vast expanse of the Atlantic visible over her right shoulder, and others of their various adventures exploring the British coast after their arrival. Then, Tower Bridge: an image of their new home.

All the time I was planning this journey down the Thames, through the estuary and out to the sea, I had this photograph in my mind. Tower Bridge signalled my parents' arrival; now it would be my point of departure. I wanted to continue the story. One Saturday afternoon, I went to see the exhibition that is housed in one of the bridge's two towers. I wasn't there to learn about the history of its hydraulic engines, however. I rushed past the exhibits to the real reason for my visit – the walkway across the top, which runs forty metres above the road below. I walked to the middle and found a spot at the rail, among the tourists taking pictures of the view, and looked east. From this vantage point, I could see the curve of the river towards the Isle of Dogs, the Canary Wharf skyscrapers just visible in the haze. I imagined that I could see all the way down the river's twists and turns to the estuary and the sea, my mind's eye racing the tide out of the city.

Before I left, I looked down at the water immediately below the bridge and experienced one of those strange moments on the Thames where different layers of time seem to slide apart for a second. I saw the grey water churn beneath the bow of a familiar white sailing boat, a young woman balancing with difficulty on the heaving foredeck, holding a camera. As I watched, she took her picture and climbed back around the mast and into the safety of the cockpit again.

2

Upper Pool to Cuckold's Point

The day of my journey down the river to the estuary, I woke up early. When I checked my phone, I found a string of text messages from my mother, sent overnight at roughly two-hourly intervals. My parents had sailed to London from the north Kent coast the night before, letting the incoming tide carry them through the estuary and up the Thames. Mobile phone coverage often extends a surprising distance offshore. As long as the boat's course skirts the coast, it is usually possible to stay in touch. There on my screen was a litany of landmarks, passed in the dark while I was sleeping, sent to reassure me of their progress and safety. Broadstairs, Tankerton, Sheerness, Grain, Hoo, Gravesend, Erith, Woolwich, Greenwich, and then into the city itself. I was to meet them at the new marina in the old Limehouse Dock, where they had found a berth to tie up and sleep for the rest of the night.

I packed a rucksack full of extra jumpers and woolly socks, shoving the tin of rock cakes I had made the night before on top. My memories of sailing on the estuary on a breezy spring day all involve wearing about twelve layers of clothing and eating stodgy food, so I thought it best to be prepared. I left my room near London Bridge and walked north. When I paused halfway across the bridge to take in the view to the east – louring grey clouds behind Tower Bridge and the water beneath bubbling like a thick pea soup – there were only a few boats to be seen on the river. A Thames Clipper passenger boat heading for Greenwich was just docking at the London Bridge City Pier, and the naval museum ship HMS *Belfast* was anchored, as usual, near the south bank by City Hall. A mixture of glass-covered restaurant and hospitality boats were rafted up on buoys by the north bank and a small motor launch bearing the orange coastguard insignia was just disappearing from sight under Tower Bridge. It was early enough to be relatively quiet, with only a few other pedestrians about, and I stood there for a while and looked at the watery space spread out before me.

In George Borrow's 1851 novel *Lavengro*, his wandering protagonist also pauses on London Bridge to take in the scene. Unlike me, he saw 'a forest of masts, thick and close, as far as the eye could reach' and 'spacious wharfs, surmounted with gigantic edifices'. The peaceful, almost lethargic tempo of life on the river that I observed is recent. The Pool of London, as the area of water stretching from London Bridge down to just below Limehouse is known, was for centuries one of the busiest shipping lanes in the world. And it was that way for a long time: in the year 1381, it is estimated that over a thousand ships came through the drawbridge in the old London Bridge. Centuries later, in 1724, when Daniel Defoe was writing *A Tour Through the Whole Island of Great Britain*, out of curiosity he tried to count all of the ships in the Pool himself one afternoon, and found 'above Two thousand Sail of all Sorts, not reckoning Barges, Lighters or Pleasure-Boats, and Yachts; but of Vessels that really go to Sea'. I repeated this exercise for myself and made it to seventeen.

There has been a port of some kind here ever since the Romans arrived in the first century AD and built a bridge across the (then much wider) Thames at the first suitable high ground inland from the sea – a site very close to today's London Bridge. A seam of gravel in the London clay here provided a suitable ford and a slight rise in the banks on either side of the river eased the construction of this first crossing. The selection of this site as London's meeting point between road and river was an immediate and lasting success, and the city grew up around the Thames. As early as the eighth century, the Venerable Bede recorded that London was 'the mart of many nations resorting to it by sea and land'. Every subsequent wave of occupants of the city, from the Saxons through to the Victorians, made use of the river to rapidly bring in goods for trade and manufacture. Standing on London Bridge in what my mother would call 'a bit of a *dwaal*' (an Afrikaans word meaning a dreamy, befuddled moment when your mind temporarily vanishes elsewhere), I tried to imagine the creaking and heaving, the yelling and splashing that would once have filled this part of the river. It was said that, at its busiest moments, it was possible to walk from one side of the river to the other just by hopping from deck to deck. It would have been a city within a city, an urban area created from a floating mass of ships rafted up in the river, awaiting their turn to unload.

I shook off my daydream and continued to walk across the bridge. I went underground near Bank and boarded an east-bound DLR train. Soon after departing the station, the box-like carriages shoot up a steep ramp and continue above ground on a track that runs just above the roofs of houses and shops. The Docklands were spread out all around me, the mixture of buildings formerly used as warehouses and dock offices now mingling in with new skyscrapers, residential developments, council estates and the run-of-the-mill corner shops and betting shops found anywhere in the UK. The first section of the Docklands Light Railway opened in 1987, part of attempts in the 1980s and 1990s to find a new purpose for this area as the docks in the Pool closed in favour of the bigger, more modern ports being built downstream in the estuary. It was partly adapted from existing railway viaducts and tracks that used to bring in goods from the docks which had fallen into disuse. Since the 1990s, the character of this part of the Thames's bank has changed completely – the great glass edifice of the financial centre at Canary Wharf looms ahead and luxury flats, entertainment complexes and gyms have filled up much of the space left by the docks. The map of the DLR network on the wall of the train carriage shows the extent to which the river and the ships that sailed on it used to dominate. Almost every single station has a name connected with London's old port enterprise, from Custom House to West India Quay, Royal Victoria to Pontoon Dock.

I got off the train after just one stop, at Shadwell. My parents were waiting for me on the boat a little further downriver, but before we set off for the estuary I wanted to visit their old home. A few minutes' brisk walk under railway arches and down narrow side streets brought me out by Tower Bridge, and I was soon following an old-remembered path towards the river and St Katharine Docks. It is as familiar to me as a much-loved home from childhood. The yellowed brick of the warehouses that encircle the two basins looks much as it did when I was waking up here twenty-five years ago. Although the swirling tidal energy of the river is just on the other side of the lock gate, the water here is smooth and unruffled. Conrad described it as 'lying overshadowed and black like a quiet pool amongst rocky crags' and it still has that appearance, of an improbable patch of water surrounded by stone.

The boats docked here now are leisure craft: motorboats, some huge and glamorous, others small and serviceable; yachts bearing lettering that indicates home ports on the English and Dutch coasts; narrowboats with pot plants on the roof and smoke just beginning to stream from their chimneys; and great wooden Thames barges. These last, once-ubiquitous boats were designed to be perfectly suited to the conditions in the estuary, with flat bottoms that allowed them to skim across the mud in very little water at low tide, masts that could easily be lowered to get under bridges and large sails that could be hoisted and trimmed by a very small crew. Famously, they could be operated by just a man, a boy and a dog, making them a very cheap and efficient means of moving cargo like bricks made in north Kent up to London. In the early twentieth century, over 2,000 barges were registered and in use on the Thames, their russet-coloured sails providing an oft-admired splash of colour against the customary greyness of the estuary. But by 1954 only 160 were still trading, as the demise of the docks in the Pool hit all the professions associated with inner London shipping. After that, improved road and rail links in the outer estuary took the cargo instead. On this particular weekend a small, informal barge rally had converged on St Katharine's, flags and pennants flying, and visitors climbed aboard to learn about the boats' past lives. All these vessels have been preserved and restored from their heyday a hundred years ago, floating reconstructions of a working life that has now died out.

Once, it was a hive of activity – 40 per cent of Britain's entire wool trade passed across these wharves, and workers once unloaded 35,000 tons of tea from China, India and Ceylon in a single year. The two dock basins are deep – nine yards down from the surface of the water in places – and cover an area of around twenty-five acres, squeezed into the north

bank of the river alongside the Tower of London and Tower
Bridge. When they were built in the early nineteenth century,
excavating such a large area was a big technical undertaking: a
visiting Swedish engineer, Captain A. G. Carlsund, writing
a decade later of what he observed during the construction,
reported that he 'frequently witnessed a thousand men and
several hundreds of horses employed in the operations,
besides several powerful steam-engines'. Soon after they
opened for business in October 1828, the proprietors were
boasting of the efficiency they provided, claiming that cargoes
could be transferred from ship to warehouse in one fifth of the
time it took in other docks and on the river itself. Aside from
a few surviving bollards on the quay that the great trading
ships would have used to moor, there's little trace of all this
industry now. St Katharine's is a tranquil, vacant-feeling place.
People either leave their boats empty here, locked up safely so
conveniently close to the centre of London, or disappear into
the privacy of the cabins below decks. The glass fronts of the
new flats and offices built here in the past few decades reflect
the light, making it impossible to tell if anyone is actually
inside. Tourists and a few curious Londoners wander past on
the wharves, but very little happens here to disturb the peace.

For a long time, St Katharine's was my focal point in London.
The docks were a home from home. When we sailed up the
Thames, this was our destination. Like the great trading ships
from centuries before, we would wait for the tide in the estuary and allow it to carry us upriver to the city and the docks.
Sometimes, we would leave our mooring late at night to catch a
double tide: that is, allow the ebb to take us out of the Medway
and then, just as it turned at low water, catch the flood rushing

up the Thames to London. If done right, this trick feels like a watery sort of sorcery – hour after hour of extra speed, long after your inner rhythm tells you the tide should have turned against you, the very water the boat is ploughing through also moving as one piece in the direction we wanted to go. My father has a decades-old atlas of British tidal streams that he still uses to make the calculations for this manoeuvre. Like a flip book, each page shows the same coastline at different stages of the tide, larger or smaller arrows in the water indicating its direction and strength. Flicked through quickly, the arrows move like the water, rushing in and out of the river. Used in conjunction with the latest tide tables, you can work out when to set off in order to maximize the amount of time the tide will be with you, rather than against you – essential in the Thames estuary, where the tide flows very fast (up to 4.5 knots on a fast spring) and where narrow channels through sandbanks, such as Fisherman's Gat through Long Sand, are more dangerous to navigate with a strong stream against the direction of travel.

Riding the tides, we would often arrive in the Thames's inner London reaches at strange times of day, such as very early in the morning or after dark. No matter what time it was, I would climb out of my bunk to sit on deck and observe city life on the riverbank. In the early 1990s, the run-down warehouses on the old quays were being transformed by developers into expensive riverside flats. At dawn I would see a solo woman in neon Lycra emerge from a converted grain store to jog along the river path – an alien activity to me, as nobody I knew exercised like this in our village in north Kent. We would keep pace with the runner for a while, gliding on the water as she bobbed up and down on the shore, before we eventually eased ahead and around the next bend in the river. At night, the small number of lighted windows would show how few people had actually moved into the former inner-dock areas. Occasionally, black cabs would pull up and discharge a group of revellers loud enough to be heard on the water. I would watch, unseen, the lights wavering on the water as we slid past.

Ten years before, when my parents made their first journey up the Thames, the riverbanks looked very different. Everything was derelict, my father remembers, with warehouse buildings unoccupied and falling down, broken windows everywhere, old cranes teetering on the unkempt wharves and the wooden structures of old piers decaying into the water. It was a melancholy vista of a formerly hectic and purposeful place. Even when I was very small, I remember the constant worry that the debris continually flaking away from the docks' structures would hit the boat. I was often stationed on the foredeck, a long-handled boat hook in hand, with instructions to repel the chunks of wood and tangles of rope that floated past us before they hit the hull. This flotsam would bob jauntily on the surface of the water, disappearing between waves and then emerging again, shockingly close. I used to grip the hook's handle tightly and thrust downwards, sometimes torn between disgust at the mess in the river and a child's curious desire to bring things aboard for examination. Once, when there was something that looked like an intact wooden chest rolling alongside us, my mother had to seize the back of my jumper to stop me tumbling overboard in my strenuous efforts to flip open its lid and see what treasure was concealed inside. Resentfully, I watched it spin away in the boat's eddying wake, destined to float out to the estuary and the sea beyond, secret safe inside.

As I grew up, so did London's derelict docks. On later trips, I observed the gradual transformation from disuse to luxury that was taking place on the river's banks. I was unaware at the time of the political dimension to all this redevelopment, although I did indulge in a childish sadness that the interesting, improbable shapes of the grasses that sometimes grew out of the sides of the old warehouses were disappearing, replaced by shiny new glass frontages. The major Docklands regeneration on the Isle of Dogs, where high-rise buildings like Canary Wharf sprouted in the middle of East End neighbourhoods that had lost their livelihoods, was headline news. The smaller, incremental changes to the abandoned inner docks happened more quietly. The relationship between the land and the water was changing before my eyes, and a long chapter of the Thames's history was coming to a close.

The site of St Katharine Docks had been designed to keep goods safely inside and undesirable people outside. At ground level on the dockside is a series of elegant brick archways, a little like an Italian *loggia*. The warehouses rise up from this, windows facing towards the water and ridged detailing in the bricks near the top storey. The design is open and practical, intended to facilitate the quick transfer of cargo and keep goods dry and well ventilated. There are no gaps between the warehouses, nor are there exterior windows. Once the high gate that led from the road into the docks was closed, the whole place became a fortress and it would have been virtually impossible to enter. Whereas today the docks are open to the public, both on foot and by water, when they were built in the early nineteenth century this was the site of a jealously guarded private enterprise.

In the late eighteenth century, crime on the water in the Pool was rife. Entire cargoes would go missing from ships that had anchored in the middle of the river, awaiting space at one of the wharves along the banks. The move to dig enclosed docks in the river's banks only started in the late 1790s; until then all commercial traffic stayed in the Thames itself, as it had done for centuries prior. The system of docking was devised by a piece of Elizabethan legislation that designated twenty so-called 'legal quays' close to the Customs House just to the east of the Monument. They ran along the north bank from London Bridge to the Tower of London. Because the law did not allow ships to dock or discharge goods anywhere else, these wharves had a de facto monopoly over trade in the Thames. The Corporation of the City of London, which owned the wharves, was a powerful lobbying body and for centuries blocked attempts to expand the quays. A few, known as 'sufferance wharves' because of the strong opposition to their construction, were built on the south bank at Rotherhithe, but they were permitted to handle only low-value cargoes.

The problems arose when London grew rapidly in the eighteenth century and therefore the amount of goods the city needed to import increased. The volume of trade at London's port doubled between 1700 and 1770 and had nearly doubled again by 1800. The British Empire was expanding: between 1794 and 1824, the number of ships arriving in the Thames increased from 14,000 per year to 23,600, and the number forced to moor in the centre of the river awaiting space on a quay doubled to 16,000 a year in the same period. Many of these were coal ships from the north-east of England, bringing fuel for Britain's increasingly industrial capital city. To alleviate congestion, a class of smaller vessels, called lighters, would slip between the moored ships to receive cargo while on the water and then deliver it to the correct legal quay, where the customs officer was waiting to receive it.

Of course, this practice was ripe for abuse, with ships crammed into the Pool and men in small boats shouting for goods everywhere. Plenty of cargo was lowered down into the wrong lighter and never seen again, or simply stolen by waterborne Thames pirates while the skeleton crew left aboard to guard it looked the other way for a cut of the proceeds. Ships were often stopped and boarded by thieves on their way into or out of the river too. In September 1782, 'a most daring robbery' was committed on the Thames just below Gravesend. Four men armed with pistols and cutlasses boarded an American ship bound for Virginia, confined the crew in a cabin and 'stole goods to the value of thirty shillings'. This is recorded in an advertisement that appeared in *The World* newspaper, in which a Mr Silvester offered a reward of £200 for information leading to a conviction. Such notices were common – there was no police force to investigate the crime, so those robbed of their goods had to retrieve them without official help.

In 1797, the magistrate and social reformer Patrick Colquhoun estimated that over half a million pounds' worth of goods were stolen on the Thames in a single year. Among the types of criminal he recorded in his book *A Treatise on the Police of the Metropolis* were river pirates, night plunderers, river pilferers, fraudulent lumbers, scuffle-hunters, mudlarks, lightermen, artificers and crooked labourers from the docks and arsenals on the Thames. In the same year, it was recorded that half a million men worked in the Docklands in some capacity or other. Smuggling wasn't the only problem: among such a large workforce, mostly drawn from casual and itinerant labourers, often on very low wages, other crimes proliferated. Assault, prostitution and petty theft were widespread. Colquhoun, along with a former mariner and Essex Justice of the Peace named John Harriott, was determined to do something about it. Together they convinced the wealthy West India traders to fund a unit of men to enforce the law on the Thames.

The Thames River Police was founded, Britain's first police force. Established in 1798, it operated a full thirty-one years before Robert Peel's Metropolitan Police. The men were recruited from professions associated with the river: former Thames watermen were hired to row the police boats, marine surveyors worked as inspectors, and 'lumpers' or dockers joined up to supervise the legal loading and unloading of cargo. In the first year, Colquhoun claimed, the police saved over £120,000 worth of goods from thieves, as well as preventing numerous other types of crime, and in 1800 the government took over funding the force, making it an official public service. Other cities around the world, such as Sydney and New York, soon followed London's example and set up their own water-based police forces.

At the same time as Colquhoun's police force was getting under way, an uneasy compromise had been reached about the future of London's overflowing port. The City of London lost its centuries-old monopoly after merchants importing goods from the West Indies, frustrated by the waiting times to get their produce ashore at the legal quays in the Thames and the security issues their ships experienced while waiting on the river for a berth, threatened to move their business to Liverpool or Bristol instead. A number of schemes were proposed, including one by the architect Willey Reveley which would have seen a wide canal dug straight across the Isle of Dogs, creating an artificially straightened Thames so that the river's distinctive bends could be used as ready-made docks. This ambitious plan was never carried out, but Parliament did pass the West India Dock Act in 1799, allowing private investors to gather funding for a new wet dock to be dug in the Isle of Dogs. There, ships could enter from the river via a canal, tie up all around the edge, away from the weather and pirates, and unload their goods in relative safety.

It was a new age for London and the Thames. In the next three decades, many more docks would be dug in east London, altering the landscape of the river forever. The engineering innovations that enabled these advances, such as the work of celebrated pioneers Isambard Kingdom Brunel and Thomas Telford, merged with a national pride in Britain's progress. The bigger the docks the bigger the ships, and the bigger the ships the bigger the clout and influence of the British Empire.

As I wandered around the two basins of St Katharine's, I looked for traces of what would have been here before the docks themselves. Construction began in May 1827 and the docks opened for business in October 1828. In the *Times* report of the grand opening ceremony on 25 October, for which 10,000 tickets were issued and a royal salute was provided by the Artillery Corps, the tone is one of jubilation bordering on jingoism. It was an 'extremely beautiful' and gratifying spectacle, the paper's anonymous correspondent wrote, speculating that all those present must have 'reflected, with national pride, on the maritime greatness of England' as they admired the docks and contemplated how they would 'produce and uphold our naval supremacy'. This glowing account continues with a description of how the first ships made their way through the lock into the docks from the river, accompanied by a military gun salute, a great waving of flags and a regimental band playing 'O the Roast Beef of Old England'.

Later, at a banquet of a 'plain but plentiful cold collation', toasts were drunk to the health of the merchants behind the enterprise and to the ladies present, as well as to, most important of all, the 'prosperity' of 'the City of London'. The writing conjures a scene of celebration and back-slapping among those present. The marine painter William John Huggins, who would later attract the patronage of both George IV and William IV for his maritime art, painted the scene at St Katharine's that day, so we have a visual as well as a written record of what took place.

Although I suspect that both reporter and artist took some liberties with the facts, the direction of their interpretation and embellishment of the scene is indicative of how it was perceived at the time. Huggins's picture shows a large but orderly and well-dressed crowd gathered on the wharf of the brand-new St Katharine Docks in the foreground. Everyone is looking away towards a great open vista of calm water (which, in its grandeur, bears very little resemblance to the somewhat cramped reality of the docks). In the background, a factory chimney and other industrial buildings over in Rotherhithe on the south bank can just be made out, pouring smoke into a bright blue sky. The focal point of the picture, though, is the *Elizabeth*, the first ship to enter St Katharine's. She is progressing through the lock from the river decked out in full ceremonial regalia, with multicoloured flags hung between her masts and from bow to stern. The picture matches the tone of the *Times* report in its loyal enthusiasm, and indeed the prevailing view on the wider dock-building project on the Thames at this time. It is a glorious, glowing scene of patriotic progress.

Yet behind this great nineteenth-century industrial success story is another, darker tale that has been all but erased from view. This area of the bank, from which the engineer Thomas Telford scooped out the dock basins for St Katharine Docks, was not empty or uninhabited when he began work on his designs. The precinct of St Katharine was a populous and ancient inner London neighbourhood. L. Grenade, a French visitor to London in the 1570s, wrote that it was inhabited by sailors and 'craftsmen of varying trades such as hatters, makers of harquebuses, shoemakers, brewers and many others' and John Stow's *A Survey of London* of 1598 mentions it as a place of 'small tenements and homely cottages, having as inhabitants, English and strangers'. Later, there was also a large Scandinavian community, which settled here in the seventeenth century to facilitate the importing of wood from Denmark and Norway to rebuild London after the Great Fire of 1666 (they even built their own church in Wellclose Square, just to the north of St Katharine's). At the heart of the precinct was the twelfth-century hospital of St Katharine's-by-the-Tower, founded in 1147 by Queen Matilda, wife of King Stephen. It was supported and enlarged by two subsequent queen consorts, and over the centuries the foundation became a traditional part of the royal spouse's charitable patronage. Astonishingly, it survived both the dissolution of the monasteries and the Great Fire (a rare medieval building to do so in the eastern part of London) and was still serving the community in the early nineteenth century.

Even this resilient hospital could not hold out against the changes that the nineteenth-century dock expansion was making upon the river's environs. In fact, the Corporation of the City of London initially applied for parliamentary approval to build a wet dock at St Katharine's as early as 1796, but it was rebuffed by a supremely polite missive from Queen Charlotte, the wife of George III, who was then the royal patron of the hospital. She wrote that while she had 'no wish to impede' the dock scheme, she hoped that 'all due care will be taken that the interest of the community under the queen's patronage shall not be prejudiced'. Demolishing a charitable hospital protected by the queen proved too great an obstacle to surmount for the developers and they withdrew their request.

But Queen Charlotte died in 1818 and, through a strange quirk of royal circumstance, the hospital was left without the protection of a queen consort – the widowed George III was mad and his regent, the future George IV, was estranged from his own wife. In addition, the twenty-one-year monopoly over wet dock management in east London that had been granted to the builders of the nearby West India Docks (who had successfully convinced Parliament of the need to protect their pioneering investment with legislation) expired in 1823. In 1824, therefore, a new bill proposing a dock at St Katharine's was put before Parliament. Objections were raised by residents, by the trustees of the hospital and by antiquarians anxious to protect the precinct's historic buildings, but they were over-ruled. The St Katharine Dock Act was passed in 1825 and demolition commenced almost immediately.

In the *Times* article, there is only one sentence that hints at the slightly less glorious version of events. 'In clearing the ground for this magnificent speculation, 1,250 houses and tenements were purchased and pulled down – no less than 11,300 inhabitants having to seek accommodation elsewhere,' it says, before going on to celebrate how this mass clearance of residents will give 'additional impetus to industry and enter-prise among other capitalists'. Contemporary accounts of the demolition are scarce, but some sources suggest that many of the houses were pulled down in a single day. The legislation that allowed the docks to be built ordered that the developers must compensate the hospital foundation (which moved to new premises in Regent's Park) and the landlords who owned houses in the area. No such provision was made for their ten-ants, though, thousands of whom were made homeless, with no right to alternative accommodation or reimbursement. The nineteenth-century dock-building project in east London, followed by the post-Second-World-War deindustrialization of the East End and the 1970s Docklands regeneration on the Isle of Dogs, displaced working-class communities, forcing them to move further along the river towards the less desirable estuary as the inner London riverbanks were refashioned.

To find out more about this astonishing demolition, I visited the parliamentary archives, housed in a tower of the Palace of Westminster. There, I found boxes and boxes of documents relating to the legislation that brought the docks into being, including a pages-long handwritten list of the residents of St Katharine's and whether they 'assented', 'dissented' or were 'neutral' to the building of the docks. Unsurprisingly, not many were in the first column, although quite a few were recorded as unable to answer because they 'declined to converse' or were 'at sea'. This fits the profile of the community at the time: the tenants in the precinct of St Katharine were poor, living and working close together in a tightly packed network of streets running up from the river. Their lives were tied to the Thames, many sailors making their temporary home there or longer-term residents engaged in trades connected with the water, like waste disposal or chandlery. In the early nineteenth century, they had few legal rights and no easy way of enforcing them. After the original bill put before Parliament proposing the St Katharine Docks scheme in 1824 met with opposition, John Hall, the leading developer, began spreading stories that the area was a hotbed of crime, full of brothels and opium dens.

There is little evidence that this area was more dangerous than any of the other Thames-side neighbourhoods, with their transitory populations and people who were hard to keep track of. But Hall's rumour-mongering was very effective, as was the petition in favour from 'residents' of the area that was appended to the legislation when it came up for consideration in the House of Commons. It was later shown that this petition (the official copy of which was almost certainly destroyed by the 1834 fire in the House of Commons) contained only 125 signatures, of which just one was from someone living in a house due to be demolished. The real householders from the precinct did voice their opposition, but too late to change any minds. The narrative was locked in place: the poor tenants were criminals or as good as, standing in the way of commercial progress, and it was only right that they should be displaced. Anyway, two of the original quartet of developers behind the St Katharine Docks scheme were Members of Parliament; one of them, John

Horsley Palmer, later became governor of the Bank of England. With such an imbalance of power between the conflicting groups, it's not surprising that these men could make 11,300 people homeless and face no consequences for their actions.

At the archive were Telford's original plans for the docks, hand-drawn on such a large roll of paper that the archivist and I had to spread it over four desks to view it properly. Every street of the precinct of St Katharine had been drawn in fine black-inked lines – whole streets that have now vanished altogether, like Shovel Alley and Cats Hole. Over the top of the street map the shape of the new docks was shaded in a light grey-blue, a watery wash drowning the houses. Around the edge, a pink area showed the extent of the required demolition, covering almost all of the intricate pattern of streets and courtyards between the Tower of London on the western edge and Ratcliff Highway in the east. It looked like the same colour pink that was used to map the British Empire – that instantly recognizable rosy hue that showed land with a disputed or violent history of possession.

The earth that was excavated to build the two basins of St Katharine Docks was loaded onto barges and towed upstream, away from the commercial wharves in the east of London. It was spread on the marshy ground between the West End's higher-class neighbourhoods and the river (the Thames had yet to be hemmed in by the embankments, so was much wider than it is today) and used to create land for what is today Pimlico and Belgravia. The dock itself was an immediate success, specializing in importing goods from Britain's growing empire. Tea from India and wool from Australia and New Zealand made up a large proportion of the goods St Katharine's handled, alongside luxuries like spices, ivory, china, ostrich feathers, tortoiseshell, oriental carpets, mother of pearl and perfume ingredients. Its investors became rich men, helping to burnish the reputation of London as a world centre of maritime trade and an imperial power.

At the end of Conrad's *Heart of Darkness* – a novel which the literary critic Harold Bloom admits 'may always be a critical battleground' owing to its ambiguous interlacing of colonial narratives – the narrator comes to a realization. Having sat in the cabin of a ship moored at Gravesend and listened to Marlow, a fellow sailor, tell a bloodcurdling tale of a voyage to the Belgian Congo, he looks up for the first time and regards the Thames as it flows past: 'The offing was barred by a black bank of clouds, and the tranquil waterway leading to the uttermost ends of the earth flowed sombre under an overcast sky – seemed to lead into the heart of an immense darkness.' The epicentre of the horror is here, on the familiar, 'civilized' shore, not out in the unknown. Even as the clinking of the slave chains that Marlow had described so vividly rings in his ears, he awakes to the idea that the origins of the abuses overseas lie not in the supposed 'savagery' of the colonies' native inhabitants, but in the hearts and minds of those who benefit from this brutal system of oppression. The evil emanates not only from the white man who encourages the natives to worship him in a remote hill station up the Congo river, but from the heart of the empire itself.

Docks like St Katharine's were built to handle the harvest of Britain's imperial project, the Thames enabling ships to bring the spoils of colonial rule all over the world right into the heart of London. The river was fundamental: it was the route via which 'the dreams of men, the seed of commonwealths, the germs of empires' came to fruition and 'the great knights-errant of the sea' began their adventures, as Conrad put it. Yet the more sinister aspects of this global commerce had roots that went back a long way. In 1555, a London merchant named John Lok – the first recorded English slave trader – brought five enslaved people to the city from Guinea. Throughout the seventeenth century and into the eighteenth, London was the northernmost point of the infamous triangular trade route, which saw British goods taken to the west coast of Africa for sale, the ships then filled with enslaved African people and sailed across the Atlantic for sale in the West Indies, before bringing cargo from the Caribbean plantations back north to the docks on the Thames. In the 1710s and 1720s alone, British ships transported 200,000 slaves across the Atlantic. The majority of enslaved people may never have sailed up the Thames, but the ships that carried them were financed and insured by the City of London, and the profits from their sale enriched the Thames-side businesses of great merchants.

The transatlantic trade was abolished in 1807, but it wasn't until 1833 that a law ordering the phased abolition of slavery in the British Empire was passed. Other forms of colonial exploitation continued well into the twentieth century and the power structures that had developed around the slave trade still persist today. In 1890, Joseph Conrad took a job as the captain of a steamer on the Congo river in West Africa and visited the continent's slave coast for himself. *Heart of Darkness* was based on his experiences on this voyage; he had long yearned to visit the 'uncharted' territories in the centre of Africa – when he was a child of about ten, he had pointed to a map of Africa, put his finger on 'the blank space then representing the unsolved mystery of that continent' and swore that one day he would go there. The Congo Free State was then under the personal control of King Leopold II of Belgium, a first cousin of Queen Victoria. His agents systematically robbed the land of its natural resources, particularly ivory and rubber, to enlarge Leopold's personal fortune, using forced labour to produce the goods that were exported to Europe. The exact death toll is hard to establish because no records were kept, but a 1919 report by a Belgian government commission estimated that half the population – perhaps as many as 10 million people – had died. While working on the Congo, Conrad met Roger Casement, an investigator appointed by the British state to produce an eyewitness account of the abuses. This report, and the two men's subsequent correspondence, informed many of the details in *Heart of Darkness*, as well as Conrad's other writings on West Africa.

The two rivers that loom large in his psyche, the Thames and the Congo, run in parallel through his journals and the subsequent novel; of the West African coast he wrote that 'every day the coast looked the same, as though we had not moved', as if one waterway overlaid the other. Conrad's juxtaposition of Africa as another world was heavily criticized by the postcolonial theorists of the mid-twentieth century; in Chinua Achebe's magnificent 1975 lecture 'An Image of Africa', he repeatedly skewers the racist assumptions that pepper Conrad's writings. Even allowing for the prevalence of contemporary racial prejudices, there is a uniquely illiberal flavour to *Heart of Darkness*, Achebe argues. The Congo natives described in the novel have no names or personalities, merely attributes that enhance their use as symbols of savagery. Conrad condemned imperial oppression but failed to identify the racism that underpinned it, Achebe concludes. And yet for all its many flaws, *Heart of Darkness* is an enduringly popular text among readers and critics. Long after Casement's worthy exposure of the atrocities perpetrated by the colonists in the Congo had been forgotten and left to gather dust on the shelf, that whisper of 'The horror! The horror!' tingles the spine and serves as a reminder. The imperial glories of the Thames are tainted.

Leaving the still waters of St Katharine's behind me, I walked east, keeping the river as close as possible. It wasn't always easy – I often found myself having to turn back behind riverside buildings onto the road when confronted with electronic gates or high fences. Wapping, the area between St Katharine's and Limehouse, was for a long time a 'filthy strait passage' – in the words of John Stow – between the many alleys on the shore and the river itself. Until the marshes that lay behind the riverbank were drained in the early sixteenth century, the whole area was pretty much cut off from the rest of the world other than via the river. After a Dutch engineer dug drainage ditches and built a wall to keep the water out, each cottager in Wapping-in-the-Wose, as it was known, was responsible for maintaining their bit of the earthworks. Like the old precinct of St Katharine, it was dominated by its connections with the sea, full of sailors, taverns, boatbuilders, chandlers and victuallers. It was a poor, sometimes dangerous place, where the boundaries between the river and the land were blurred. The buildings were precarious and frequently patched up. Stairs led down to the river everywhere.

Wapping Old Stairs, which still survive next to a pub on Wapping Wall, lead down to the river just where it begins to curve north around Rotherhithe. The tide was approaching its full height, so I stood near the top, watching the motion of the water as it slowed now. This point is one of several likely locations for the old Execution Dock, which once stood on the Wapping foreshore (the exact spot is disputed, with no definitive evidence surviving). For 400 years, convicted pirates (or those guilty of other maritime crimes, such as mutiny) were brought here in procession across the river from the Marshalsea Prison in Southwark and hanged on the foreshore, 'there to remain till three tides had overflowed them'. The corpses swinging by the neck from a short rope were intended as a deterrent to anyone considering a career of crime on the Thames. The final executions took place in 1830, meaning that all of the pilferers on the river identified by Patrick Colquhoun in the eighteenth century would have known this to be their fate if caught.

Today the riverfront at Wapping – and that of many other Docklands boroughs – is a desirable place to live. The same wealthy class of people who would have found the prospect of living on the river east of the Tower laughable even fifty years ago now pay millions of pounds for tiny apartments built on the site of former wharves and tenements. Much of this transformation took place under the auspices of the London Docklands Development Corporation (LDDC), a controversial body set up in 1981 by Margaret Thatcher's government. In his autobiography, the then Secretary of State for the Environment, Michael Heseltine, wrote about the moment that inspired him to transform the area. He saw it from the air, travelling along the path of the Thames in a small plane. He observed 'vast expanses of polluted land left behind by modern technology and enhanced environmentalism' and declared that the Docklands was 'a tip: 6,000 acres of forgotten wasteland'. The residents of this area felt differently. Although they were aware of an acute need for new employment opportunities to replace over 80,000 jobs lost as the inner docks closed, there was, unsurprisingly, little local support for a wholesale transformation of the area into a giant business park for private companies.

The LDDC had the power to override local planning authorities, acquire land via compulsory purchase and relax regulations in order to attract developers to disused former industrial areas. Under its jurisdiction, the financial centre at Canary Wharf was constructed, as well as London City Airport, the ExCel centre and numerous shopping and housing developments throughout the area. In Wapping, an early consultation with residents in 1981 showed that chief among their concerns was that new housing would be unaffordable other than for the very wealthy. In a pattern that is still happening with new housing developments in London today, the corporation pledged that 40 per cent of new accommodation would be designated 'affordable', only for house prices to rise steeply during construction as the area suddenly became more desirable. The LDDC's solution was to offer interest-free loans of up to £10,000 to local people wishing to buy in the new developments – an amount that was often too low to outbid wealthy buyers moving in from elsewhere.

The new developments erased the architecture of the industrial buildings that had been there before. Along Wapping High Street, a parade of yellow-brick and glass low-rise apartment and office buildings stands where once there would have been warehouses, shops and boatyards. The exception is the surviving waterfront pubs, like the Town of Ramsgate, the Captain Kidd and the Prospect of Whitby, this last now squeezed onto the end of a street of generic modern buildings. The developments also had a social as well as an aesthetic impact. The new, well-heeled residents of Wapping and other Docklands areas did not necessarily want to integrate with the working-class communities around them, often citing concerns about safety and security. Gated apartment buildings and high walls have become the norm. Views of the Thames are an important selling point for the new flats, along with a feeling of privacy and self-contained isolation – hence the river path being in some places entirely blocked by private walkways and terraces. The land acquisitions that took place under the LDDC's authority confused the question of who owns the riverbank here, and although there is often a theoretical right of way, in practice it is very difficult to walk unimpeded next to the water.

I crossed the bridge over the canal that leads into the Shadwell Basin. From here, it used to be possible to access the series of linked basins known as the London Docks, which ran east through the Eastern Dock, Tobacco Dock, Western Dock and Wapping Basin and covered about thirty acres of the bank. On nineteenth-century maps of the area, Wapping itself is a small white sliver of land almost completely surrounded by blue water, the Thames to the south and the docks cut through to the north – isolated just as it was before the marshes were drained. Shadwell is the only dock to survive intact from this complex; the rest were mostly filled in to provide land to build on. Part of the infilled Western Dock was used by Rupert Murdoch to build the infamous 'Fortress Wapping' printworks, where he moved his newspaper operation, News International, in 1986 to break a strike by the printworkers on Fleet Street. The 6,000 striking workers held out for almost a year in a running battle with management and the police, in what became, along with the 1984–5 miners' strike, a symbolic labour struggle of the Thatcher years. The former dock site suited Murdoch's purposes – being newly reclaimed land, it was easily protected from the surrounding roads and buildings with razor wire and prison-style security systems. The journalists and printers picketing outside had little chance of getting in to sabotage the new high-tech presses now being used to print the newspapers, which only required a workforce of 670.

When I was a student, I won a place on what was known as the Murdoch Scholarship Scheme, a work-experience programme funded by the newspaper magnate. For a few weeks one summer holiday, I slept on a sofa in London and worked in the newsroom at *The Times* – then still based at the Wapping plant, although News International has since relocated to an office by the Shard at London Bridge. One of the educational trips organized for us as part of that scheme was a tour of News International's brand-new printworks at Broxbourne in Hertfordshire, just north of the M25 and a couple of miles from the path of the Thames tributary the River Lea. We were shown the presses, the storeroom with hundreds of giant rolls of paper, and the control room, from which the whole high-tech operation was run. As the process was explained to us, I gradually realized that I had seen maybe five people working there, in total – almost all of the work was now automated, directed from the computer terminals in the control room. Later on during my brief stint working at News International, I was sent with some urgent parcels to the courier dispatch point. This was quite a way from the office building in Wapping, where the newspapers' journalists then worked. I found myself walking down the path by the old print sheds, now deserted and denuded of equipment after the recent switch to Broxbourne. One of the sliding doors was slightly open and I peeked in. When my eyes had adjusted to the gloom, I could just make out the vast space, empty except for the litter and debris left behind.

The stretch of the Thames Path to Limehouse is passable. There, my parents were waiting for me on the boat, ready to set off downriver. I passed an old wooden jetty and walked in front of brick-built apartment blocks, unremarkable and square in design, with bright blue metal balconies facing the river. As the pub by the lock into the Limehouse Basin came into sight, I had to leave the riverbank and follow the road up to the bridge at the entrance. Soon, I was on the quay at the edge of the dock, looking for a familiar red sail cover and silver mast. In the more than thirty years since they first sailed up the Thames, my parents have upgraded from the boat they built themselves to a slightly larger, more comfortable Swedish sloop called *Cantilena*. She's thirty-eight feet long with a white fibreglass hull and a wooden, Scandinavian-style interior. She was moored to a pontoon on the quieter eastern side of the basin, near to where the Limehouse Cut enters the dock. The Cut is a short canal, running for two miles north-east from Limehouse up to a lock at Bromley-by-Bow, where it joins the River Lea. It was opened in 1770 and used by barges moving goods between the Thames and the Lea (the latter becomes Bow Creek in its lower reaches and joins the Thames to the east of the Isle of Dogs). Limehouse is a canal junction and was once a vital transfer point for cargo – the Regent's Canal enters the basin on the western side, which in turn connects to the Grand Union Canal at Paddington, meaning that a vessel could leave the Thames here and travel all the way to Birmingham.

Cantilena's deck was empty, but when I climbed down the steps to the cabin my mother was spooning porridge from a large metal pot on the gas hob into plastic bowls decorated with tiny boats. I took one and sat at the table, while my father read aloud to me from the course he had plotted on the computer while I had been walking the fringes of the Docklands. Paper charts and almanacs were laid on the desk in front of him, but the recent addition of this digital version makes it possible to see the movements of other boats (particularly the huge ships in the ports downstream) overlaid on the chart – it's a very sophisticated blend of mapping and radar. Other than the occasional speculation about what the weather might be like in the

estuary, we ate our porridge in silence. I felt a strange mixture of anticipation and tedium – we were about to set off on a trip to the estuary that I had been planning for months, but at the same time everything about this was so familiar that it was difficult to force myself to pay attention to the specific details. Already, I felt myself slipping back into the role I used to play when I was a teenager and we sailed together like this most weekends. The itchy, prickly frustration I used to experience when explaining to friends yet again that, yes, my parents had built a boat and sailed it thousands of miles to be in Britain crept over me. Of course we would leave London by water. How else do you get to the sea?

The breeze was stiffening, even in the dock where the apartment buildings around its edge sheltered us from the worst of the wind. I helped with the usual pre-departure chores – putting any loose possessions or crockery away in the

lockers around the walls of the cabin so that nothing would fall
if the boat suddenly heeled over, making sure the valves in the
hull that allowed water for the sinks and toilet in and out were
secure, and putting on three extra layers of clothing and a hat.
I climbed back into the cockpit and helped my mother cast the
boat off from the pontoon, while my father stood at the wheel
to start the engine and used the handheld radio to notify the
lock-keeper that we wanted to leave. The lock at Limehouse,
which leads out to the Thames, is like many of the others that
separate the river from the basins dug out of its banks: two
pairs of rounded black metal gates moved by hydraulic levers,
with an area of water in between big enough to contain several
boats. We motored slowly through the open first one and tied
up against the wall so that the boat would be held firm as the
water level in the lock changed. The inner gates closed behind
us and the outer gates opened just a crack to allow the water
to trickle out between them. It was shortly after high tide now
and the level in the basin was slightly higher than that of the
river. Once the two were level, the outer gates opened. My
mother and I, waiting on either side of the mast, removed the
mooring lines from the bollards we had secured them to with
a practised wrist flick that I had forgotten I knew. My father
eased the throttle open, *Cantilena*'s speed increased and we
passed between the outer lock gates into the river.

As soon as we cleared the dock, the wind picked up and I was
immediately grateful for my extra jumpers. The swell increased
too, as the boat moved into the tidal stream rushing out east to
the sea. I climbed onto the foredeck for a better vantage point.
Already the buildings I had threaded my way through to reach
Limehouse looked smaller. It was as if the river, now breaking into small waves that slapped against the hull, had come
into sharp focus, while everything on the banks receded into

a blur. I thought of Conrad, piecing together a portrait of the Thames from all of his different memories of sailing into the Docklands from the estuary. This stretch of the river 'is a thing grown up, not made', he wrote in a chapter of *The Mirror of the Sea* entitled 'The Faithful River'. It was a confused place, he felt, which looked as if it had 'sprung up by accident from scattered seeds'. Nothing made sense except the smooth simplicity of the Thames, flowing through this changed and changeable landscape of docks and wharves and quays.

Ahead, I could see the sharp angles of Canary Wharf rising from the Isle of Dogs. Cuckold's Point, the apex of the Rotherhithe peninsula, bulges out into the river to the south, the first of many turns we had to take before we would reach the open water. The wind is funnelled between the buildings on these reaches where the river is still relatively narrow, so it isn't worth hoisting a sail just to have to trim it every five seconds as the direction changes. The motor kept the boat moving steadily in the channel, the heavy thrum vibrating through the deck beneath me. Already the sky was opening up, pushing down towards the water ahead of us. I took a deep breath. Somewhere in the air was the scent of the sea.

3

Woolwich Reach to Silvertown

Following the river around the Isle of Dogs is a disorientating experience. As we gently guided the boat around the meander, my father standing at the helm, the familiar skyline of angular glass and towering grey concrete appeared first on one side of the deck, then ahead, then on the other side, before finally we left it behind to the stern. This is just one of the strange tricks of perception the Thames plays on those who navigate its lower reaches – the way east to the sea requires you to turn through every different compass point along the way. It can leave you baffled and dizzy.

Although it curves into the graceful arc so familiar from the *EastEnders* titles, the river essentially forms three sides of a square here, boxing in the high-rise buildings at Canary Wharf. Seen from above on a chart or map, the land looks like a raindrop about to detach and fall into the water of the river below, a pendulous protrusion forever dangling. The West India Docks slice through near the top, the access canals hinting at the fourth side of the square. Further down, near the curved south bank of the Isle, is the L-shaped gap of the Millwall

Dock. None of this is visible from the river – from the water, skyscrapers dominate, the watery expanses of the docks hidden behind the modern flats and former industrial buildings that line the banks.

The day of our journey, the clouded sky shone a bright pearly grey. This kind of light is common in the estuary; it casts strange shadows and makes it difficult to judge what is near and what is far. It makes the Isle, which in reality is now a well-connected eastern suburb of London, look more remote and distant. The tops of the skyscrapers disappear behind a gradient of low-lying haze and the low-rise buildings between them and the river seem flat and disinterested. The place is turned in on itself, focused on the offices and restaurants that now encircle the old docks.

It wasn't always so. This was once a marsh, drained and dyked over the centuries to create firm land for farming. A 1745 map of the Isle of Dogs drawn by John Rocque shows windmills all along the Isle's eastern shore, on the outside of the marsh wall. Similarly, in the background of Hogarth's 1747 engraving *The Idle 'Prentice turn'd away, and sent to Sea* there are mills all along the deserted shore of the Isle, which is seen over the shoulder of the lazy young man being rowed upriver to Deptford to join the navy. Before the docks were dug and people settled here to work in the nineteenth century, this was prime agricultural land, where wealthy London merchants would build their country houses. On Rocque's map, the Isle is divided into many fields. From the small hamlet of Poplar at the northern edge, workers returning home at the end of the day from the shipyards at Blackwall could look south across lush grazing grounds to the distant Thames.

As we moved slowly past, I climbed out of the cockpit and onto the foredeck, perching in between the handrail that runs across the top of the cabin and the taut halyards alongside it. I could feel on my cheek that the breeze was stiffening, but there was still no point in raising a sail, because to get round the Isle to the relatively straight east–west reach at Woolwich, we would have to head in three different directions in a short space of time. Once upon a time sailors would have steered this course solely under wind power, constantly tacking and adjusting their sails to cope with the shifts in wind direction following the Thames's meander. Now the luxury of the engine does the work for us, so I sit idly and watch the land slip by, staring up at the edifices of Canary Wharf as they rise from the horizon.

The origin of the name 'Isle of Dogs' is disputed. Some say that it refers to the fact that the bloated carcasses of drowned dogs would wash up on the Isle's eastern shore as the tide flowed out of the city; others that it relates to Henry VIII's hunting dogs, which were kennelled here while he resided at a palace across the river in Greenwich. It has long been a low-lying, watery place – from the fifteenth century onwards, records show that every century or so a major breach would occur in the sea wall and the area would, temporarily, be inundated. Smaller floods were even more common and basements on the Isle were constantly damp. I have seen modern maps which show the effect of storm surges of various heights, even taking into account today's flood defences: in one projection for a 5.9-metre flood, almost the entirety of the Isle of Dogs disappears under blue shading.

Like the more westerly areas of the Docklands that I explored on my way to Limehouse, this part of the Thames landscape has a fraught and political history. 'The Island', as it has long been affectionately known among the working-class communities that have inhabited it since the West India and Millwall Docks were built in the nineteenth century, was at the heart of the Thatcherite redevelopment projects of the 1980s and 1990s. When the docks on the Isle of Dogs closed in 1980, thousands of people became unemployed and many more peripheral businesses laid people off (it is estimated that for every job lost in the docks, a further three disappeared in the supply chain). At its peak in 1955, the Port of London employed 32,000 dockers, but by 1985 it had just 3,000 on the books. The peninsula was poor: 95 per cent of housing was rented, over 80 per cent of it from the council. In the previous two decades, the docks accounted for almost 20 per cent of all employment in the five East End boroughs: Greenwich, Lewisham, Newham, Tower Hamlets and Southwark. At the same time as the docks were closing, the area was designated by the government an 'enterprise zone' which offered tax loopholes to business developments, and had the effect of killing off attempts to redevelop the dock areas for affordable and social housing. House prices trebled here between 1984 and 1987. Meanwhile, the LDDC was aggressively pursuing opportunities for private investment, hoping to create at Canary Wharf a financial centre to outdo the City of London. The first and most distinctive skyscraper – One Canada Square, with its well-known pyramid-shaped roof – was completed in 1991.

When I moved to London in 2009, I found the atmosphere of this almost-island grimly fascinating. I had seen it many times from the water, but it wasn't until I had a weekly Travelcard and weekends to kill that I began to explore it on foot. I would take a train east, not caring about the destination, and sit with my face glued to the window as historic warehouses and mirrored high-rises flashed past. I knew a little of the history, but when I got off the train by the West India Docks, I was shocked to find myself in what appeared to be a perpetual building site. The headline-grabbing clashes over development on the Isle of Dogs might have happened fifteen years earlier, but the problems they had caused were still very much present. Council housing and multi-million-pound apartment blocks sat side by side and people with a historic, lifelong connection to the area found themselves moving away as prices rose beyond their means. Often I would walk north, from Canary Wharf to Bow, say, or east across the River Lea towards Barking and find that what had looked like a straightforward route on the map was complicated by abandoned building sites surrounded by hoardings or roads with concrete barriers across. Temporary footbridges sometimes allowed me to climb up and peer down at the great holes bored into the ground to hold the foundations of some new tower block, but usually I would have to retrace my steps and try again another way.

The resentment and disturbances that followed the dock closures linger in the landscape here, in poorly maintained civic buildings or high streets full of betting shops and payday lenders. But when opposition to the LDDC began to grow in the early 1980s, it wasn't a simple matter of residents versus newcomers, or ex-dockers versus the bosses – although those conflicts did flare up too. Relations were complicated by class resentment, as the predominantly white working-class communities of the Isle of Dogs suddenly found themselves living among wealthy bankers who moved into warehouse-conversion penthouses to be close to their jobs at Canary Wharf. A group of anarchists even set up a movement called Class War, which, among other things, advocated vandalizing new residents' fancy cars and protested against 'yuppiefication'. Existing residents found that there was little call for the expertise they had gained through decades of working on the docks in the new local industries of finance and law. The racial politics in the area became ugly when the local authority moved Bangladeshi families into council flats. The Labour Party's 'homes for local people' slogan from the early 1990s could cut both ways: a rallying cry to socialists against the incoming bankers, or a dog-whistle signal to those who objected to non-white families moving into social housing ahead of white residents. In 1993, Derek Beackon was elected the BNP's first-ever councillor when he won a by-election in the Millwall ward on the Isle of Dogs. His campaign had focused on housing and 'rights for whites'. He lost the seat eight months later, when an increased turnout brought Labour back to power, but his brief term in office was hailed as an early victory for a resurgent far right, which would go on to have greater successes in riverside areas further out in the estuary in the early 2000s.

Local communities felt powerless in the face of the LDDC and the Thatcher government's privatization agenda. One of the ways they expressed their discontent was through a series of petitions, delivered to Parliament at Westminster by what was called the People's Armada. Pleasure boats were hired for the trip and a barge was decorated with a huge blue banner depicting a red dragon with a body curved like the river around the Isle of Dogs and the words: 'Docklands Fights Back – Homes, Jobs, Healthcare, Schools, Shops, Parks for the People'. The leader of the Greater London Council, Ken Livingstone, met the Docklands group at Westminster and hosted a rally, where the 'People's Charter for the Docklands' was presented to all the politicians in attendance. In his 2005 book *The Thames*, the American historian Jonathan Schneer compared this fledgling protest movement, which was eventually snuffed out by the sheer power of its opponents and growing apathy in its own ranks, to the Chartists of the

1830s and 1840s. 'The latter-day Chartists likewise faced an unyielding powerful government, and likewise a situation that, in some ways at any rate, began to improve,' he writes. The nineteenth-century Chartists consciously drew their name from the Magna Carta, signed on the Thames at Runnymede in 1215. With the People's Armada, the Chartists' ideological descendants in the East End in the 1990s harnessed the political symbolism of the river to add weight to their own cause.

We rounded the southern bank of the Isle of Dogs. The clouds darkened as the boat swung north, up into the reach that runs along the western side. Although the sky was still blue in places, it felt like rain was coming. The breeze ruffled the surface of the river, shivering pointed waves in the direction the tide was pulling us – round the curves and out of the city. From my vantage point sitting on the cabin top, I could see a couple of canoes launching from a concrete slipway in the area known as Mudchute and a few small speedboats buzzing about ahead. The skyscrapers at Canary Wharf were still visible, looking as if they had shuffled places now that I was seeing them from the less familiar eastern perspective, rather than the usual view from the centre of London.

I stood up and climbed around in front of the mast. The low-lying north Greenwich peninsula was visible off the starboard bow, the stony foreshore still gleaming wet where the tide had just receded. A concrete sea wall ran along most of its edge, holding the tide at bay, while wooden piles and steel netting enclosed part of the bank. As on the Isle of Dogs, high-rise glass-and-steel blocks of flats speckled the bank, high cranes hovering behind holding the promise of more to come. The most striking component of this part of the Thames's bank, though, was the Millennium Dome. From my viewpoint, it was just a crescent of white, with the yellow tips of a couple of supports looming above. Only as the boat was pulled round the top of the peninsula by the tide did its sheer scale became more apparent.

The Dome loomed large in my childhood journeys along the Thames. It was constructed between 1997 and 2000, and every time we sailed past I would stare up in wonder at the brightly coloured pillars and the cables that were gradually strung from them to support the vast white fibreglass fabric that covers the structure. I didn't often see things being built in the estuary or the outer reaches of the Thames; I was far more likely to witness a demolition or a slow, inglorious collapse. A half-term visit to the exhibits the Dome housed during 2000 was a disappointment and I would rather have toured the exterior than queued to see a *Blackadder* film inside. Still, I vividly remember the thrilling day in 1999 when *EastEnders* updated the aerial view of London to include the Dome in its title sequence.

For all that, the Dome, now part of the O2 music venue, has become synonymous in British culture with failure. The eventual cost of its construction is estimated at £750 million, its poorly reviewed exhibits attracted only about half the projected number of visitors and it stood empty for years while politicians tried in vain to convince private companies to find a use for it. But in its construction is also something hopeful. It was originally conceived in the mid-1990s by John Major's Conservative government as a successor project to the great constructions for the Great Exhibition in Hyde Park in 1851 and the Festival of Britain on the south bank of the Thames in central London in 1951. Rather than a well-known central London location, the tip of the North Greenwich peninsula was chosen. The intention was to use the publicity and investment the millennium celebrations would attract to transform this post-industrial brownfield site on a largely unloved section of the river. In addition, part of the project's ambition was environmental: the 170-acre site on which it was to stand was contaminated by toxic sludge from the East Greenwich Gas Works, which had ceased operation here in 1985. Before anything could be built, the land had to be purified – an undertaking that added greatly to the overall expense but which with hindsight is a far greater achievement.

'It will be a triumph of confidence over cynicism, boldness over blandness, excellence over mediocrity,' Tony Blair declared during a speech in December 1999 in which he pledged New Labour's commitment to the Dome. He might have been wrong when he went on to say, 'It will last for generations to come,' but I have always cherished that moment nonetheless – it crystallized a brief moment of optimism in the future of the outer Thames.

On this trip, we didn't linger alongside the Dome. We had soon slipped around the narrow point of the peninsula and were heading almost east again, into one of the straightest reaches of the winding Thames. I heard a shout from behind me and turned from my scrutiny of the shore to see my father was waving at me from the cockpit, signalling that I should come down off the foredeck. I edged around the cabin, holding onto the wire lifelines that surround the deck because the water was choppier now that we had moved out of the protective shadow of the north bank.

As I stepped down into the cockpit, where my father was steering and my mother, wearing a thick jacket and a navy-blue fleece deerstalker, was scanning ahead with binoculars, the Thames Barrier came into sight ahead. This unique flood defence stretches between Silvertown (the run-down industrial area between the Royal Docks and the river) to the north and Woolwich to the south. I borrowed the binoculars and saw that the hydraulic gates between the barrier's piers were open, to allow the river to flow freely through. Every passing craft is required to radio the barrier control room to request permission to travel between the piers. At my father's signal, I pulled the throttle lever almost upright, so that the engine was quietly ticking over but our speed slowed right down. He took the VHF handset from its holster on the steering column, depressed the button and spoke in his slightly clipped South African accent. 'Thames Barrier, this is *Cantilena*, repeat *Cantilena*, over,' he said, carefully enunciating the boat's name, which nobody ever pronounces correctly. The crackly response from the unseen operator in the control room high up in the building next to the barrier on the south bank came almost immediately, as loud as if he was suddenly on deck with us. '*Cantilena*, this is Thames Barrier, go ahead, over.' My father explained that we were heading out to the estuary and the operator confirmed that we could safely pass through between the third and fourth piers. Just in case of any confusion, he also turned the traffic light from red to green, indicating the gap we should use.

The barrier looked suddenly enormous as we made our way through. Each pier rises twenty metres above the riverbed, higher than the very top of our mast. In the fleeting moment when I could look down inside the structure, I saw part of the hydraulic apparatus that controls the vast cylindrical floodgate, currently resting out of the way far beneath us. The barrier is open most of the time for boats to travel through as we did, but it still represents a dividing line on the Thames. It is closed when the Environment Agency's forecasters consider that there is a substantial risk of the city flooding – whether from a large volume of water flowing down from the upper Thames, an unusually large tide or storm surge coming in from the estuary, or – in rare cases – both. Its gates create a block on the river, preventing the usual ebb and flow of the tide and effectively turning the area upstream into a vast temporary reservoir. It's hard to appreciate the scale of what it does while actually on the river. Only aerial photographs taken while it is closed show the calm, smooth river upstream and the higher, broiling water below that the barrier is repelling.

The Thames Barrier began operation in 1982. When my parents made their first journey up the river from the estuary, it was a brand-new landmark. It took eight years to build and required several groundbreaking engineering processes to get the enormous hydraulic swing gates in place. The design of the parts we see above the water is striking in its simplicity, with gently curved silver metal casings. It looks futuristic, like something from a 1970s sci-fi film. Unlike many other civil engineering projects, the barrier is highly visible. It has a symbolic as well as a practical purpose: it reminds the people who live along the Thames that they are protected.

That the Thames Barrier was constructed only towards the end of the twentieth century would seem to suggest that flooding is a relatively recent problem on the river – perhaps linked to climate change and rising sea levels. This is far from the case, however. For all the solidity and apparent permanence of London (and its vital importance as a growing capital city of millions), it has always been at risk of inundation. In 1099, the *Anglo-Saxon Chronicle* recorded, 'On the festival of St Martin, the sea flood sprung up to such a height and did so much harm as no man remembered ever before.' *The London Encyclopaedia* records many such subsequent floods. In 1237, the marshes at Woolwich were completely swamped and many people drowned. The water surged up the river and flooded Westminster Hall; the lawyers who worked there rowed around the building in boats. This happened again in 1515, and once more in 1579, when one contemporary description mentions that once the waters had receded from Westminster, fish were left on the floor of the hall. On 7 December 1663, Samuel Pepys wrote, 'There was last night the greatest tide that ever was remembered in England to have been in this river, all Whitehall having been drowned.' The so-called Great Storm of 1703, during which thousands of chimney stacks blew down in central London and the lead was blown off the roof of Westminster Abbey, caused huge damage on the river as well. In his book *The Storm*, published the next year, Daniel Defoe wrote, 'It was a strange sight to see all the Ships in the River blown away, the Pool was so clear, that as I remember, not above 4 Ships were left between the Upper part of *Wapping*, and *Ratcliff Cross*, for the Tide being up at the Time when the Storm blew with the greatest violence.' Like Pepys, Defoe was astonished by the storm and the floods it caused: 'unless a like Occasion had happen'd could never before be heard of,' he wrote, a common sentiment in those who have written about the Thames floods down the years – every time is the worst time in memory, but it is never quite bad enough to prompt radical action to prevent it from happening again.

The first recorded attempt to codify flood prevention on the Thames in legislation was in 1428, when Parliament passed an act that obliged riparian landowners to maintain flood defences on their property. Down the centuries, a long succession of similar bills followed, with limited success. Weirs for fishing and mills were everywhere on the upper Thames, and those who used them were reluctant to remove them in favour of permanent flood defences. Later, the great port enterprise in London and the lower Thames was too profitable to consider any barrier that would affect the tides or – heaven forbid – make part of the river inaccessible to ships. And yet the floods kept coming. In 1809, the central arches of the medieval bridge at

Wallingford collapsed under the immense pressure of the flood waters. As the nineteenth century wore on, the population of London grew and the river began to be narrowed and confined by Joseph Bazalgette's embankment projects. This had the triple effect of funnelling the flood waters further and faster along the course of the Thames, raising the level of the water and increasing the potential for casualties because the explosion of urban poverty meant more people were living in unsafe dwellings near the river.

On 7 January 1928, all of this came to a head. The coincidence of a high spring tide, sustained heavy rain in the Thames Valley area, a snowy Christmas and mild New Year, and a storm in the North Sea caused the highest water levels and speeds in the Thames to date. A fifty-foot stretch of the embankment at Lambeth broke and the water rushed over and up into the drainage system. Fourteen people drowned in basement flats, unable to escape from the rapidly rising waters. An estimated 4,000 more were made homeless, several underground stations were flooded and the ground-floor storage area at the National Gallery of British Art in Pimlico (now Tate Britain) filled with water. Five works by J. M. W. Turner, all of which depict scenes from the Thames or the estuary, were damaged. The complete list of pieces affected, made on a typewriter but dated by hand to September 1928, records 101 paintings and three miniatures that were 'submerged but not damaged'. As well as Turner's Thames watercolours, the list includes works by Corot, Pissarro and Daubigny, as well as a work from 1848 by William Westall appropriately entitled *The Commencement of the Deluge*. A photograph taken the morning after the flood shows five men in shirtsleeves with waders up to their thighs carrying a massive canvas out of the gallery to safety.

This flood, which caused such tragedy and upheaval in the

capital, ignited the debate about how to protect London from the rising waters of the Thames. Its effects had been worsened by the recent practice of dredging the riverbed around the Isle of Dogs and removing mud and silt to make the channel deeper, so that bigger ships could enter the docks there, because London's port enterprise was still going strong. For the same reason, despite calls for some kind of action – which ranged from a plan to turn the whole of the Thames into a giant tideless reservoir to moving the capital city away from the river entirely – very little was done, beyond reconstructing the embankment that had broken and replacing some of the most unstable housing in that area. It took another even bigger and more disastrous flood to spur government to action.

The Thames was a drab gunmetal grey and the sky barely a shade lighter on the summer afternoon a couple of months after the trip down the Thames with my parents when I set off to walk from the tip of the Greenwich peninsula to the Thames Barrier along the southern bank. When travelling by water, this stretch of water goes past very quickly. On foot, I had more time to absorb its details – the silty stretch of foreshore that extends out towards the river's channel, the eccentric collection of small boats moored in parallel lines just downriver from North Greenwich Pier, the determined optimism of the volunteers growing vegetables in perspex greenhouses on an old jetty. I walked along the tarmac path that follows the bank, mostly uninterrupted, east from the O2 entertainment complex around the Dome.

At one point the path left the riverbank and I walked through the grounds of a factory producing aggregate and cement, protected on either side by barriers of barbed wire and wire mesh. Thick clouds of dust hung in the air, the machinery oddly close as the footpath cut near to the works. It was a sudden and strange contrast to the open, paved path along the bank of the Thames I had been following just moments before, where tourists wandered and children rode bicycles up and down.

In the distance, I could see the silver piers of the Thames Barrier gleaming above the darker grey of the river's surface. As I got closer, they became more distinct: seven alien-seeming protrusions strung out from bank to bank, five larger ones in the middle and two smaller either side with low-lying bridge-like structures joining them to the land. Once I emerged from the cement works back onto the final section of the river path, I was shocked by how near they were. It is difficult to judge

the scale of things on the river – the perspective between land
and water always seems to shift and change – but I knew from
passing between the piers on the water how high they really
are. A four-storey house plonked alongside them would still
come up shorter than their peaks.

Once I had passed the point on the bank where I was level
with the barrier, I found the cafe I was looking for. I had
an appointment to keep with Andy Batchelor, the manager
of the Thames Barrier. He works for the Environment Agency,
the government body that oversees flood defences on this river
and elsewhere, and has spent his entire career working in the
Thames estuary. He's tall, spare and self-effacing, although
obviously passionate about his job. Before he gave me a proper
tour of the barrier's operations, we went into the visitor centre
to see the educational exhibits the staff use to explain their
work to visiting school groups.

In particular, Andy was keen that I watch a short film in which he and other barrier employees explain how their work fits into the overall system of flood protection measures in the estuary. We also examined a cross-sectional model of the barrier itself, which had mini versions of its cylindrical hydraulic gates rotating slowly up through imitation river water. Only once I had seen all of this and Andy was satisfied that I understood the basic tenets of his work did we climb up to his office high above the southern end of the barrier. From this vantage point, we looked out straight across the 520-metre span to Silvertown on the other side of the Thames.

As a young engineer, Andy told me, his dream was to work on the Thames Barrier. It was still under construction when he graduated in 1979, so he got a job as part of the team improving flood defences in the outer Thames estuary – raising the level of sea walls and erecting other flood gates on tributaries like Barking Creek. Then, in 1984, he joined the barrier's maintenance team, before becoming its overall manager in 1999. He leads a team of eighty-seven people who work on a variety of day-to-day tasks, from servicing the barrier's moving parts and forecasting future floods to leading tours for school groups around the site. He feels a great sense of duty to do his job well. Although the Thames has flooded repeatedly throughout history, everything that Batchelor and his colleagues do here is informed by one particular inundation.

Late at night on 31 January 1953, a heavy storm erupted in the North Sea. By the early hours of the morning, strong winds combined with low pressure and fast currents had produced a surge that devastated the UK's east coast. The storm caused damage all over the country – 30,000 people were evacuated from their homes – but it was particularly intense in the Thames estuary. The river was already full to the brim after days of rain and the extra water pushed into the estuary by the surge broke sea walls and flooded thousands of properties. More than 320 people in the UK died that night, many of them in Essex and the other coastal counties north of the Thames estuary. The water came in the dark; people awoke to find the river rising rapidly into their houses and many were unable to escape in time. Some drowned, but others died from the cold as they huddled on roofs in their nightclothes while the water rose all around them. It remains one of the country's worst ever natural disasters.

There was little or no warning of what was about to happen, which added greatly to the terror and confusion. Despite the flooding the Thames had experienced down the centuries, the modern state had little infrastructure to help deal with a disaster on this scale. 'What a lot of people don't appreciate,' Andy told me, 'is that in 1953 there were no systems. There was no real way of telling local authorities and police groups along the coast that something was coming. They all saw it for the first time separately, and because of the lack of preparation, that's what added to the loss of life.' Afterwards, policymakers and legislators decided that something finally had to be done, that the priority of a clear shipping lane in the Thames had to accommodate better flood defences for the people and businesses on the river's banks. As well as containing homes at risk, the estuary was now a major industrial centre – gasworks, oil refineries, brickworks, boatbuilders, landfill sites and cement works like the one I'd walked through on the way here were all situated on its banks and in danger from future flooding on this scale.

In his essay *The New English Landscape*, the writer Ken

Worpole, who grew up on Canvey Island in the estuary, moving away just a year before the flood, recalls the quiet horror the great tide of 1953 caused. Land was cheap on the Essex coast and hundreds of flimsy prefabricated bungalows like the one his family occupied had been built in the years following the Second World War to meet the demand for housing in east London and Essex after the devastation of the Blitz. Streets of such dwellings ran right next to the sea walls, the roads muddy and perpetually wet. The corpses of the fifty-nine people from Canvey who had died during the night were retrieved from their houses and laid out on the pavements to be identified, their family and friends walking the length of the streets to find out if the worst had happened. A further 13,000 people were evacuated from their homes, but in the chaos relatives and friends lost track of each other. A blackboard was placed at the crossing point over Benfleet Creek to the mainland and anyone who left safely was supposed to write their name in chalk so they could be removed from the list of the missing. But these weren't the stories that appeared on the television news coverage of the flood, Worpole points out. Instead, it was pictures of the tens of thousands of farm animals that had been washed out to sea that became the iconic image of the tragedy.

Central London was largely spared from disaster, although the water came extremely close to overtopping the embankments at Lambeth and Millbank, as it had in 1928. The Thames broke its banks at the point near where the barrier stands today, though – 1,100 houses were flooded in Silvertown and Canning Town on the north bank. The total cost of the damage in Britain was estimated at £50 million (over £1 billion in today's money).

In the wake of the 1953 flood four options for the future were considered: do nothing, move the capital out of London, raise the walls along the Thames by three metres, build a flood barrier on the river. By this time, the port operation in the Pool of London was slowing down, with the Royal Docks and the port at Tilbury taking more of the traffic as ships became larger and less able to navigate the upper reaches. The eventual solution, Andy explained to me, was a combination of the third and fourth options: better defences throughout the estuary and a flood barrier on the Thames. A lengthy debate ensued, the competing interests arguing for different priorities: any barrier must be movable, to allow ships to pass into London and the remaining docks unimpeded, but it must also be completely effective at stopping another flood or storm surge, and it mustn't cost too much. The wrangling dragged on; by 1966 still nothing had been decided upon. A proposal in 1958 for a guillotine-like drop-gate barrier with two openings for ships had been rejected, as had the Port of London's preferred option for a simple barrier with 150-metre-wide openings. To break the deadlock, the government commissioned the Anglo-Austrian physicist Hermann Bondi to provide feasibility studies for better flood defences in the Thames.

In his report, Bondi concluded that a movable barrier was the best option and also restated the urgency of finding a workable solution. 'A major surge tide in London would be a disaster of the singular and immense kind ... It would be a knock-out blow to the nerve centre of the country,' he wrote. A breakthrough occurred in 1969, when the engineer Charles Draper conceived of the cylindrical rising sector gate, reputedly inspired by the gas taps on his parents' cooker. His design allowed for a strong, impenetrable barrier that could withstand great force, but which could also be rotated completely out of the way of shipping when not required. In 1972, Parliament passed the Thames Barrier Act, and the stretch of river between Silvertown and Woolwich was selected for the barrier's construction – partly because of its relative straightness compared to the rest of the Thames and partly because of the firmness of the chalk beneath the riverbed, which could support the hundreds of tonnes of concrete that would be needed to take the barrier's weight. Construction began in 1974 and involved over 3,000 people. Huge concrete sills reinforced with steel were built in a dry dock on the north bank and then moved into position in channels dug in the riverbed. The biggest ones are sixty metres long and weigh 9,000 tonnes. The project eventually cost £535 million (about £2 billion in today's money). Meanwhile, sea walls and defences were reinforced and expanded for eighteen kilometres below the barrier site on either side of the Thames – the part of the project that Andy worked on when he first graduated in 1979.

On the wall in Andy's office is a framed photo collage. Appropriately, it depicts flood barriers (given his passion for his work, it would be hard to imagine him displaying anything else). These great edifices of steel and concrete are the nearest thing the Thames Barrier has to sister structures and the people who operate them are Andy's global colleagues. He's in regular contact with his counterparts in Italy, Russia and the Netherlands, and together they share data and advice about flood management around the world. The Netherlands is a particularly important partner, because what happened on the Dutch coast in 1953 still informs all flood defence efforts in Britain. There, what is known as *de Watersnoodramp* hit the southern part of the country's coastline just as it was breaching sea walls in the Thames estuary. The dykes that were supposed to keep the water out broke in sixty-seven places, flooding an area about 900 miles square, including nearly 10 per cent of all Dutch farmland. An estimated 1,800 people died on the night of 31 January and a further 70,000 were evacuated as their homes were submerged under the flood waters.

In the Netherlands, the 'never again' attitude continues to dominate everything they do. The country spends 0.1 per cent of its entire GDP on continuing improvement of flood defences, aiming to be prepared for a once in 10,000 years level of disaster (the UK's own preparedness is for a once in 1,000 years flood occurrence). Another effect of the 1953 flood was to remind the people living along the east coast and the estuary of their connection with those living on low-lying land across the North Sea. That night, national boundaries and differences mattered less than the fact that they were coast dwellers and faced the same horrifying wall of water.

The connections between the two places go back centuries. Dutch engineers were responsible for many of the drainage and land reclamation projects in the estuary, including on the Isle of Dogs, at Barking and on Canvey Island. Worpole remembers how at carnival time on Canvey in the early 1950s people would dress in Dutch costume and parade past streets with names such as Delft Road and Kamerdyke Avenue.

The 1953 flood changed the character of the landscape on both sides of the North Sea. In the estuary, when the sea walls were raised, the northern side of the Thames became known as 'the walled fortress of Essex'. More recently, a somewhat more forgiving and ecologically judicious attitude towards flood protection has been developed, with some areas of marshland allowed to flood to reduce the pressure of the tide trying to squeeze through narrow gaps. When I ask Andy about the risk today, he's calm and professional in his answers. The safety of important landmarks and infrastructure – such as the Houses of Parliament, 10 Downing Street, several major hospitals and parts of the London Underground, as well as thousands of homes – depends on him making the right call. 'It's 375,000 properties, something like £300 billion worth,' he told me, with a slight smile.

But unlike in 1953, when there was no advance flood warning system, he's constantly fed forecasts and data on the amount of water in the Thames, and although the decision whether or not to close the barrier and activate the estuary's other defences (such as the gate at Barking Creek) rests with him, he has dozens of people backing him up with their expertise. The barrier costs around £8 million a year to maintain and operate.

As of early 2018, the barrier has closed 181 times since it began operation in 1982. Fifty of those times occurred within a three-month period in the winter of 2013–14, with twenty of the closures on consecutive tides. Extremely heavy rain caused flooding all over the country – particularly in the Somerset Levels – and Andy and his team worked round-the-clock shifts to keep the water level in the Thames below the critical point. The decision to close the barrier (a process that takes about an hour and a half) is deceptively simple. Andy explains it to me patiently, drawing diagrams on a piece of scrap paper on the table in front of him, in what I sense might be his habitual laid-back, logical tone. If A, the amount of rainwater forecast to flow down the Thames, plus B, the height of the next incoming tide, equals more than C, the amount of water the river can contain without flooding, the barrier must be closed. 'We can't stop the rainfall, but we can stop the tide,' he says. During that winter, there was nothing he could do to stop the rain from further soaking the flood plains or filling up the water table, but by closing the barrier he could prevent the tide from flowing over the top and possibly putting sea walls under strain. Only twice since 1953 has a similar combination of spring tide and storm surge in the North Sea threatened to trigger a similar disaster: once in January 1978 and once in January 1983. In both cases, the water came close to breaking through, but better warnings and preparedness staved off serious damage or loss of life. With the barrier now in operation, Andy hopes that there will never be another close call.

The barrier can't last forever, however. It's made of concrete and steel, and sits on a muddy riverbed constantly immersed in salt water. In addition, when it was conceived in the 1970s, terms such as climate change and global warming 'weren't even in the dictionary', as Andy says. It was originally designed to be superseded by other flood defences by 2030, possibly even a second barrier further out in the estuary, but more recent studies have shown that the current structure is robust enough to remain at the heart of the Thames's flood prevention strategy until 2070.

There are more than 8 million people living in London itself and another 1.3 million in the wider Thames estuary. Although the barrier isn't hard to access (unlike many of the other landmarks in the estuary area, it's possible to reach it on foot or by public transport from the centre of the city), it isn't exactly a popular or even well-known destination among Londoners. The Environment Agency runs a constant public engagement campaign, inviting the public to events like the annual maintenance closure and encouraging schools to bring pupils for educational visits, but it's not really a fixture on the tourist map, like the London Eye, say, or Tower Bridge. Most of the people I've ever mentioned it to had a vague awareness that it was on the river somewhere and had perhaps seen pictures in the news or passed through it on a ferry trip to Woolwich, but very few had ever seen it with their own eyes, or cared to do so in the future. Yet in the decades since the Thames Barrier has been in operation, there hasn't been a single tidal flood in central London. It's so successful, we are able to forget that it's there. And as long as it doesn't fail, the barrier and the people like Andy who work on it will carry on being invisible.

As the boat passed through the Thames Barrier on our journey towards the estuary, it felt as if we had crossed over a border into a different place. Everything looked the same, but passing between the piers *Cantilena* had left behind another of the markers that define the river's relationship with London. Boundaries in the river and the estuary are fluid and hard to define – the mud moves, the tide flows in and out, and nothing feels permanent. But of all the lines that men have tried to draw here, this is the easiest to comprehend. Sea levels in the south-east are rising at a rate of approximately 1mm every year, both because of climate change and because of the gradual downwards tilt of the southern tectonic plate that holds the British Isles. If another great tide comes, like the one in 1953, this will be the frontier where the water is turned back. The raised sea walls protect some areas downstream, but others are now managed as flood plain, with strategic areas designed to absorb and hold the water and stop it reaching areas of housing or industry. I sat down in the back of the cockpit to look over *Cantilena*'s stern at the piers. The barrier is there to protect the city and its surrounding suburbs and industrial areas. We were now on the outside, closer to the sea.

The curved silver backs of the piers grew gradually smaller as I stared at them – this reach of the Thames between Silvertown and Woolwich is relatively straight, so I could keep them in view. The gates were open and the tide ran swiftly with us, creating a swirling mass of rushing water at the foot of each one. It seemed as if the barrier was filtering something from the river, catching it before the rest of the water flowed on, bearing us to the estuary. As we moved further away, the engine just ticking over and the tide pulling the boat forward, I remembered how Neb, a character in Iain Sinclair's 1991 novel *Downriver*, likens the barrier's piers to 'dream helmets', their curved shape similar to the 'igloos' he haunts in Victoria Park, east London. These rounded lumps of masonry are actually the remains of alcoves salvaged from the old medieval London Bridge, demolished in 1831 after the five granite arches of the new Victorian bridge had been completed 100 metres upstream.

In much of his writing, both fiction and non-fiction, Sinclair is concerned with psychogeography: thinking about the psychological effects of a place and its past on inhabitants or observers.

This field became popular in the 1980s and early 1990s – Sinclair said at a V&A event in 2008 that in Thatcherite Britain 'everything was being wiped out, and writers had to resurrect tools of resistance from the past', an explanation with particular relevance in the light of the radical changes happening in the Docklands and the estuary at the time. In *Downriver*, Sinclair's excavations result in Neb's obsession with hidden connections and Masonic symbols, declaiming about them to uninterested passers-by. For him, the alcoves from the old bridge still contain 'all the nightmares that have ever flowed down the river'. Their shiny silver lookalikes that support the barrier's great gates have this quality too – they act as a dreamcatcher, Neb says, filtering Londoners' sleeping visions from the water and keeping them safe. The image resonates with the Thames's ability to absorb memories and experiences from different times.

The Thames Barrier neutralizes the dangerous qualities of the river, making it a safe – and sometimes invisible – presence in the city. I don't think it can stop dreams from escaping, though, or even strain them temporarily out of the water. The attraction of a river as a vehicle for our unspoken memories and desires is in its inexorable progress towards the unknown sea. The further we drifted away from the barrier, the harder it was to discern. In the muted light of a grey afternoon, the piers blended back into the landscape, as if they had always been there. With an effort, I dragged my searching gaze away and climbed out of the cockpit to sit on the deck again. Ahead, the river curved away to the left, the Tate & Lyle sugar refinery, now sold to an American conglomerate, dominating the northern bank with its blue sheds and miles of external silver piping. My father eased the throttle forward and the boat's speed increased. There was still a long way to go.

4

Gallions Reach to Frog Island

The river was a dull grey but at times, when the clouds parted briefly and shards of weak sunlight fell down onto its surface, it looked almost navy blue, shimmering and secretive. Small pointed waves ruffled its surface, whipped up by the wind. The boat was turning slowly to the left, following the river's next curve. The Woolwich ferry disappeared from sight behind the bank. I looked up and saw a plane, shockingly low, flying over my head. It ripped across the sky, crossing the river with wheels already extended, in order to land at London City Airport, which occupies part of the old George V Dock on the north bank.

The tide was running strongly now and from where I sat on the cabin roof, with my feet dangling down towards the deck, I could see that the contents of the river were on the move. The speedometer in the cabin showed that we were doing about five knots now – the nautical equivalent of just under six miles an hour – but I knew that the boat was travelling much faster than that. The speed-measuring instrument works by calculating how quickly water is rushing past the boat as it moves forward, because that usually gives an accurate figure for how fast you are travelling. But when the tide is flowing in the same direction as the boat is moving, the hull isn't slicing through the river in order to go forward, but rather sliding along with it, invisible to a speedometer set up to measure the quantity of water coming from the opposite direction.

When the engine and the tide are working together to move the boat along, the bank slides by astonishingly quickly. I looked down for what I was sure was just a few seconds to change a setting on my camera, but when I flicked my gaze back up an entirely different view greeted me. There's something restless and even invigorating about the river's motion at this state of the tide: as if it has decided on a destination and is eager to set you on your course. The boat is pushed inexorably towards the sea. In that moment, I am sure I felt what hundreds of thousands of departing sailors had felt before me: the jittery nerves of a fresh journey begun, coupled with the anticipation of what is to come. It gave me a small flashing notion of Conrad's excitement at this place, the route to the rest of the world, which he described in *The Mirror of the Sea* as the 'road open to enterprise and courage [that] invites the explorer of coasts to new efforts'.

The plane had descended beyond my view now and the boat was finishing its pivot out of the relatively straight stretch that houses the Thames Barrier. The bulge that marks the eastern extent of the old Royal Docks is known as Gallions Point, a name borrowed from the fourteenth-century Galyons family, who once owned all the land along the river here. The straighter stretch beyond the point also takes their name: we had arrived at Gallions Reach. Once past the former entrance to the docks, the north bank is full of low-lying warehouses and sheds. This used to be a major industrial area, with a huge gasworks and other trades that supported the docks. Much of that has gone now. Some of the brownfield land that was left has been turned into housing estates and a giant retail park, but the rest of it is undeveloped. The colour palette reminds me of what I saw from the train in the Thames Valley on my way to the river's source – the buildings a uniform blend of grey, faded blue and rusty brown, a near-perfect reflection of the sea, shore and sky further out in the estuary.

The same shades are echoed in the Barking Barrier, which comes into view as the boat moves along the reach. Its two grey pillars rise forty metres above the river's surface, supporting a steel barrier thirty-eight metres wide that is held high above the water unless needed to prevent a storm surge or particularly high tide from flooding back up Barking Creek into the River Roding beyond. As we slipped past, I could see through its open space up the river beyond, as if it was a picture frame. Behind, the low-lying acreage of the Beckton Sewage Works spreads across the Thames bank and flood plain. I used to ignore structures like this on our journeys in and out of the estuary – waste disposal wasn't something I particularly wanted to dwell on, it was the river that held interest for me – and other than when the smell was inescapable, I remained ignorant of what was going on in the huge round pools on the other side.

Just a little further on from Beckton, on the south sound of the river, there is another sewage works, at Crossness. This one is a little harder to ignore. The original pumping station, with its humbug-striped chimney and graceful, arched brick facade, stands out from the low-slung modern sheds of the sewage works that surround it. Opened in 1865 by the Prince of Wales, along with the embankments along the river in central London, it was a key part of Joseph Bazalgette's scheme to clean up the Thames. It is a beautiful and elaborate structure which the influential mid-century architectural historian Nikolaus Pevsner once described as 'a masterpiece of engineering – a Victorian cathedral of ironwork'. Some of the same Gothic flourishes are visible upriver in the design of the Palace of Westminster: vaulted arches and crenellated exterior decorations.

It looks out of place on this reach of the river, where empty factories and tumbledown sheds cluster on the banks – as if it belongs several miles further west. Even from the deck, I could see that this was a building designed to exhibit and celebrate the devices it housed: it wants to be looked at and admired. I scrambled back into the cockpit to grab the binoculars and study it in more detail. 'Oh, that's the old pumping house,' my father said, when he noticed what I was looking at. 'It's where they housed the engines that pumped the shit into the river.' I stared as the building receded further into the distance. The disparity between form and function was intriguing. Even after all this time, the estuary could still surprise me.

On 7 July 1855, the eminent scientist Michael Faraday took a trip on the Thames. He travelled by steamer at low water upstream from London Bridge, the boat surging through what he later described as 'an opaque pale brown fluid'. He tested the pollution level in the water as he went by dropping fragments of white card into it at every pier he passed and observing how long it took for the pieces to disappear from view. Such was the terrible state of the river water that 'before they had sunk an inch below the surface they were undistinguishable'. Later the same day, he wrote a letter to *The Times* in which he pointed out that the whole river was a 'real sewer' in which 'the feculence rolled up in clouds so dense that they were visible at the surface' and expressed his astonishment that such conditions persisted at the heart of the nation's capital city.

Faraday's letter was widely reprinted and his observations

caused a public outcry. Soon after, *Punch* printed a cartoon
showing a top-hatted Faraday holding his nose and leaning out
from a boat to hand his pristine white visiting card to a filthy
depiction of Old Father Thames standing waist-deep in the
river. 'And we hope the Dirty Fellow will consult the learned
Professor,' the caption read. Faraday had merely recorded pub-
licly what everybody who went near the Thames at the time
knew: the river was overflowing with human faeces. As London
had grown – the population of the city at the 1841 census was
1.8 million, up from a million thirty years before – so had the
scale of the problem. The filth of the entire city's population

FARADAY GIVING HIS CARD TO FATHER THAMES;
And we hope the Dirty Fellow will consult the learned Professor.

was flowing into it, as was industrial waste from the numerous gas and chemical works situated on the banks alongside the booming docks. It was the age of the buccaneering industrialist and growth was so rapid that the little sanitation infrastructure that existed could not keep pace. Frequently, people had no alternative but to dump their waste by the river and hope it would just disappear. A sanitary commissioner's report from 1857 recorded that 'large quantities of objectionable matter are frequently left on the foreshores to be washed away by the tide'.

At the time when Faraday wrote his letter, the river was the principal and final outlet for sewage in London. From the mid-eighteenth century, sewers had begun to be constructed beneath the streets of the city, but they were primarily intended to carry away surface water to prevent flooding and were frequently allowed to crumble and become blocked. Inhabitants tried to use them for rubbish disposal (an 1844 sanitation report recorded that workers sent down to unblock clogged sewers found 'coals, cinders, bottles, broken pots' and 'old hats, dead cats, scrubbing brushes', as well as masses of mud). The city was running on a primitive system that had been in place for centuries whereby domestic privies drained into brick-lined cesspools dug beneath streets and houses – there were 200,000 of them in the city by the turn of the nineteenth century – which were emptied, irregularly, with shovels by so-called night-soil men employed by the nearest vestry or parish board. The resulting muck was then conveyed by cart to farmers on the outskirts of London to use as fertilizer for crops. But the city was growing too, the suburbs rapidly expanding. With more people to collect from and further to travel to reach the countryside, the night-soil men couldn't keep up. Parish authorities in east London began to buy up cheap Thames-adjacent marshland in Essex and Kent in order to dump their waste. This technique of outsourcing the city's filth downriver, where it became some-body else's problem, was increasingly popular. As one council report put it, 'The most natural solution is to shoot it in some sparsely inhabited district where public opinion is not strong enough to effectually resent it being deposited.' In other words: send it to the estuary and let it rot there.

Even this eastward-bound procession of dung carts and barges was not enough to keep the city clean. By the mid-nineteenth century, over 200 tonnes of faecal matter were entering the Thames in London every day. Ironically, the widespread adoption of one of the great innovations in hygienic living, the flushing water closet, in the 1830s actually made the pollution in the Thames much worse. When the waste had festered underground in cesspools, occasionally seeping into cellars and poisoning wells in poorer areas, it was at least rela-tively static. In some grand houses in the West End, the owners would brick up the cesspool when it was full and have a new one dug, rather than deal with the unpleasantness of having it emptied. According to the Metropolitan Sanitary Commission's first report in 1847, the foundations of some of the grandest houses in the city were 'literally honeycombed' with subter-ranean caches of filth. But all the moving water from flushing water closets resulted in cesspools overflowing far more often, causing run-off into the sewers. At that time, all the sewers ran straight into the river.

The river was also the city's main source of drinking water. Unregulated private companies competed to supply households with the cheapest service. Drawing from the Thames, both upstream and in its tidal reaches, was a key factor in keeping their prices down, as was cutting out steps like running it through filter beds and settling tanks. John Wright, the editor of *Hansard*, was one of the earliest people to raise alarm at the state of the Thames – in a pamphlet published in 1827, he revealed that one company was pumping water from the Thames to sell, untreated, for household consumption just a few yards away from where a major sewer entered the river. Wright claimed his investigation proved 'that Seven Thousand Families in Westminster and its Suburbs are supplied with Water in a state offensive to the sight, disgusting to the imagination, and destructive to health', and this caused a city-wide panic.

In response, a parliamentary commission produced a report into alternative sources of drinking water in 1828, and several companies (fearful of the consumer backlash, no doubt) moved their pumping operations further upstream to the cleaner reaches above London. No legislation was passed making it illegal to draw drinking water from the polluted urban Thames, though, or to dump excrement or industrial waste in the river. In 1831, Wright wrote to *The Times*, saying that while he had no wish to add to the 'existing alarm', he felt it was his duty to point out that thousands of families in Southwark were still receiving water drawn from 'the very spot in the Thames ... at which the great common sewers of London discharge their disgusting and noxious contents'. St Thomas's Hospital, he explained, consumed 5 million gallons of this polluted water every year and, during their attempts at purification, they were skimming off large quantities of 'liquid mud'.

It seems extraordinary now that such terrible pollution ever existed in London, let alone so recently in the history of the river and the city. For all that the Thames was key to the Victorian vision for imperial expansion and global glory, it was also a source of shame. Wright referred to the polluted river as 'evil', and in 1859 the publisher Thomas Wood wrote despairingly that the Thames was 'the largest navigable sewer in the world', and that the decomposing ooze along the tideline was 'discreditable to the great Metropolis of England'. Yet no single public body had the authority or the jurisdiction to mastermind a clean-up effort. The conflicting interests in the Thames of the Corporation of London, the dock companies, the water companies, the Admiralty and Trinity House (the body that supervises navigational marks and lighthouses in British waters) stymied parliamentary efforts to improve the situation. Besides, at this point, nobody realized how dangerous the muck in the river was. Germ theory was still in its infancy; the vast majority of scientists in Britain still believed that many infectious diseases were caused by the spread of a noxious 'miasma', which emanated from rotting refuse and general filth. The pollution in the Thames was considered unpleasant, but was not seen as the vast public health risk it actually represented.

By the early 1850s, there had been three major cholera outbreaks. More than 36,000 people died of the disease in London in the nineteenth century and a further 1,500 people a year died of typhoid between 1850 and 1870. In 1861, Queen Victoria's husband, Prince Albert, died at the Thames-side castle at Windsor of suspected typhoid, possibly caused by polluted drains – ever the progressive, Albert had recently had them redug in an effort to cleanse them. It wasn't until the 1854 cholera outbreak that the physician John Snow was able to prove his theory that the disease was waterborne, by mapping cases in Soho according to their proximity to water pumps in the street that he suspected were delivering water infected by the fetid river or nearby leaking cesspools. Famously, he vandalized the water pump in what is now Broadwick Street, removing the handle so no more water could be drawn from it, and the number of new cases of cholera in the neighbourhood immediately began to subside. Snow published his findings, but they weren't widely accepted for at least another decade, during which time disease continued to tear through the city's poorer neighbourhoods, where people lived close together, filth was piled up everywhere and there was no clean water available. Tellingly, the further downriver you lived, the more likely you were to be infected: in the 1849 cholera outbreak, eight in every 10,000 people at Kew died, while it was seventeen at Hammersmith, forty-seven at Chelsea and 163 at Waterloo. Out in the estuary, where the city's excrement had been dumped by the river, conditions were even worse.

The water in *Cantilena*'s wake had a silvery sheen to it, clear drops thrown up as it foamed and surged behind the boat. I leaned over the railing at the back of the cockpit to take pictures, trying to capture the way the shadows shifted as the clouds moved. In the camera lens, the water looked almost azure – a colour I have never before associated with the Thames. My memories of the river in the early 1990s are all steeped in yellows, greys and browns – depending on the light, it could be an almost mustardy yellow or an olive-green brown. I've been trying to photograph it my whole life, pointing a cardboard disposable camera at its surface when I was a small child and clicking constantly, only to be disappointed when the developed pictures came back and I had thirty-six prints of the same drab-looking waves.

It had a smell too, which in the brisk, breezy conditions of this new journey out to the estuary I couldn't distinguish. When I think back to the sailing trips we took during my sulky teenage years, it seems that there was always a rotting, brackish note to the air – a smell I used to pretend to despise, but which secretly made my stomach clench with excitement when I caught it for the first time as we approached the boat, ready to embark. Linking a scent to a memory, I was like a collector pinning a butterfly to a card. When I re-encounter a particularly treasured fragrance, it's a transporting experience. A combination of dusty spring rain, leather and a particular man's cologne, if I smell it in the wake of a passing stranger, can whirl me back to a dismal day in Oxford when I was eighteen and falling out of love. The hospital corridor where I had my first round of chemotherapy had such a powerful odour of saline, plastic, strong tea and gentle concern that, long after, I would gag as I walked past its entrance and the smell hit the back of my throat. I could immediately feel the sharp sting of a needle in my hand and the creeping drowsiness of a powerful drug filtering up my arm.

The smell I've squirrelled away for the estuary is complex, with mud, decay, salt, smoke and soggy foliage all swirled together. I can remember how newcomers to the area would respond when it hit them for the first time – friends of my parents invited on a weekend sail with us, or a school friend of mine dragged along to keep me company. They would waft their hands in front of their faces, rolling their eyes and half laughing at how horrible it was. After a while, you become accustomed to it and stop noticing, breathing perhaps a little more shallowly to keep it out. The smell is an intrinsic part of the estuary's landscape. To savour a proper lungful of its air, to turn your face into the wind and breathe deeply, is to admit something difficult – that this unarguably ugly place, where the grey sea meets the grey sky with barely a smudge of mud in between, is beautiful.

The river is a sewer, but it is also a symbol. In many religions, water stands for the sacred and pure, and immersion in it is a way of coming closer to the deity it represents. In Christianity, ablution has always been linked to absolution – ritual foot washing or the use of holy water represents purification. To cleanse the body is to cleanse the spirit. 'You were washed, you were sanctified, you were justified in the name of the Lord Jesus Christ and by the Spirit of our God,' St Paul tells the Corinthians in the New Testament.

This connection took root strongly in the eighteenth century in the theology of the Methodist John Wesley. In a sermon 'on sin in believers' that he wrote in 1763, Wesley directly addressed the connection between cleanliness and holiness: 'A man cannot be clean, sanctified, holy, and at the same time unclean, unsanctified, unholy. He cannot be pure and impure, or have a new and an old heart together.' It is not good enough just to wash off the exterior dirt and sin; true godliness requires moral purification too. For the Methodists, and other evangelical Christian sects active in Britain in the eighteenth and nineteenth centuries, pushing for improvements in the moral tone of 'depraved' cities like London was closely linked to campaigning for social justice. Lift people out of poverty, find them steady work, persuade them away from drinking and dissipation, and – most importantly – clean up their dwellings, and the chance of saving souls increased.

Charles Dickens was one of a number of prominent nineteenth-century figures pushing for sanitation reform. He was a member of the Metropolitan Sanitary Association, a body formed in 1849 when the Public Health Act that had been passed the year before (it was supposed to clean up drinking water, sort out the sewers and provide more medical care) was not applied to London. On 10 May 1851, Dickens addressed the association's annual dinner and reaffirmed his belief in the fundamental necessity of improving sanitation as a means of bringing about societal change: 'Sanitary reforms must precede all other social remedies ... neither education nor religion can do anything useful until the way has been paved for their ministrations by cleanliness and decency'.

In this context, the crisis of the polluted Thames in the mid-nineteenth century stood for much more than just fetid water. It was a calamity in plain sight; the social evil that everyone could see and yet no politician would solve. Dickens included references to the disastrous state of the river and its effects, observed with his own 'eyes and nose', in his fiction. The famous opening of *Bleak House*, which began monthly serialization in March 1852, portrays London as a never-ending mound of filth, built 'crust upon crust' from 'as much mud in the streets as if the waters had but newly retired from the face of the earth'. The corruption of the Court of Chancery, the novel's principal subject, is expressed through the static sludge of the city's streets and the 'fog down the river, where it rolls defiled among the tiers of shipping and the waterside pollutions of a great (and dirty) city'. Later on in the story the busybody social worker Mrs Pardiggle takes heroines Ada and Esther to visit the house of some impoverished brickmakers. The father of the house belligerently shows them their dire sanitation facilities, saying, 'Is my daughter a-washin? Yes, she IS a-washin. Look at the water. Smell it! That's wot we drinks. How do you like it, and what do you think of gin instead! An't my place dirty? Yes, it is dirty–it's nat'rally dirty, and it's nat'rally onwholesome.' The reference to gin is telling; Dickens believed that the connection between poverty and alcoholism – rife in poorer districts at the time – wasn't because of some essential depravity or sinfulness among the lower classes, but because people living in these areas had no alternative. If the water is foul, what else can they drink?

This idea appears again elsewhere in the novel, when Esther observes 'some pewter pots and a milk-can hung on the area railings' at the house of another misguided philanthropist, Mrs Jellyby. Even in this otherwise fairly middle-class neighbourhood, beer and milk are all that is safe to drink.

Sanitary reform was a decades-long preoccupation for Dickens. Back in 1844 he had said in the preface to *Martin Chuzzlewit*, 'In all my writings, I hope I have taken every available opportunity of showing the want of sanitary improvements in the neglected dwellings of the poor.' His novels sold hundreds of thousands of copies in his lifetime (*Bleak House*, collected together into a single volume in 1852 once its initial serialization was complete, had sold in excess of 700,000 copies by the time Dickens died in 1870). Still, although the focus in his fiction on cleanliness as a way of alleviating the suffering caused by poverty and squalor certainly raised awareness of the problem, he and his fellow campaigners were unable to shift the political consensus towards action. A widespread belief at the time was that it was not for politicians to intervene in commerce or trade; for Parliament to pass legislation regulating the behaviour of water companies or factory owners would have been a major expansion of state power in an era that strongly inclined towards small government. 'The British nature abhors absolute power,' thundered an editorial in *The Times* in August 1854. 'We prefer to take our chance of cholera and the rest than be bullied into health . . . There is nothing a man hates so much as being cleaned against his will, or having his floors swept, his walls whitewashed, his pet dungheaps carried away, or his thatch forced to give way to slate, all at the command of a sort of sanitary bombailiff.'

It took a heatwave in June, July and August of 1858 to convince London's political establishment that something had to be done about the Thames. The hottest summer on record to date, temperatures regularly reached the mid-thirties centigrade in the shade in the city centre and hit nearer fifty in the sun. It was also dry, and after weeks without rain the water level in the river was so low that nobody could deny it was an open sewer full of excrement. At the Palace of Westminster, the fetid river flowed right past the windows. A newly formed Tory minority government had the difficult job of marshalling support for legislation to tackle the cause of the dreadful stench that wafted in during debates and committee sittings against vested interests ranging from the water companies to MPs anxious that they would lose their seats if constituents were burdened with the expense of new sewers. As the capital heated up through June, the wealthy fled from their riverside homes and the newspapers began to clamour for a solution to the problem, declaring that London was living through a 'Great Stink' and decrying the delaying tactics of politicians in endless committee hearings. Curtains soaked in chloride and lime were hung at parliamentary windows to block the noxious river fumes, but the stink was overpowering. On 30 June, the Chancellor of the Exchequer, Benjamin Disraeli, with 'his pocket handkerchief ... applied closely to his nose, with body half bent, hastened in dismay from the pestilential odour' of the riverside committee room, followed by others.

Finally, parliamentarians had experienced the revolting fumes endured for years by those who lived by the malodorous river, without the option of fleeing in disgust. It was a turning point. On 3 July 1858, *Punch* produced another cartoon of the Thames, captioned 'Father Thames introducing his offspring to the fair city of London', suggesting that it could be a design for a new fresco in the Houses of Parliament. In it, the disgusting river deity heaves three emaciated, filthy, skeletal

infants, representing diphtheria, scrofula and cholera, out of
the water and shows them to a pristine goddess drawing her
immaculate robes back from the stream while bloated corpses
float past. Thousands of pounds were being spent every week
pouring lime into the river where the sewers dispersed their
deadly contents in a futile attempt at purification; men were
also employed to spread lime on the foreshore at low water, to
dissolve some of the solid filth building up there. Eventually,
the tide of political opinion turned. On 15 July, the Thames
Purification Bill was introduced by the prime minister, Lord
Derby, and just a few weeks later, on 2 August, it passed into
law, all delaying tactics and opposition dissipated by the sheer
force of the fumes emanating from the river. Disraeli, who has
been given much of the credit by recent historians such as
Rosemary Ashton for the canny political operation that ensured
the bill's swift passage, described the Thames during this
period as 'a Stygian pool reeking with ineffable and unbeara-
ble horror'. His reference to the River Styx hinted at the harm
already done by earlier inaction: people had died because of the
filth in the river; London had descended into the underworld,
the sweet stream of the river's upper reaches polluted by sin.

The pumping station at Crossness that I could still just about
see through the binoculars was a key part of the clean-up operation that followed the Great Stink. Joseph Bazalgette, chief
engineer for the Metropolitan Board of Works, had already
submitted a proposal for a sewerage system that would stop raw
sewage flowing straight into the river in central London and
so alleviate the terrible stink. Under new legislation he forged
ahead with construction, employing hundreds of draughtsmen
to draw up the plans for his new network of intercepting and

outfall sewers, and instituting strict quality-control measures for the Portland cement that would form the walls of his new tunnels beneath the city. His design created three levels of sewers on either side of the river, to which all existing drainage tunnels would be connected. These would then join the Northern and Southern Outfall Sewers respectively, running all the way east to Beckton on the north bank and Crossness on the south, before their contents were pumped into the Thames, at the eastern edge of the city, where it was hoped that they would flow straight out to the sea rather than being brought back into London on the tide. The great embankments on both sides of the river in the capital's centre provided space for the sewers beneath and roads on top, as well as riverside promenades and gardens. New artificial banks for the Thames

were constructed on the foreshore out of cement, the sewers were laid down behind and then more cement filled around them. By the time the scheme was complete, there would be an extra 1,300 miles of sewers under London. It was an enormous undertaking and cost millions of pounds – £4 million (£240 million in today's money) for the sewers and £2.5 million (£150 million) for the embankments, a sum far in excess of the £3 million (£180 million) Disraeli had estimated.

Bazalgette's work was described by the *Observer* in April 1861 as 'the most extensive and wonderful work of modern times'. Like the opening of St Katharine Docks four decades before, the inauguration of the Victoria Embankment by the Prince of Wales in 1870 was hailed as a great triumph for progress, a step forward for London as a modern city. It irrevocably altered the character of the Thames in London. The old foreshore and its associated trades and residents were swept away in favour of the concrete riverside promenades already popular in Continental cities like Paris. The sewage no longer ran out into the river but through tunnels in the embankments on either side, meaning that the Thames once more became a popular place of recreation, both for riverside walks in the city and for boating further upstream. By narrowing the river, Bazalgette had also intentionally increased its speed, which had a 'scouring' effect and carried away far more of the debris that had previously eddied about on the tideline. But a divide had been instituted between the river and those who walked on its banks. Bazalgette's embankments created a hard, definite edge where previously there had been soft, mutable foreshore. It was no longer so easy to get down to the river itself; a psychological barrier had been put in place.

The improvement works of the 1860s were considered a tremendous success. Bazalgette was knighted and his scheme hailed by politicians and newspapers alike as the beginning of a new, more sanitary age for London. Miasma theory remained the predominant explanation for diseases like cholera and typhoid, but by removing the sewage from the river, Bazalgette had inadvertently helped to reduce the spread of waterborne diseases. It wasn't a universal solution, though, and soon there were hints that the improvements were benefiting the richer suburbs in the west and centre of the city more rapidly than elsewhere. In 1866, there was another major cholera outbreak, this time concentrated in the East End of London between Aldgate and Bow. It was another hot summer and the Abbey Mills Pumping Station on the River Lea, which would eventually lift the waste from the low-level sewer into the Northern Outfall Sewer and so divert it away from the river, was not yet complete.

In July and August 4,363 people died of cholera in this one small area. Investigation by Bazalgette, Snow and others concerned with sanitary reform showed that the East London Water Company had not been complying with new regulations about filtering and treating water. Their outfall into the River Lea was just half a mile downriver from where the drinking water reservoir was situated and it was eventually proved that infiltration and contamination had taken place. Nearly 6,000 people died in this outbreak, 93 per cent of them in parishes served by the East London Water Company. It was to be the last major incidence of cholera in London and did at least finally convince the scientific establishment of the truth of John Snow's theories about the disease's transmission by infected water. The statistician William Farr, previously sceptical of Snow's work, wrote after the 1866 epidemic that 'the theory of the East wind with cholera on its wings, assailing the East End of London, is not at all borne out by the experience of previous epidemics' and only the bravest adherent of the miasma theory 'would have dared to drink a glass of the waters of the Lea'. Soon afterwards, the influential medical journal *The Lancet* also announced itself persuaded that the water supply was to blame. Then, in the late 1860s, Louis Pasteur's work on the spread of infectious diseases and his observations of micro-organisms provided the basis for a theory of epidemics based on germs rather than smells. Supplying clean water for London continued to be a problem, though. One bizarre proposal made in 1869 involved damming Thirlmere and Haweswater in the Lake District and constructing a 240-mile canal to bring the contents to the capital. But at last the relationship between a cleaner river and a healthier population had a scientific, rather than a moral, basis.

On a sunny, blustery Saturday in early September I set out on the train to visit a friend who lived in the Royal Arsenal, Woolwich, just upriver from the Crossness sewage works. A tall ships festival was taking place and there were several historic sailing vessels moored on the jetty, excited children climbing the rigging. We wandered around the various stalls selling nautical paraphernalia and peered at the ships from the shore, but not being sufficiently fascinated by maritime history, we decided against queuing to go on board and instead settled for a walk downriver along the Thames Path. It is paved here and runs on top of a concrete embankment. Blue-painted railings divide the walker from the water and there's a narrow strip of scrubland between the path and the boxy blocks of flats behind.

The path was busy with people exercising, walking dogs, cycling, playing with children and stopping to enjoy the view across the river. We walked briskly to keep warm as the wind swept across the water. Occasionally, we passed a disused jetty jutting out into the river; perhaps it had served a factory or warehouse long since demolished to make way for housing. Behind the scrub and the riverside flats is the eastern extent of what used to be the 1,200-acre Royal Arsenal site – a major military installation since the eighteenth century and, during the First and Second World Wars, home to a number of munitions and ordnance factories. It was badly damaged during the Blitz, and although weapons research continued here until the early 1990s, the buildings gradually fell derelict or were demolished. Belmarsh, the high-security men's prison, was built on part of the site and lies just behind the river path. On the opposite bank, we could see the round, bulbous gas holders at Beckton and the electricity pylons marching across the horizon. The further we got from Woolwich, the fewer people we passed. Soon our only encounters were with the occasional runner or dedicated Thames Path walker with rucksack and map.

For once, it was pleasant to walk without an agenda or a route to follow. Much of the journey along the Thames that I had undertaken on foot I had done alone, constantly consulting my notes and imagining myself back in time. Here, enjoying a companionable walk, I felt present – a part of the life of the riverbank today. The contrast between the dull concrete and the lush green vegetation creeping along its edge is a reminder of both the rural origins of the river and its industrial past. For long minutes, we didn't talk, listening instead to the steady tread of our feet on the path and the gentle rush of the river as the tide flowed in. A quiet kind of joy crept up on me as the water filtered higher against the concrete wall beneath us; a golden moment of sheer pleasure at being in a place where I felt at home. Although I was still upriver from the estuary landscape of my childhood, in the transition zone where the Thames begins to widen and solid banks give way to marshes, I recognized it everywhere – from the salt-toughened grasses to the dusty cloud hanging above the concrete plant across the river at Creekmouth.

Eventually, we approached Margaret Ness, the point at which the river curves east again before the fresh southerly meanders further downstream at Erith and Greenhithe. 'Ness' is a common suffix in place names in the estuary. It denotes a triangular formation of land that juts out from the shore, usually formed by longshore drift or silt deposits. Here, centuries of such erosion and deposition have created the equivalent of a blind corner on the river, where a boat proceeding towards it would struggle to see if another craft was approaching in the opposite direction around the bend. As we came near, the scrub by the path gave way to denser woodland – it used to be a landfill site for hazardous waste and infrastructure spoil (some of the earth moved to create the Olympic Park in Stratford was dumped here), but in the early 2010s it was reclaimed and transformed into Gallions Park, a landscaped open area of grass, undergrowth and sandy paths. The paved way ahead of us bent away from the river's edge, running between the scrub and trees. We took a dusty fork off to the left to stay near the water and found ourselves walking around a square red metal fence boxing in the small lighthouse that warns ships of the river's turn. Harking back to the age of sail, this place is known as Tripcock Point, because it marks the place on the river above which it was forbidden for ships to carry their anchors 'cocked' – that is, hanging freely from a cable rather than safely stowed aboard.

Out on the point itself, there is a small clearing amid the scrub. The Margaret Ness light is supported on a nine-metre-high iron frame and when lit is visible up to eight miles away. The fence around it is hung with barbed wire and warnings about vandalism. We had passed a fair amount of rubbish in the undergrowth by the path – old clothes, rusting bits of metal, even part of a chair – suggesting that this was a popular place for fly-tipping. Once around the light itself, it is possible to clamber right out to the edge of the water. The hard concrete of the sea wall we had been walking parallel to disappears, giving way to a gentle slope of mossed stones and rubble, with the familiar silty mud of the estuary beneath. Most of this was underwater because of the rising tide, but as I stood and peered down, the movement of the waves occasionally exposed a secret line of weed and sand. The salty, spoilt scent in the air down at the waterline was intoxicating; I barely heard when my friend called over to me to come and look at an information board she had found on the other side of the light.

I walked over to join her and started to read. The board explained, in a few straightforward and matter-of-fact sentences, that Britain's worst public transport disaster occurred just a few hundred metres from this spot on 3 September 1878, when a passenger steamer named *Princess Alice* collided with a coal ship called *Bywell Castle* in the middle of the river. The steamer took less than five minutes to sink and an estimated 650 dead bodies were eventually pulled from the water. The tragedy was made all the worse by the location and timing of the accident: it occurred an hour after high tide, when the Beckton and Crossness sewage works had just pumped one of their twice-daily outfalls of 75 million gallons into the river, ready to be swept out to the estuary by the ebbing tide. The *Princess Alice* broke up and dumped hundreds of people into the water at its highest concentration of toxicity and pollution. Only around 130 passengers survived. After reading this, I stared out across the river, which was glinting innocently in the afternoon sun, and tried to imagine myself in the place of those terrified people for a second. I knew better than most how quickly the tide could flow in the Thames, but even then if I fell in here, where the banks were much closer together than they were in the outer estuary, I would rate my chances of swimming to the shore, or at least staying afloat long enough to be rescued. Except it wasn't water that these people fell into; it was a revolting brew of concentrated sewage and industrial waste. They never stood a chance.

As we turned to begin our walk back, chastened by what we had read, I racked my brains for some previous knowledge of the *Princess Alice* disaster. Even with all my years on the estuary and my obsessive reading about the river, I was sure it had never come up before. To me it seemed like a vital part of the story of the Thames's great clean-up in the nineteenth century – after all, the sewage would not have been at that point in the river in such a concentrated and lethal form if it hadn't been for Bazalgette's great sewer scheme. But it had obviously dwindled in importance, overshadowed by John Snow's pioneering work on cholera and the imperial glories of the new embankments.

As soon as I started delving into the background of the *Princess Alice* disaster – it was a huge story for the many newspapers that covered London in the 1870s – one thing became apparent. This was a tragedy that predominantly affected working-class people, from both the East End and Woolwich. In those places 'every street had lost somebody'. The steamer was a pleasure boat, returning that evening from an excursion to Gravesend. The trip cost two shillings, an affordable treat for people on lower incomes in poorer neighbourhoods, many of whom were visiting the Rosherville Pleasure Gardens, which had its own pier and was easily accessible from the river. Many of the passengers were women and children, enjoying their day out on the water. The *Princess Alice* had departed from London Bridge and picked up more passengers at Woolwich before heading downriver. She was overcrowded and top

heavy – estimates vary, but it is thought that there were about 900 people on board. On the way back, as they approached Margaret Ness against the tide, her captain followed the old Thames waterman's technique of 'working the slack' – that is, sticking to the south bank, where the point sheltered that side of the reach from the strength of the current and the water was therefore smoother and allowed for easier passage. The *Bywell Castle*, a much larger and heavier ship, came around the point and steered to the same side, expecting to pass the *Princess Alice* on the left, in accordance with the standard shipping protocol when ships meet mid-channel.

The coal ship hit the steamer on her right-hand side. The *Princess Alice* broke in two and sank almost immediately. In *Downriver*, Iain Sinclair imagines what it would have been like on board at the moment of collision as the general merriment on board became terror and passengers disappeared under the water just a short distance from the bank. 'Layers of muslin belling into strange shapes, wrapping them in cement.' Other boats in the vicinity, attracted by the *Bywell Castle*'s whistle, came to the aid of those in the water and did what they could to help with the rescue. But most people drowned in the sewage-filled river, many trapped in the cabins or caught in the crush at the stairways in the rush to escape. Some of the survivors later died from infections caught from their immersion in the foul waters. The clothes on the corpses that were recovered from the river were discoloured and bleached by the chemicals the pumping station had just spewed out. In his book *The Thames*, Jonathan Schneer records some of the horrors that emerged in the days that followed, including how undertakers had to make extra-large coffins for some of the bodies, because the sewage had caused them to bloat and swell far beyond their natural size. The recovery effort continued for several days after the collision, with Thames watermen earning five shillings per corpse they brought to the banks. The police had a difficult time managing the crowds of 'sensation seekers' who made their way out onto the marshes and foreshore on both sides of the river to gawp at the scene. The *Illustrated London News* recorded that 'the original shock of the disaster was giving place to a holiday mood of curiosity and rapaciousness', and that pickpockets filtered through the throng, relieving people of their money and watches, a grim parody of the joyful river pageants of years past.

Around 120 of the 650 or so bodies recovered were too decayed or disfigured to be identified, and a further 130 passengers were never accounted for – it was presumed that their bodies had sunk into the mud or been swept out to sea by the tide. The sheer scale of the tragedy and loss of life reverberated through the city over the following days. *The Times* called the wreck 'the most terrible disaster of the kind which has ever been our duty to report'. Relatives and survivors toured London's mortuaries, hoping not to find the swollen remains of those they loved. The crash was so sudden and the loss so absolute that they lingered for years afterwards, with some who were never even on the *Alice* to start with claiming to have swum ashore. Elizabeth Stride, or 'Long Liz', was one such: she told acquaintances in the 1880s that she had been on the steamer with her husband and children and that she alone of the family had survived, the tragedy leading to her descent into poverty and prostitution. In *Downriver*, her plight is one of the tales that is woven through the contemporary narrative, her sorrow and anger after the disaster limitless. She 'drank in revenge. Diluted the Thames with gin.' In reality, Stride was never aboard the ship, her estranged husband died of tuberculosis in an east London hospital six years later and they had no children. But in September 1888 Stride was found dead with her throat slashed and the case was subsequently linked to the Jack the Ripper investigation in east London. She has since become one of the five murdered women at the centre of that long-running urban legend – a pathetic, infamous figure, known only for the manner of her death and the shadowy figure that killed her. Her apocryphal link to the *Princess Alice* is one of those connections that are too fitting, too apt to dismiss in the face of the real facts. The idea that she survived the filthy waters of the sewage-choked Thames, only to fall into sin and die at the hand of a depraved serial killer, seems to be straight out of a penny dreadful, or from the shores of Disraeli's 'Stygian pool'.

Bazalgette may have received a knighthood and a grand memorial in recognition of his great work in cleaning up London, but he had merely done what the city has been doing for centuries: sending the problem downstream, to a place where nobody of significance can complain. It's the way of rivers to flow past us, gathering up our secrets and desires as they move through the landscape. Moving water flushes away knowledge; once something is downstream, it's as if it never was. The *Princess Alice* disaster was a reminder: the sewage that had caused politicians in Westminster to hold their noses in the 1850s had been relocated, not eradicated. The collision's high-profile fallout, with the inquest reported in lengthy newspaper columns and debated in editorials, increased public awareness of what was actually happening to London's waste – millions of gallons of it still being pumped into the river every day, just further east than it had been before. Throughout the 1880s, public concern that a second Stink could occur grew. Eventually, in 1887, the Metropolitan Board of Works extended the processing at Beckton and Crossness to begin filtering solid waste before pumping the liquid into the river at high tide. The remaining sludge was loaded into one of six specially designed barges (the first one commissioned was named the SS *Bazalgette*) and taken out on the ebb tide to be dumped in the Black Deep, a particularly deep channel in the estuary between the Knock John and London Sands sandbanks. It took about twenty minutes for the waste to disperse into the water once the ship's valves had been opened. The dark, spreading stain it caused on the water earned the vessels their nickname: 'Bovril boats'. Once again, the waste was just being taken further east, away from where it could trouble life in London and its environs. Astonishingly, this process continued unchanged for over a hundred years. It wasn't until 1998 that EU regulations put a stop to the practice of dumping sludge into the Thames estuary and instead it was incinerated or treated to become fertilizer.

From the 1880s onwards, the cleanliness of the lower river and the estuary began to improve. The twelfth-century chronicler William Fitzstephen had talked of 'the fishful Thames', and many accounts down the years mention the different fish to be found – herring, plaice, mackerel, smelt, salmon and many more. Fishing villages once existed all along the estuary's shores: when Daniel Defoe visited Barking in 1727, for example, he found it to be 'chiefly inhabited by fishermen'. The fish market at Billingsgate had been the focus of the trade for centuries, but when the toxicity of the river began to increase in the 1830s, the fish disappeared. The last salmon was caught in 1833, and in *Three Men in a Boat* Jerome K. Jerome jokes, 'I never knew anybody catch anything up the Thames, except minnows and dead cats.' The collapse in the fish population brought many fishing families to the brink of starvation. Boats were left to rot in the mud on the foreshore when it was no longer worth taking them out as there was so little left to catch. Reliable rail links between London and the east coast affected fishermen on the Thames too: fish from Grimsby and Great Yarmouth, for example, could be sent to the capital without too much effort, replacing the meagre haul from the polluted river in the city itself.

Fish and other river-dwelling species have long been considered a good barometer of water's health. They sit in the middle of a river's ecosystem, bacteria beneath them and predators like seals and birds of prey above. Without any one element, the ecosystem collapses. This is what happened in the Thames in the mid-twentieth century, when bomb damage to London's sewers from the Second World War went unrepaired and the noxious brew that had once flowed safely underground began to leak out again. The river was declared 'biologically dead' by the Natural History Museum in 1957, after research showed that there was no oxygen in the water for miles to either side of London Bridge. The naturally occurring bacteria in the water that break down sewage and suchlike do so aerobically: that is, they require oxygen for the reaction, taking it from the water. The Thames was so polluted that the bacteria could no longer function.

A succession of laws passed in the following decades improved matters, making it illegal to dump agricultural by-products in the river and strictly regulating what waste could be added to the landfill sites on its shores. Other factors contributed too: for instance, heavy-metal poisoning used to be a big problem in the Thames, particularly silver, which was used for developing photographs, but the advent of digital photography did away with it. There was no one organization or moment that created a cleaner river, but rather many individual threads like this that brought it about, from the death of industry in east London to the improvement of the old sewage works as they expanded to keep pace with the city's ever-growing population. The first salmon in over a hundred years was caught by Thurrock Power Station in 1974; many other fish have since returned, including sea bass, flounder, dace, bream and trout. The Zoological Society of London (ZSL) has recorded over a hundred species living in the estuary and lower reaches of the river, which has become a crucial nursery and breeding habitat and provides an essential transition zone between salt and fresh water for migratory species like the European eel. In 2006, a bottlenose whale swam up the estuary and was eventually stranded and died on the shore at Battersea. Pods of porpoises and dolphins have been sighted, as have otters and herons. There are now nature reserves on the river's banks where once there was derelict land or rubbish dumps – at Rainham Marshes, Cliffe, Erith and many other places. Environmentalists still have concerns about the impact of dredging practices in the outer Thames on fish, but more habitats are protected and wildlife populations are documented now, enabling conservationists to make the case for more resources and bigger reserves. The river is alive once again.

Once the boat had passed Crossness, there were no more Victorian pumping stations for me to gaze at through the binoculars. Tired of watching corrugated-metal sheds and dusty tarmac pass by as we slid beyond the industrial estates of Belvedere and Lessness Heath, I turned the lenses on the water ahead, chasing rills and waves with my eyes as the river eddied around another bend. I lighted on a patch of golden brown on the smoky surface of the water. Peering closer, I identified a pair of eyes and some whiskers bobbing about as the boat moved, and then another pair nearby. The tide was more than half out now, exposing the foreshore in the shelter of the river's curve. A pair of harbour seals were perched on it, at water level. They were flopping around gently, basking in the cool mud exposed by the receding tide. As I stared, they seemed to look back at me, almost insouciant. This was their home; I was just passing through.

Speechless with shock, I thrust the binoculars into my mother's hand and gestured in their direction while I grabbed my camera and tried to get a picture. Looking back later at the shots I took, it's clear that the sandy bank was too far away for my amateur's lens, but I treasure those wobbly, blurry photographs anyway. It was the first time, in all my years on the estuary, that I had ever made such a sighting. Seals are top-level predators, able to survive only where there is sufficient stock of fish like salmon, mackerel and herring to sustain them. The ZSL Thames Marine Mammal Survey now records an average of 113 seal sightings a year, and although the data is difficult to gather, this points towards increases in the estuary populations of both harbour and grey seals. To me, their presence confirmed what I had been observing all day: the river had changed for the better.

The slightly sulphurous smell of my memories was gone. The water, although still silty and drab in appearance, was unmistakably cleaner.

The problems of pollution in the Thames are by no means over, however. Plastic, not sewage, is now the major threat to life in the river. Broken toys, traffic cones, water bottles and endless plastic sticks from cotton buds litter the tideline, and do not biodegrade. In 2015, researchers from Royal Holloway, University of London, found that 75 per cent of the flounders in the Thames that they tested had plastic fibres in their guts. Around 300 tonnes of rubbish are removed from the river every year, via special barges or passive waste collectors (floating U-shaped structures tethered at one end that collect the plastic as it floats past on the tide). But they can't catch everything: the Thames21 charity reports that discarded wet wipes, made from plastic fibres, are forming their own drifts and banks at slower-flowing bends in the river. A 2018 survey of the foreshore at low tide found an average of forty wet wipes per square metre. Industry body Water UK says wet wipes make up 93 per cent of the material blocking sewers.

Slowly, legislators are moving to combat this deadly detritus. The 5p charge on single-use plastic carrier bags introduced across the UK in 2015 has reduced their use by 90 per cent, a ban on plastic microbeads in cosmetics came into force at the start of 2018, and a similar prohibition on plastic straws and cotton bud sticks could soon follow. In a speech at the London Wetland Centre in January 2018 – created from four disused Victorian reservoirs on the banks of the Thames at Barnes in west London – Theresa May launched a twenty-five-year plan to eradicate unnecessary plastic use in the UK. 'We don't want to go back to being the "dirty man of Europe",' she said, in a reference to the polluted state of Britain's waterways when the country first joined the European Economic Community in 1973, before directives on water quality and industrial waste helped to clean up rivers like the Thames. I had seen the odd piece of plastic flotsam from the boat on the journey so far, but I knew that it was on the banks that most of the detritus collected, stranded by the falling tide. The banks were lying lower and I could see the exposed mud of the foreshore now that the tide had ebbed further away. Reeds and grasses poked through at the edges and jagged, rotten pieces of wood thrust up at odd angles, the remnants of long-forgotten jetties and posts. Through the binoculars, I could see the tangled mess of waste at the tideline.

Eventually the seals receded from sight, even through the binoculars. The river bent south again around Frog Island, the curved point of land between the water and Rainham Marshes on the north bank. Although there were still buildings on the banks – the East London Waste Authority's treatment works and recycling centre is on Frog Island – we were finally beyond the limits of the city. London's hold on the river had loosened and the contradictory sensations of the estuary were in evidence. The gleaming mud, shifting through greys and blues and browns as the clouds moved overhead, was captivating. This place was for so long valued so little that an entire city's worth of sewage was spewed into it. It was considered a kind of black hole on the map – a place where nothing of consequence existed. But the recovery of the river's ecosystem in the past five decades, and the sheer beauty of what I was observing from the deck, show how wrong this was. As Ken Worpole says in *The New English Landscape*, 'We have been throwing things away for centuries, only recently realizing that there is no such place as away. We all live downriver now.' The river may carry off our mistakes as it flows on, but it will never let us forget them.

5

Crayford Ness to Coalhouse Point

It was barely light when the train pulled in at Slade Green Station. I was the only passenger getting off at this sleepy suburb on the very south-eastern edge of London at seven in the morning and it wasn't hard to see why: spidery fingers of frost iced the edges of the platform as I walked towards the road and my breath hung in the air. I had woken early on a chilly Saturday morning in February, a month or so after making my New Year's Eve resolution on the foreshore, in order to come here, where the River Darent marks the boundary between London and Kent as it flows north into the Thames. Wrapped up warmly, I had slipped out of the city before it awoke. The semi-detached houses of this commuter district had a blank, drowsy look to them as I wandered about the car park, looking for the lane I had identified on the map the previous night which would take me north-east to the Thames.

I found it eventually, branching discreetly off amid a tangle of bare branches where the main road curved around yet more pebble-dashed facades. I walked for what felt like a long time between spiky high hedges denuded of leaves and muddy pools at the edge of the crumbling tarmac, until the lane dwindled to a track. A path turned off to the right and then the unmistakable mud of an estuary foreshore was ahead, sloping down from the grassy bank to the silty, dark stream of the Darent below. I turned slowly on the spot; the land all around was flat. Huge electricity pylons stalked across the horizon in every direction, and the dun-coloured cylindrical chimney of Littlebrook Power Station in the distance to the east told me how far I still was from the banks of the Thames. Everything was quiet and grey, with only a very faint sound of rushing water as the tide ebbed out of this little tributary.

The track continued along the bank and I followed it around the Darent's final curves, wedged between the foreshore and the huge industrial park that had appeared without warning on the other side of me. I remembered this from elsewhere in the estuary – there are fields, scrubby brown earth open to the louring sky, and then there is tarmac with timber stacked on it and forklifts everywhere. The juxtaposition is jarring, the lack of transition unfamiliar. We're so used now to rural areas and significant vistas being protected. But nobody thinks this silty spit of land that separates the Darent from the Thames is worth preserving. It could be lost under concrete.

As I approached the end of the track, a great floodgate came into view, its two towers and open shutter framing the river like an open portcullis on a castle. As with the one at Barking, this arresting, almost Brutalist structure was built in the aftermath of the 1953 flood to protect the land here should there be another extraordinary surge. Its simple design – two upright columns and a horizontal bar between them – is like a distorted echo of Tower Bridge, from another world upstream.

But I had come here to see the Thames and when I finally reached the end of this little tributary river it was there waiting for me, the olive-green and grey water partly drained away with the tide. I climbed the slightly raised, sloping earth embankment, now covered in thick-stemmed grasses, and looked across to the other shore. I was on the border here, with London on one side of the Darent, Kent on the other and Essex across the Thames. My life on the river was bound up in these places – Kent, and the towns further along the south bank where I was born and first got to know the water; London, where I had floated after my time studying upstream; and Essex, the unknown land over the water, which was so similar to yet so different from my childhood home. The river connected them all, and me. Even though I was right at water level, with no vantage point over these flat, estuarine lands, I felt that grand, expansive sensation usually associated with surveying the prospect of what is to come – like Keats's explorers, 'Silent, upon a peak in Darien'. To my eyes, the view from the Paul Nash's Wittenham Clumps has nothing on this.

There is no such thing as untouched wildness in Britain, no matter how much clever design or marketing might try and make you think otherwise. All landscapes are a result of the interaction between humans and nature. Everything around us is affected by man's intervention or neglect, yet today's conception of nature is one that prioritizes solitude and a sense of 'untouched beauty'. In an essay about the Bosnian Alps, the writer Fiona Sampson once commented that 'our landscapes are not innocent'. The reason that Britain is particularly prone to commodifying ideas of 'nature' and 'heritage' – for sale on tea towels and calendars – she says, is because the combination of Romantic ideas about transcendent individual experiences of nature and the cultural tourism of the Grand Tour 'encourage us to think about landscape as a series of natural tableaux removed from daily life'. The ideal landscape is an uninhabited one, unspoilt by human activity and preferably featuring a few sublime crags.

The vista laid out before me could not have been more different from this abstract idea. The traces of industry were everywhere: the petrol refinery, the container depot, the oil storage facility and many other such buildings in Thurrock, the Essex borough across the water. In the distance to my right, I could just make out the angular cables of the Dartford bridge, the eastern-most Thames crossing that takes the M25 with it over the river. I was standing on an embankment created as part of the flood defences protecting the factories and warehouses behind me. And it was flat; flat, marshy land as far as the eye could see. For Wordsworth and his fellow Romantic poets, 'sky-pointing peaks' were symbols of the connection between man and God, an earthly manifestation of the divine that aroused strong emotions in the observer. To an extent, today's nature lovers still think like this: it's the supposed wildness of the Scottish Highlands and the Lake District that inspires the most passionate reactions in writers, walkers and tourists. There is little inspiration to be found out here, in the marshes.

The wind was getting up, and an icy chill was blowing into my bones. I turned away west and began to walk along the river path, so that I could loop back gradually towards the station and a train back to the city. It ran away from the bank a little, so there was scrubby grass between me and the Thames, the water just out of view. On my other side, the industrial buildings soon gave way to fields again. I felt lonely walking here – not because I was alone, but because this was an experience that I wouldn't share with many others. I wouldn't come here on day trips with friends and I wasn't taking pictures to share on social media. It was as if I had walked off the edge of the map. The prevailing wisdom that a landscape such as this is best ignored gives it an uncharted, mysterious quality. It feels left behind.

On their first journey into the estuary in 1984, my parents sailed non-stop from Brighton, through the night, to catch the tide. By the time they reached this point, on the outskirts of Greater London, it was past three in the morning and they were tired. The hardest navigation was behind them – the sandbanks and currents in the broader estuary giving way to the more defined river that eventually narrows to become the Thames that flows into central London. Rather than press on through the night to the city, they decided to stop where the river bends around the Swanscombe peninsula, between Gravesend and Dartford. The Thurrock Yacht Club has its base on the north bank of the river here and provides moorings for visiting boats on the edge of the channel. Having safely tied up in the dark, they retreated into the cabin for much-needed food and sleep before continuing upriver to Tower Bridge later that morning.

Sailing this course in reverse with them was an enlightening experience. Like most children, I am used to thinking of my parents as fixed in time by me, forever settled in the way they were when I was growing up. Many young adults find them-selves surprised to realize that their parents had a life of their own before the arrival of children. For me, as I embarked on this journey back to the estuary, it was my parents' past that preoccupied me. Other than the well-rehearsed words of their emigration story – told so many times in explanation to new friends and acquaintances that the surprising edges have long since been rubbed off it, like a pebble worn down by the sea – I have little sense of what they were like when they were the age I am now, deciding to trust their lives to a boat and their futures to a new continent. To me they have always been supremely confident, practical people with an unshakeable belief in the power of reason and logic to solve any problem. I find it difficult to imagine them as inexperienced, unsure twenty-somethings finding out about this place for the first time. I still remember how shocked I felt when, helping my mother sort out some old photographs for a new album, we came across a picture of my father wearing denim jeans – something I can't remember him ever doing during my lifetime. Suddenly, awfully, I was aware that he had once been young too.

Conversation, sometimes stretched out over hours, is an aspect of sailing trips that I always found tedious as a teenager. There's not really anything to do while the boat is under way except sit in the cockpit, help with navigation, trim the sails and keep lookout. The motion has always made me feel nauseous if I go down into the cabin or read a book, so hour after hour would be spent on deck, huddled in eight layers of clothing, keeping an eye on the horizon for the specific sequence of flashing lights that would denote the next buoy on our course. Sometimes, we would play cards or a board game with stuck-down pieces like Battleship or Mastermind, but more often we would just talk – about school, work, where we were going, what we had been reading, or anything else that came up. Looking back, it was a way of being that did not exist anywhere else in my fourteen-year-old life: forced to sit still in a confined space for hours on end, with nowhere to run to, no television to watch and no books I could read. And yet still, with the ignorance of teenagers the world over, I rarely took the chance to ask my parents about their own experiences.

Now, more than a decade after the last of those sulky teenage sailing trips, I know better. It's rare these days for me to sit uninterrupted with my parents for as long as our journey from

central London down the Thames to the sea has taken. I used
the time to quiz them about their memories of the places we
passed along the way, and felt a little like I was stepping back-
wards into a time before I existed, when my parents saw the
river's banks for the first time. As we passed the point where
the River Darent joins the Thames and the Queen Elizabeth II
Bridge came into view, my father put *Cantilena*'s helm on autopilot, so that he could sit down opposite me and properly take
in the view. He started pointing to parts of the bank that had
been landfill sites when they first sailed this way – dusty, grey
holes in the land barely visible from the water, many of which
were now grassed-over hummocks hovering above the muddy
gradient of the foreshore. The breeze was stiffening as we slid
down the relatively straight stretch of the river by the town of
Purfleet (a former military base and gunpowder production site,
and, from 1889, the place where the borough of Kensington
dumped its rubbish) on the north bank, the power station tower
I had seen on my wintry walk up the Darent to the south. Soon,
we would be able to cut the engine and hoist a sail.

Cantilena passed under the bridge with plenty of space above
the top of her mast – I always think when approaching such
obstacles that she won't fit, but we've never hit anything – and
the autopilot automatically altered the course slightly to starboard to make sure that we left clear water between the boat
and the Stone Ness Lighthouse on the north bank. This is
another ness, a roughly triangular point on the bank formed by
the silt and mud dumped by the river in the curve as the flow
slackens. Like the beacon I had examined at Margaret Ness,
Stone Ness is a light on an openwork steel frame, horizontally
striped in red and white paint to make it visible in all the grey-
greens of the river and topped with a wind turbine. It marks the
southernmost extent of the Thurrock Marshes, which although

drained and dyked to provide space for the bridge's ramp, a huge oil storage depot, a vast lorry park and many other similar businesses, because of the shallow slope of the foreshore could still be hazardous to shipping wandering out of the channel in poor weather or at night. Several of the depots have long jetties over the shallows to the very edge of the deep water. Two huge tankers were moored by the oil depot pier head as we slid by, their cargo being invisibly pumped ashore to the serried ranks of white cylindrical storage drums on the shore. This was a familiar sight in my childhood on the estuary. We would pass several power stations regularly, and my father would do his best to satisfy my insatiable curiosity about everything I saw by explaining the intricacies of how each kind of fuel – we passed coal-, gas- and oil-fired plants on our various voyages – was unloaded safely and stored. I loved staring up at the big ships, awestruck by the vertiginous surface their hulls presented from where I sat below, almost on the water in our little boat, and learning why they had such odd names and exotic points of origin (under a tax-avoidance system known as 'flags of convenience', many big ships are registered in countries like Panama and Liberia, rather than the owner's actual country of origin, to get around tax rules and labour regulations).

Once past the lighthouse, we entered the stretch of the Thames known as Fiddler's Reach, where the bank falls away sharply to the north as the river cuts into the land. On a foggy night here in October 1964, an East German cargo ship called MV *Magdeburg* carrying forty-two British-made Leyland buses bound for Cuba collided with an empty Japanese vessel just before 2 a.m. The *Magdeburg* was holed below the waterline and rapidly filled with water as she heeled over, eventually coming to rest horizontally on the riverbed, her smashed cargo in disarray. She remained like that for months, as initial attempts to raise her failed. It was the worst collision in the Thames since the Second World War, but nobody was injured and no blame was apportioned. Yet it has remained a live case for those fascinated by the proxy skirmishes of the Cold War, and in 2008 a historian named John McGarry claimed to have found evidence in an East German archive that lent weight to long-held suspicions that the crash had been deliberately orchestrated by the CIA to prevent the buses reaching Fidel Castro's Cuba. The collision certainly occurred at a febrile political moment. US president Lyndon Johnson was unhappy with British companies for circumventing sanctions on Cuba and reportedly summoned the British foreign secretary, Rab Butler, for a dressing-down. Johnson is said to have waved a wad of dollar notes at Butler as a humiliating offer to lend him some cash if Britain was so hard up that it needed to sell buses to the communists. The involvement of the American intelligence services in the collision has never been proved, although some academics have said it isn't completely out of the question. Debate rages on conspiracy-theory websites and forums to this day: you only have to search 'Fiddler's Reach' for the whole thing to tumble out across your screen.

On the north bank are the villages of Thurrock, which are now connected in a kind of coastal suburban sprawl character-istic of this part of Essex but were once separate rural entities with evocative, ancient names like Chafford Hundred, Badgers Dene, and North and South Stifford. Somewhere deep beneath the bed of the river runs the tunnel that carries the Eurostar and high-speed domestic trains under the Thames on their way between the Kent coast and London. These trains can reach speeds in excess of 200 mph and are some of the fastest in Britain. They didn't start running until after I had left Kent to go to university, and even now when I take one to visit my

parents for the weekend I marvel at how quick the trip from
London is – just over half an hour, rather than the two hours it
used to take – and how for so many years I thought that coming
upriver by boat was the only way to get to the city.

When my parents moored here in the middle of the night
in 1984, they knew nothing about the place on the riverbank
a few metres from where they had stopped. Thurrock Yacht
Club is in Grays, the largest town in the borough, which has
always had strong connections to the sea and to the river. It's
a large conurbation, linked to the main roads that head east
from London to the coast, and its fortunes are tightly bound
to the industries I could see from the other side of the river.
Around the time that my parents were sleeping there, the
area began to go through a drastic economic and social transition – not dissimilar to what is happening in other industrial
areas of Britain, such as the north-east and south Wales. The
docks at Tilbury, just downstream, were the biggest employer
in the area for the first half of the twentieth century, with
school leavers naturally following their fathers into the steve-
doring trade without the need for further education or travel.
But the combined effect of more mechanization at the port and
the advent of containerization, where cargo was transported
in huge metal boxes that could be loaded and unloaded by a
vastly reduced workforce, meant big job losses in a short space
of time. Around a fifth of the population were unemployed and
on benefits by the middle of the 1980s. Just as on the Isle of
Dogs further upriver, a government drive towards glitzy new
development to replace the downsizing industries associated
with the docks and a lack of attention to the long-term needs
of the existing population – such as better skills and access to
new employment opportunities – fuelled resentment.

The south-east has long been the most prosperous region of

Britain, but Thurrock and other places like it in the Thames estuary stand out against the trend. They are tiny pockets of deprivation – the most recent research shows that more than twenty of its wards are among the bottom 10 per cent in the whole country for indicators like antisocial behaviour, poor health and school-age pregnancies. They have more in common with the deindustrialized towns further north, like Doncaster and Grimsby, than they do with the wealthier conurbations immediately inland. This economic isolation intermingles with the loneliness in the landscape I felt on the banks of the Darent. Without jobs to go on to after school, young people leave the area altogether or commute to London for work. The remaining population is ageing, with the number of men aged eighty-five or over expected to rise by 220 per cent by 2028 and women by 115 per cent – an increase considerably higher than for the country as a whole. An estimated 32 per cent of house-holds in the borough contain a person with a limiting long-term illness and the demand for carers is outstripping the supply of people currently employed in the profession.

All of this has political consequences. After decades of seeing it across the water, I first visited Grays in April 2015 during the general election campaign. I was far from the only journalist to do so: the area, usually ignored by the national media, was in the spotlight because polling had shown that, against the nationwide trend, UKIP was in the lead in the Thurrock constituency. I spent time wandering around the market in Grays, chatting to stall holders bitter about 'newcomers' apparently getting council flats ahead of their own relatives, and in the council estates that surround the town, knocking on doors with Labour activists who feared that their own voters were turning away from them and towards Nigel Farage's anti-immigration rhetoric. Between the end of the Second World War and the 1987 election, the overwhelming majority of people here had voted Labour, an affiliation bolstered by the strong trade union tradition in the docks and associated workplaces. Then, lured by Margaret Thatcher's promise of homeownership for the working classes and rapid economic renewal, coupled with the decline of those labour structures as the traditional industries laid people off, Thurrock turned blue. Now, with unemployment still high and immigration a hot topic, the incumbent Conservative MP was defending a tiny majority of just ninety-two and was considered easy prey for the insurgent far-right party.

For a brief moment, this place became the embodiment of Britain's wider political anxieties. My fellow journalists expressed shock at the deprivation and decay they found here, just a thirty-five-minute train ride from central London. 'The industrial skyline stretching out into the distance looks more like the Urals circa-1935 than a provincial Essex town,' one wrote in the *New Statesman*. In the political establishment awareness was growing that perhaps globalization and Britain's increasingly service-orientated economy weren't delivering benefits for everyone. In 2014, *The Economist* had described nearby Tilbury as containing 'a polyp of hard-up, mostly white, grumpy people,' and this particular working-class demographic now seemed to be shifting the political norms by rejecting the main political parties in favour of UKIP, which had policies expressly designed to appeal to their insecurities and fears.

These white working-class people in the estuary felt left behind – by evolving industries that no longer required their skills or labour and by politicians who hadn't formulated policies to heal the wounds this left. A sense of collectivism, of everyone in the community working together towards the same object, was fractured and eventually destroyed by the economic changes that blew through here in the 1980s and 1990s. It's the same in lots of places like this. People who were once proud of being from a 'steel town' or a 'port city' would find that identity no longer available to them. It particularly affected older men, who laboured for decades in their chosen trade, only to be cut off from the solidarity and security it offered when they reached late middle age, too late to retrain or acquire new skills for a different profession. Research undertaken by a team from Sheffield Hallam University found that 41 per cent of 'very aged' men in Thurrock live alone. In the past few years, the government has started talking about a 'loneliness epidemic', estimating that 9 million people in Britain 'always or often feel lonely'. The impact of deindustrialization on mental health is only now beginning to be studied, so the stress, anxiety and depression it caused have gone largely undocumented and untreated. In his 2016 study on the effects of declining manufacturing in the West Midlands, *Cut Out: Living without Welfare*, the journalist Jeremy Seabrook argues that part of this stems from the fact that the communities in former industrial areas were never permitted to grieve for the passing of their old way of life. 'There was no space for any acknowledgement that human lives were rooted here, with all the grace and sadness that accompany them,' he writes. 'Obsessed with an ideology of progress, few have paused to ponder on the subjective experience of those whose world and whose emotions, for five or six generations, were shaped by, and rooted in, this environment, with all the sorrow, pride and pain it imposed on them.' His words resonate strongly in relation to the Thames estuary, where progress and forward momentum are tied to a sense of Britain's self-image: the river is part of the capital's glory and therefore all changes and developments along its banks are for the better, no matter what the reality might be. When I visited in 2015, many people spoke about Grays and the wider Thurrock area in the past tense – 'It's not how it used to be' or 'It was a good place to live' – even though the actual fabric of the place remained relatively unchanged. Something less tangible than the solid concrete and brick and earth had disappeared.

In Thurrock, the political expression of this thwarted grief followed a familiar pattern. High unemployment and few job opportunities among the white working class, many of whom had origins in the working-class neighbourhoods of London's East End, from where their families had moved out to the estuary in the hope of a better life after the destruction and dilapidation of the Blitz and the hardship of the Second World War, led to frustration and anger. The arrival of immigrants, from both the European Union and elsewhere in the world, fostered resentment and the perception that newcomers were 'jumping the queue' when it came to council houses or school places. An ugly strain of nativist sentiment emerged in towns on both sides of the estuary: in Barking, Dagenham, Erith, Purfleet, Dartford, Gravesend, the Medway towns and Southend, the racist belief that the white majority were somehow being disadvantaged grew. The black, Asian and minority ethnic population of Thurrock doubled to almost 20 per cent between the 2001 and 2011 censuses – a rapid alteration for an area that had previously been relatively racially homogeneous. The 2011 census also showed that just under 15 per cent of people in the borough were foreign-born, slightly more than the 12.4 per cent average for Britain as a whole.

In the early 2000s, the neo-fascist BNP rapidly increased the number of candidates they fielded in local council elections nationwide, from seventeen in 2000 to 217 in 2003. And in 2003, the BNP's Nicholas Geri won the Grays Riverside ward in Thurrock in a by-election with 38 per cent of the vote. By 2006 and 2007, the party was coming a close second to Labour or the Conservatives in many wards across the borough, sometimes missing out by just a few dozen votes, before securing their second council seat in Tilbury in 2008. This mirrored the trend in Lancashire, the West Midlands and West Yorkshire – all places with a similar economic background. As his profile increased via appearances on various television and radio programmes, BNP leader Nick Griffin became a national figure, condemned by politicians of all mainstream political parties but adored by the crowds who turned up to his rallies in places like Stoke and Blackpool.

The rise of the BNP and then, in the latter part of the 2010s, of UKIP – another insurgent right-wing party that carefully dissociated itself from the racist street tactics of Griffin's movement yet appealed to a similar sense of dissatisfaction and disenfranchisement among parts of the white working class – became the dominant narrative in British politics. The estuary was at the core of UKIP's electoral strategy: Nigel Farage, the party's one-time leader, stood unsuccessfully, once in 2005 and once in 2015, as a parliamentary candidate for Thanet, a marshy former island on the eastern end of the Kent shore. Among the Westminster establishment, there was a tendency to dismiss the growing popularity of such parties as an anomaly or aberration, as in the 2005 general election when the BNP achieved 17 per cent of the vote in Barking, their highest ever. Some in the Labour Party, in particular, were reluctant to accept that the move towards greater globalization and integration with Europe overseen by the Blair government was in some part responsible and that it hadn't been a universal good for the people of

Britain. To understand a bit more about this division, I went to see Margaret Hodge, the MP for Barking, who had served as a Labour minister under both Tony Blair and Gordon Brown, to ask her about her campaigning tactics against the BNP. She had been severely criticized in 2006 by leading Labour politicians and the left-leaning press for saying that eight out of ten white families in her constituency were 'tempted' by the anti-immigration rhetoric of Nick Griffin's party, and many times since for her approach to tackling this most divisive of subjects.

Hodge is a diminutive, impeccably groomed woman now in her early seventies, who came to Britain as a child from Egypt, which is where her Jewish family had taken refuge when fleeing from Nazi Germany in the 1930s. She told me of her initial shock at visiting Barking for the first time in 1994, having lived in the far more ethnically diverse north London borough of Islington for decades. 'When I went there it was white, it just hit you coming out of the tube station, it was white,' she said. 'Now, it's more like the rest of London. It's an area in transition, and change is difficult. It's that transition which the BNP exploited.' We were speaking in the beautiful front room of her elegant Islington town house, her treasured grand piano standing a few feet away from the armchair she occupied. Hodge had worked for several major corporations and had been a council leader before she became an MP; her late husband was a high court judge. Part of her constituency consists of the Becontree estate, the largest council estate in the UK, which was built in the 1920s and 1930s to provide accommodation for families from east London displaced by slum clearances. It's not hard to imagine why her constituents might have felt alienated by the brand of politics Hodge represents – her life was very different from theirs. 'I really think [the BNP] had a chance of taking over the council and taking my seat,' she told me. Labour had 'failed to connect' with people struggling with the way their lives and homes were changing. 'We looked inwards, not outwards. We thought we could weigh the votes in because this was a traditionally safe Labour seat. We didn't think we had to earn them,' she said.

Her solution, and the core of the campaign she began in 2006, was to not brush off people's fears as merely racist and therefore not worthy of attention – something which was controversial in her party at the time. She went door to door, not talking about the Labour Party overall, but rather asking what the small, local issues were that she could help solve. There was no point making promises based on numbers when it came to immigration, she said, because inevitably targets would be missed and people would feel let down. What she could do was help with day-to-day problems with school places or benefit forms, and rebuild trust that way. In addition, she made it clear that she believed that economic migrants needed to 'work their time and earn their rights' before being entitled to benefits like social housing, to counter the widespread impression that newcomers were jumping the queue ahead of the existing population. 'When I originally said it [in 2008] people went bananas,' she said. 'I started talking about how access to social housing ought to be based on how long you've lived in the area, not just your need. That was very controversial, but that's the way you deal with racism. You've got to earn your rights.' In the years that followed, as more and more safe Labour seats in former industrial heartlands were threatened by insurgent far-right parties, her party adopted a similar stance. In 2014, the Labour leader, Ed Miliband, declared, 'It is not prejudiced to worry about immigration. It is understandable.'

Hodge's critics were silenced on 6 May 2010, when she doubled her majority to 16,555 and beat the BNP leader, Nick

Griffin, into third place. She was the undoubted victor of what had been dubbed by the media 'the Battle for Barking' and had been supported by hundreds of anti-fascist activists from all over the country, who had travelled to her Thames-side constituency in the months and weeks before polling day to lend their support and help canvass. However, the conditions that brought about that febrile moment haven't disappeared, she insisted: 'The underlying concerns that led to that are still there. I haven't given up. I haven't taken my foot off the accelerator ... I still get that "It's changed, it's not the same round here" thing, which is code for it's become a mixed borough.' She is vigilant now, she told me, following up every time someone attends one of her regular coffee mornings to express dissatisfaction, and makes sure she helps them. Paging through the recent editions of local newspapers in Barking and the rest of the estuary's towns provides plenty of stories to back up Hodge's concerns. In 2014, a former UKIP MEP and local council candidate in Gravesend declared that there were 'no-go zones' on the Kent side of the Thames because of gangs of eastern European immigrants; in 2017, another UKIP MEP and former parliamentary candidate, Tim Aker, said the same thing of Grays. Over the past half a dozen years, the phrase 'immigrant crime wave' has come regularly from the mouths of both the party's candidates and its supporters.

The ethnographer Lisa Mckenzie, who helped to conduct the London School of Economics' Great British Class Survey, has written of repeated incidences of white working-class subjects telling her that they don't just feel 'left behind' by contemporary politics, but completely invisible. 'We don't exist to them, do we?' one young woman from London's East End said to her in 2016, the day before Britain voted to leave the European Union. Just as UKIP followed the BNP in focusing on the effects of the estuary's post-industrial malaise, the Brexit campaign inherited much of the same support. The links that were made during the referendum campaign between high levels of immigration and membership of the European Union resonated throughout the estuary. Although London defied the national trend and voted strongly to remain, downriver it was a different story. On the Essex side, in Barking and Dagenham, 62.44 per cent of people voted to leave, with that proportion rising to 72.28 per cent in Thurrock and 72.7 per cent in Castle Point, the next borough east, and there were similar results on the north Kent coast too. These results emphasize that the people of the estuary still feel cut off, invisible to the great liberal metropolis upstream. When you are already an outsider, it can feel like there's nothing left to lose.

Nearly three years after my election-campaign visit, I went back to Grays. My mother and I drove from Kent, through the tunnel under the Thames at Dartford. We flew down the roads in the car I learned to drive as a teenager, which now whistles slightly alarmingly at high speeds but is still going. It was a hot spring day, the sun beating down hard through the windscreen. We navigated the tangled motorway junctions on either side of the river using crumpled Ordnance Survey maps rather than a road atlas, with me in the passenger seat covered by several layers of crinkling cartographic carapace. It had been years since we made an expedition like this together, but I fell back into the family habit of giving directions by compass points and landmarks, rather than road names and road junctions. This way of approaching all navigation as if at sea was another thing I only realized was strange when I grew up. Most people were a bit baffled when told that they should 'walk north-north-east

from the station and bear west at the war memorial' to find my
house. My mother always knows where north is, like she has
her very own compass floating in her chest. She doesn't have
to think about it, consult a map or check the position of the
sun; she just knows, and always has done – though this left
her disorientated when she first arrived in Britain from South
Africa. While living on the boat in St Katharine Docks, she
had a temporary job as a programmer at Shell's headquarters
on the south bank of the river. Sometimes, while walking about
the city, she would find herself going in the wrong direction to
get to her destination. The celestial landmarks of the northern
hemisphere were the other way around to her, and until she
had recalibrated herself to her new home, it was as if the world
had turned upside down.

The traffic was busy around Grays and we inched past betting shops, takeaway joints and charity shops until we found
a shady parking spot under a crumbling concrete flyover. We
crossed the railway line at a crowded level crossing and then
walked south towards the Thames. Many of the things I had
observed on my previous visit were still there – the shops
boarded up now that residents have less disposable income,
the flashing lights of mobile phone repair shops in window after
window on the high street – but there were positive changes
too. We passed the Thurrock campus of South Essex College,
built at a cost of £45 million in the centre of Grays as part of
ongoing attempts at regeneration, where diverse groups of students were eating packed lunches and relaxing in the sun. The
huge glass and steel facade of the building behind them held
strange, bright rainbow glints, a welcome change from the dull
grey of the rest of the town.

Soon after, we reached the approach to the river. Under a
metal arch outlining the words 'Grays Town Wharf' against the

sky, huge steel gates emblazoned with yellow and black stripes were swung open – a reminder that the chance of a flood like the one in 1953 is still taken very seriously. That night, the water overtopped the sea wall, as it did all along the riverbank from Tilbury round to Rainham Marshes. The council buildings in Grays became the makeshift headquarters of the local rescue operation, evacuations and temporary refuge for the homeless coordinated by volunteer telephonists who waded through the town to help. Beyond the gates, a paved quay surrounded three sides of an old dock let into the bank. I went over to the railing and looked down: the mud in it was almost liquid, difficult to distinguish from the river water that was just skimming across its surface as the tide rose. The mingled debris of the estuary was partly visible, with clumps of seaweed tangled around plastic flotsam. A shopping trolley was half buried, its handle deep in the mud and the front wheels still swinging above the surface as if it had been plunged into the dock just moments before. The trolley in the water is a classic image of dereliction and hopelessness, seen all over the UK in disused waterways and canals. But here I felt it looked oddly appropriate – even intentional. The silvery-grey grid of the trolley's basket contrasted perfectly with the fluid lines of the mud obscuring it, and the colours – rippling between pearlescent grey and mustard yellow as the clouds changed the angle of the sunlight – were a mirror image of those in the estuary itself. It was a perfect, accidental sculpture – a work of found art.

We walked around the dock and onto the sea wall. From here, we could see the yacht club where my parents caught their brief moment of rest on their first journey up the Thames – a businesslike little building with a beacon and a slipway leading down into the water. Several larger boats bobbed in the stream just offshore, tied up to the moorings that my parents had fumbled to find in the dark. My mother was delighted to be back, and to find it relatively unchanged. So much is impermanent in the estuary, a place that remakes itself with every ebb and flood of the tide, but here was a little reminder of her past self – a waypoint on the voyage that ended with a new life in a new country. Our excited exclamations attracted a few politely curious glances from the people enjoying the sunshine on the quay – the river here was far from a lonely place, despite the dock being full of liquid mud. People were eating their lunches on benches, looking at the view across to Kent or sunbathing by the water. It reminded me of the atmosphere by the Thames in central London on a fine evening – a feeling of carefree recreation.

To the east, beyond the cluster of masts by the yacht club, I could see the towers and cranes of the port at Tilbury. From here it looked small, but I knew that this was just the misleading perspective of the river's curve – the port covers an area of over 1,000 acres, with an enormous U-shaped basin dug out of the Essex bank where the river makes a great loop to the south to pass Gravesend. A lot of the land to the east of Grays used to be marshland, especially where it lay in the bend of the river, and it was progressively drained to accommodate the arrival of industry. As the docks upstream were closing throughout the twentieth century, Tilbury was the growing hope of the shipping business, being big enough to accommodate the larger vessels that could no longer make it all the way up to the Pool of London. Road and rail links were progressively improved to enable the goods unloaded at Tilbury to reach the city quickly, but the same changes that were closing other docks hit here too. A new container terminal was opened in 1967 and dock workers were laid off because nothing like the same numbers were needed to operate it. Unemployment is still high. From my position upstream, the docks looked deserted, although a crane was silently moving back and forth, effortlessly lifting containers from an unseen ship.

The estuary is a man-made landscape, created out of material abandoned or dumped, and shaped by what those upstream choose to conceal. At Thurrock, it is revealed as a place in motion, with no fixed identity, where the ugly truths of human existence are laid bare. There has been no holding back here, no tempering the demands of industry or waste disposal with a desire to preserve something beautiful. Here, our flaws are writ large, layered in the land. It isn't just sewage or refuse, although there is a lot of that, still. In 2015, the expanse of rubbish that had been fly-tipped at Cory's Wharf in Purfleet was a mile long. In the nineteenth century, as expanding railways required more space in central London, churchyards were dug up and the bones dumped into barges that were towed downstream to be disposed of in the river at Tilbury. This is still happening, in a way – as recently as 2015, when the excavations for Crossrail disturbed a burial ground of 3,300 skeletons underneath the former site of the Bedlam Hospital in east London, they were reburied in reclaimed land on Canvey Island. Examination showed that these people had died of the plague; there were rumours locally that they would bring the Black Death to Canvey, but residents' objections weren't considered worthy of regard.

That the estuary is unhealthy and best avoided is an idea that has lingered for a long time. In his immense three-volume survey of Britain, published between 1724 and 1727 as *A Tour Thro' the Whole Island of Great Britain, Divided into Circuits or Journies*, Daniel Defoe wrote that gentlemen going out into the nearby marshes to hunt 'often return with an Essex ague on their backs, which they find a heavier load than the fowls they have shot'. He had local knowledge – he had moved to Essex from London in the 1690s, after one of his many stints in a debtors' prison, and ran a brick factory just inland from the present Tilbury Docks (it used Thames mud to manufacture the bricks from which the Royal Observatory at Greenwich was built). He is still celebrated as one of Thurrock's most notable residents (there used to be a 'Robinson Crusoe' pub and a shopping parade named 'Defoe' in his home village of Chadwell St Mary). He also commented on the 'strange decay of the [female] sex here' and wrote that 'it was very frequent to meet with men that had had from five or six, to fourteen or fifteen wives' in these parts. His explanation for this high mortality rate among women in the Essex marshlands was that when men married women from elsewhere who were not 'seasoned to the place', they tended to sicken and die soon after arriving in the estuary: 'When they came out of their native air into the marshes among the fogs and damps, there they presently chang'd their complexion, got an ague or two, and seldom held it above half a year.' The widowers would then head back to the uplands inland to find another wife; Defoe recorded that he met one man living with his 'fifth and twentieth wife' and whose thirty-five-year-old son was already on spouse number fourteen.

Epidemiologists subsequently identified this 'ague' as a strain of malaria, spread by the mosquitoes that thrived in the marshes that fringed the estuary's coast, to which some longtime marsh-dwelling families had developed a resistance. Britain experienced a period of climate cooling (sometimes known as the Little Ice Age) from the sixteenth to the mid-nineteenth century. The Thames froze repeatedly and the English mosquito, *Anopheles atroparvus*, moved south to breed in the sluggish, brackish waters offered by marshes such as the ones at Thurrock and Tilbury. As many as one in ten children in coastal Essex died, and vicars refused to take up positions in marshy places, fearing the ague. The source of the fever was unknown until the late nineteenth century; in areas where it was prevalent, it was an everyday terror, so common that it became unremarkable. In her Canvey Island novel *Behindlings*, Nicola Barker eloquently summed up its horrors: 'Concealed in the perilous but stealthy fog which constantly tiptoed around this fractured isle like a ravenously phantasmagorical winter mink, slipping, unobserved, between plump and tender post-nuptial lips, slinking, unapprehended, through the spirited flair of passionated nostrils.' The malarial parasite, *Plasmodium falciparum*, stiffens infected blood cells by up to fifty times, causing the blood to become more viscous and flow more slowly. In the early seventeenth century, the physician William Harvey, who was the first to accurately describe how the body's circulatory system functions, observed that patients suffering from fever often had blood that was 'rendered thick' – an indication that the parasite was present.

The last recorded outbreak of malaria in Britain occurred just downstream from Tilbury, at Cliffe on the Hoo Peninsula (the long spit of land that runs from Cliffe out to the Isle of Grain and divides the outer Thames from its final tributary, the River Medway). The area had long been troubled by the disease – in the tiny village of Cooling, just a couple of miles further east along the peninsula, the churchyard contains a row of thirteen tiny gravestones, marking the burials of child malaria victims in the nineteenth century. A group of soldiers with malaria were sent home from Greece to recuperate at the barracks in Cliffe at the end of the First World War, in defiance of their doctor (Ronald Ross, who had won the Nobel Prize in 1902 for his work demonstrating how mosquitoes spread malaria). Soon, mosquitoes in the estuary were transmitting the milder version of the malarial parasite, *Plasmodium vivax*, to local residents. Over 500 cases of malaria were reported on Hoo the following year, although there were no fatalities. Since then, widespread schemes to drain the estuary's marshland and reclaim the land for industry have destroyed the mosquitoes' habitat, while better understanding of the disease in the medical profession has prevented another outbreak. However, there are concerns that the 'ague' could return, as global warming helps to produce the warmer, wetter conditions in which mosquitos thrive. Georgia, Turkey and Azerbaijan have all experienced fresh malaria outbreaks in recent years, and mosquitoes carrying dengue and yellow fever have been spotted in Italy and Belgium. Watery areas like the Thames estuary, the Somerset Levels and the Norfolk fens have seen an increase in people reporting multiple bites and pet rabbits suffering from myxomatosis, another mosquito-borne disease. Places near large sewage treatment works – like the huge sites in the Thames estuary that handle most of London's waste – are especially at risk as the planet warms.

The once-marshy banks where molten shadows used to track the tide's imperceptible movements in and out have been hardened to support the firm concrete quays and perfectly square metal warehouses of modern industry. Observing Tilbury as we pass by on *Cantilena*, I could see temporary edifices built by cranes from brightly coloured shipping containers adding a strange new contour to the horizon. Above, everything is squared off, definite, the perpendicular lines of the cranes echoed in the straight sides of the ships and the perfect facade of Tilbury Fort's seaward bastion. Through the binoculars, the containers look like so many precisely positioned Lego bricks, slotted together into colourful stacks. Yet alongside all of this imposed order the river still runs riot, an untamed reminder of this place's fluid identity – it becomes whatever is demanded of it. Joseph Conrad felt that the docks here had a different character from those upstream – St Katharine's was 'cosy', but Tilbury was full of 'vast gloom'. In *The Mirror of the Sea*, he observed of the new docks here, which opened in 1886, 'Nothing in those days could have been more striking than the vast, empty basins, surrounded by miles of bare quays and the ranges of cargo-sheds, where two or three ships seemed lost like bewitched children in a forest of gaunt, hydraulic cranes. One received a wonderful impression of utter abandonment, of wasted efficiency.'

Tilbury is hard to pin down. As the autopilot made tiny

adjustments to our course to account for the tide, I became aware that the river is narrower here (about 700 metres across) than the more estuarine reaches upstream of the Queen Elizabeth II Bridge, tricking the eye into believing that the sea must still be a long way off. Like Conrad, I find the sheer size of the cranes and basins at the Tilbury Docks difficult to comprehend. This was the first place that he lived outside London after settling in Britain. In October 1896, he and his wife, Jessie, moved into a 'damned jerry-built rabbit hutch' – a small semi-detached villa – down the road from the railway station in the village of Stanford-le-Hope, just round the point from Tilbury. Not long after, they moved round the corner to a medieval farmhouse with a view of the river. They needed somewhere cheap but still within easy reach of London, where Conrad could make the connections that might advance his nascent literary career. But he had not entirely given up the sea and would go on occasional trips down the estuary with his friends, including on a beamy sloop called the *Nellie*, a boat which would go on to make an appearance in the opening of *Heart of Darkness*. This place suited him – near to the city for convenient trips yet far enough away that property was affordable on his meagre income, and close enough to the sea that he could still feel the salt spray on his face. He was a creature of the in-between.

The estuary is flat and open to the sky here, and it is very hard to gauge distance or size. After a while trying to make sense of it, I too started to feel like a bewitched child. My mother was in the cabin making mugs of tea and slicing up a fruit loaf – it was almost lunchtime, but we had decided not to have our meal until we had hoisted the sails. I sat on the same side of the cockpit as my father, both of us looking towards the docks and the jetties at Tilbury as *Cantilena* chugged steadily past. It was here that Elizabeth I regendered herself in the face of the threat of the Spanish Armada in 1588, saying, 'I know I have the body but of a weak and feeble woman; but I have the heart and stomach of a king.' This point on the river where both the city upstream and the sea feel so remote affects people strangely. The writer Antonia Fraser once described to me an 'extraordinary experience' she had when visiting Tilbury for the first time, while researching a possible biography of the Virgin Queen. 'I had never been in that area, and I was absolutely staggered by it, the flats and Tilbury itself,' she told me over coffee in the living room of her west London house, her cats sniffing around by the French windows. 'To have lived all my life and never had any sight of it, it left a permanent impression ... I felt like Alice, because it was so quick – I'd gone through the mirror.' A lifelong Londoner, she had slipped somehow into another country, even though she was just a few dozen miles downstream from her own home.

For many, Tilbury was the gateway to a new world. As well as the place where goods from the Empire were unloaded, it was also the point of transition for a different kind of cargo: people. It is London's answer to New York's Ellis Island – the point of entry for those starting a new life, and of departure for those leaving Britain behind. Many passenger and cruise liners docked here, and in 1930 the prime minister, Ramsay MacDonald, formally opened a brand-new landing stage, complete with a domed baggage hall and its own railway station, so that passengers could transfer easily into and out of central London. This is where, on 29 September 1888, 'an Indian teenager with a mild case of ringworm and a fine head of hair' named Mohandas Gandhi disembarked to spend three years studying law in London, having been at sea for weeks as his ship steamed all the way from Bombay, little knowing that decades later he would be agitating to liberate his country from the imperial British rule that these very docks helped to uphold. George Orwell embarked here in 1928, on his way to be down and out in Paris, because the steamer from Tilbury to Dunkirk was 'the cheapest and not the worst way of crossing the Channel'. It's also where those leaving Britain for a new life on the other side of the world took a final glimpse of their homeland – whether they were being forcibly deported to the colonies or joining the 'Ten Pound Pom' scheme that provided subsidized emigration for Brits going to Australia or New Zealand after the Second World War. As Ken Worpole put it, 'The watergate at Tilbury [is] thick with shades of the transported.' In 2014, his words took on a new, more literal, meaning, when thirty-five people were found inside a shipping container at the port. These were Afghan Sikhs, thirteen of them children, who had travelled across Europe by lorry to seek asylum in Britain. One man, Meet Singh Kapoor, had died on the voyage across the North Sea from Belgium, and several others had to be hospitalized. The footage of their release was shown on the news, with a warning that 'some may find these images distressing'; as if the notion of people being treated like freight wasn't upsetting enough. A criminal syndicate was accused of illegally smuggling vulnerable people for profit and four men were prosecuted. It was an uncomfortable discovery that something so vile could go undiscovered here, so close to the centre of London and the seat of authority. While I followed the progress of the investigation and trial, it reminded me just how remote the estuary can feel.

Perhaps most famously, though, it was at Tilbury that the HMT *Empire Windrush* docked on 22 June 1948, carrying 492 Caribbean people who had responded to adverts in their local newspapers from employers seeking workers to help boost the struggling British economy in the wake of the Second World War. It was a homecoming: the ship itself was named for a tiny tributary stream that flows into the upper Thames near Abingdon in Oxfordshire and the *Evening Standard*'s front-page headline was 'Welcome Home!', as the 'sons of Empire' disembarked in their new land. In the *Guardian*'s report of the ship's arrival, one of the immigrants pre-empted the 'them and us' narrative that still dominates political discourse today. 'Surely then, there is nothing against our coming, for we are British subjects,' he told the reporters waiting at the Tilbury quayside for a glimpse of Britain's newest residents. 'If there is – is it because we are coloured?' The British Nationality Act of 1948 had confirmed that all Commonwealth subjects had the right to live and work in Britain – a freedom that had been abolished by the time my parents arrived here from South Africa, owing to the disproportionate hostility to immigration that greeted the so-called '*Windrush* generation'.

The status of migrants from the British Empire has always been fraught and complex. Britain colonized vast swathes of the world, shipping precious natural resources back from these places to the docks on the Thames and oppressing the people they had displaced from their land. When the imperial tide finally ebbed and the Empire began to be dismantled in the twentieth century, British citizenship was one of the few compensations offered – after all, if people had been born under British rule, it made sense that they were British subjects. Yet as the response to the *Windrush* passengers and the hundreds of thousands who followed in their wake from India, Pakistan, the Caribbean, Australia and South-East Asia showed, the prevailing opinion in Britain was that these former imperial subjects weren't *really* British, even if they did provide a handy boost to the struggling domestic workforce in the late 1940s and 1950s. Like the estuary itself, they were neither one thing nor the other. By 1968, the Commonwealth Immigrants Act had restricted citizenship rights to those with a 'substantial connection with the United Kingdom' – defined as having a parent or grandparent who was a UK national – and in 1972 (partly as a result of the response to Enoch Powell's infamous 'Rivers of Blood' speech), a work permit requirement was introduced. In 2018, it was revealed that dozens of *Windrush*-era immigrants had been wrongfully deported under a government policy known as the 'hostile environment', which was designed to make accessing services like health care and housing as difficult as possible for those who could not prove that they were in the UK legally. It was an abrupt reminder of how much more closed off Britain has become in the last half-century, because the very reason many of those who arrived at Tilbury on the *Windrush* and other similar ships can find it difficult to prove their status is that, at the time when they were invited to travel here, their status as British citizens seemed too obvious to require comprehensive documentation.

I've struggled a bit with my own national identity. I was born in Chatham, by the River Medway, but my parents are South African by birth, upbringing and education. I have never lived there and, unlike many children of immigrants, I have never been particularly attracted to my parents' national identity. Being a white South African is a surprisingly complex matter, especially given their politically dominant position in that country for so long. It's not a homogeneous category, though, and between the Afrikaners (who are primarily descended from the original Dutch settlers in southern Africa in the seventeenth century and have their own established language and culture) and the British South Africans, there is a lot of hostility. These two groups were on opposite sides during the Boer Wars, and it was an Afrikaner political party that enacted the racist and segregationist laws known as apartheid. My father has often talked about how, as a young white man descended from British immigrants growing up in a working-class family in apartheid South Africa, he felt alienated and separate from what the world saw as the tyranny of the white minority in his country – that the political power wielded by the Afrikaner government had nothing to do with him. On both sides, my South Africa family came originally from Britain and Ireland, and my parents were brought up to think of themselves as British, distinct from the Afrikaners. To many in the UK, though, they are foreign (although, by virtue of being white and well educated, they have never been subjected to the kind of discrimination that many others in similar circumstances face).

What are we? I have never been sure, and at times I have found that uncertainty troubling. But no longer. As the cranes of Tilbury disappeared to the stern, I felt content. I sipped at the scalding-hot tea my mother had passed up to me from the cabin – the specially insulated mugs she used for sailing trips are so efficient at keeping the heat in that you never get to the shore without a burnt tongue – and wriggled around in my seat so that I could keep a lookout over the starboard bow for boats coming upriver that might need to cross our course. Coalhouse Point, where the river curves north and widens again, was just coming into view. My father had climbed out onto the foredeck and was freeing halyards and undoing sail covers. This is where we belong, in our in-between place.

6

Mucking No. 5 to Lower Hope

When sailing, especially in the Thames estuary, there is a lot of sitting still while waiting for things to happen. I am always surprised by how much my muscles ache at the end of a day on these waters, because to my recollection I have done nothing but sit in the cockpit and occasionally pull on a rope. But in fact I have been in motion all the time: tense and vigilant for possible obstructions in the water, my body imperceptibly responding to the movement of the boat and the river, making tiny, unconscious adjustments to stay upright. Since I became aware of this, I have started trying to tune my mind in to this frequency, to feel myself imitating the water beneath the hull. This effect was particularly noticeable as *Cantilena* rounded the right-angle corner beneath Coalhouse Fort, heading north past the edge of east Tilbury on one side and the marshy expanse of the Cliffe Pools, where the Hoo Peninsula begins to branch off from the Kent coast on the other. We left the red-and-white-striped structure of the Shornemead Lighthouse behind us to the right, marking the shallow waters close in by the southern shore, just opposite the wooden groynes stretching out from the Tilbury side. The effect of the ebbing tide was weakening as we neared low water, but the wind was still coming strongly from the south-west and as it blew perpendicular to our course it whipped up ruffled peaks in the water that slapped insistently against the hull.

The final bend of the Thames lies on a reach known as the Lower Hope. Once we turned east to come into the channel that runs along the north bank of Hoo, I would be able to look straight out into the North Sea. This sense of openness, though, is accompanied by a greater awareness of the obstacles under the water and near the river's banks – the mud, the silt and the sand. Already, the water was wider and the banks harder to make out, but I knew they were still there. The hard edges of the concrete sea walls are more difficult to perceive, even through the binoculars, as the mud and gravel have built up over the course of many tides to form a gentle slope, mimicking what would once have been the natural silty foreshore. At Cliffe, the boundary between land and water is further blurred by the bank, which looks solid enough from my vantage point in the middle of the channel, but is in fact a narrow isthmus between the river and the marshy pools of the nature reserve behind. As we move further north along the reach, the ribs of a beached wreck come into view where the end of this narrow spit of land meets the place where Cliffe Creek flows out through the marshes and joins the Thames. These are the mossy, rotten remains of the Danish schooner *Hans Egede*, built in 1922 and damaged by fire off Dover in 1955. As with many partially destroyed ships, she had a brief afterlife as a hulk in the estuary: because her three masts and rigging had been destroyed beyond repair but the wooden hull was still intact, she was used as a makeshift container in the shallows of the Medway for goods like grain and coal. But then she began to take on water while being towed up this stretch of the river in 1957 and so was beached. She has been here ever since, sinking gently into the mud, the planks of her hull gathering a greenish sheen of weed and gradually peeling away from their struts – a rare visible reminder of the other hulks and wrecks that have been stranded on the estuary's shores down the years. Behind her silhouette, I could see the spoil heaps from the gravel and aggregate works that still operate at the mouth of the creek. Such extraction has long been a feature of the estuary's landscape. General Gordon, who famously perished in Khartoum in 1885, was in charge of the defences in the estuary in the 1860s; he is said to have complained about the fumes drifting across to the military base at Gravesend from the cement slurry works at Cliffe.

The closeness of the sea has long made this part of the river crucial to military efforts to defend Britain's capital. Although it feels further after travelling along the twists and turns of the Thames, we are still only thirty-three miles from London Bridge. An invading fleet sweeping in through the estuary from the North Sea could strike at the heart of the nation with deadly rapidity, as had been proved throughout history from the Romans and the Vikings to the Dutch raids during the Anglo-Dutch Wars of the seventeenth century. During one of these, in 1667, the Dutch fleet diverted into the Medway and burned the British naval ships moored at the military dockyard at Chatham. This was such a symbolic blow to the authority of the British crown that Samuel Pepys, a naval administrator, recorded in his diary, 'The truth is, I do fear so much that the whole kingdom is undone.' The fear of invasion in the Thames persisted for centuries: the fort at Cliffe, which I could see over the starboard bow through the binoculars, its windowless walls now gaping towards the water, was built in the 1860s, and a state-of-the-art torpedo missile system was added thirty years later.

Operation Sea Lion, Hitler's never-enacted invasion plan for
Britain, involved the German forces occupying the land around
the Thames and Medway rivers first, to isolate London from
military assistance, and then pushing north into the rest of the
country. The defences out here in the estuary, often unknown
and invisible to those upriver, kept millions of people safe.

While I had been scanning the shore of the Hoo Peninsula,
my mother had been keeping a steady eye on the water
ahead. The deep-water channel through Lower Hope is relatively narrow, dredged continually by the Port of London
Authority to ensure that the cargo ships heading for Tilbury
have enough water beneath them. It is marked by green and
red buoys on either side – green for starboard, red for port as
seen when entering the river from the sea – and smaller vessels
are supposed to stay just outside them so as to keep clear of
the commercial traffic. Occasionally she pressed the button
on the autopilot control panel to adjust our course slightly,
counteracting the effect of the tide that was trying to drag the
boat eastwards even as the engine pushed us north, avoiding
a possible collision with the hard metal shell of a buoy. These
look like tethered metal birdcages floating on the surface of
the river, about three metres in diameter and about six tonnes
in weight. Each one has its own name and position, marked on
charts and in almanacs, and is used by those at sea to determine their position and safety relative to the obstructions that
lurk under the water. These days, they often have solar panels
on top that power their night-time lights. They each have an
individual flash pattern, also noted on the charts, so that a
navigator can work out where they are in the dark. In daylight,
and with the assistance of modern electronic charting and
satellite technology, it is much easier to know where the boat
is at any moment (and also these waters are so familiar to my

parents that they barely need to check). Still, just to be sure, my father kept jumping down the cabin steps to have a look at the computer. He would then shout a description of the next mark in our course up to us on deck: 'Green, on the starboard bow, Mucking No. 5!' My mother, scanning the horizon more out of habit than necessity, would then indicate that she could see it and was ready to take avoiding action if needed.

The rhythm of this, the division of responsibilities between my parents, is very familiar to me. My mother has always had sharper eyes, and so lookout duty has long been her speciality when we are sailing, especially in hazardous coastal waters like those in the estuary. When we were sailing at night, trying to see the next set of lights was a game my sister and I enjoyed, thrilled to be allowed to stay on deck way past our bedtimes when on shore, as long as we stayed wrapped up in many layers of wool and oilskin. My father would tell us that we were looking for 'white, a pattern of three flashes in every seven seconds', and we would kneel up on the cockpit seat to gaze into the darkness, desperate to be the first to spot it. And yet it would always be my mother, quietly pointing, who would see it first, a faint glimmer across the dark water, growing stronger with every heave of the hull. This time, while the boat gradually crept closer to the green buoy, I found myself asking her about what it had been like doing this in reverse on that first trip into the estuary, without the aid of satellite navigation. She laughed, adjusting the chin strap of the fleece deerstalker she wears while sailing to keep her ears warm, and just said, 'Different!' Night-time navigation in the estuary while under sail in the early 1980s had involved a fair amount of near misses. Working only with paper charts and rudimentary navigational instruments, they had no certain way of knowing where they were other than via their own skills of observation and navigation.

They used to shine a torch on the buoys as they loomed out of the darkness, trying to read the names painted on them, to have some idea how far up the channel they had reached.

The names of the buoys have always fascinated me. In preparing for this journey, I spent hours poring over the paper charts I pinned to my walls, murmuring the strange, incongruous phrases to myself as I tracked the river's paper journey out to sea. Sometimes the buoys run in numbered sequences, as in this stretch of the river – we had now passed Mucking No. 7 and were heading for Mucking No. 5 – and sometimes they are orphans, like the one called Diver Shoal, which we had given a wide berth before turning north into this reach. The names usually refer to the hazard beneath the water that the buoy is there to warn sailors of, in this case the Mucking Flats (an area of saltmarsh set into the curve of the north bank just opposite the north-western corner of the Hoo Peninsula). The buoys and their lights form a kind of safety net laid over the landscape, now manifested in a very modern, high-tech form, but still connected via their names to the same courses that sailors of centuries past would have sailed.

The same words appear again and again when navigating here: 'ness' for a headland or promontory, 'gat' for a narrow but deep passage between two areas of shallows, 'deep' for a clear channel. Their spellings might have varied down the years – the place now known as Goldmer Gat was Goldemore Gatt in 1671 and Goldmers Gatway in 1824 – but in essence they have remained the same, at least to those bawling them down the deck to a fellow crew member in a storm. The Thames estuary, because of its unique combination of fast-flowing tide, its huge expanse of water and the fact that it combines with the North Sea and the English Channel, has an abundance of shoals, sandbanks, marshes and other hazards lurking beneath its surface. Many ships have fallen foul of its dangers – there are more shipwrecks per square mile here than anywhere else in Britain. My parents always made sure to impress upon me from my earliest years that the estuary was not a place to take risks or skimp on navigational precautions. Even now, when we were retracing a well-worn route out to sea, they were still keeping an eye on the depth sounder and the eddies in the water around each buoy to check on the strength and direction of the tide. In all the years I sailed with them, we never had a serious accident or ran aground for more than a few seconds. They wear their seamanship lightly, but the depth of it can still surprise me. This is a strange place to feel safe, yet I have never doubted for a second that I could cross the estuary and remain unharmed.

As if trying to shake me out of my reverie, the wind strengthened a little and the loosened halyards at the mast cracked. I stared ahead over *Cantilena's* bow to the green can bobbing in the waves, the light glinting off its solar panels. Beyond, the shallows at Mucking lurked, invisible.

Even when the estuary looks like a vast expanse of empty water, it's hard not to be aware of the earth beneath, flowing like the tide and forming new shapes and patterns on the riverbed. The meeting point of the North Sea and the Dover Straits, plus the discharging rivers Thames and Medway, is a turbulent and unpredictable place. Regular surveys are carried out by the UK Hydrographic Office, the government body responsible for ensuring safety at sea for both military and civilian personnel, which show that although the major mudflats, sandbanks and shoals have remained fairly constant in their shape and position down the years, the whole complex sedimentary system is dynamic, the sand moving in ribbons across the outer estuary as the waves move west, eventually joining up with and enlarging existing sand formations. The water on the southern side of the banks is deepening, while to the north it is shoaling progressively shallower as new sand piles up. Unlike in other coastal areas of Britain, these formations are comprised almost entirely of sand and particles of the London clay that lies under much of the soil in the Thames's drainage area, with very little gravel at all. These sandbanks are huge too – the one known as Long Sand runs for twenty miles north-east from opposite the mouth of the Medway between Black Deep and Knock Deep, two deep water channels used by ships leaving the Thames and heading out into the North Sea. There are plenty of others too, as R. M. Ballantyne recorded so evocatively in his 1870 novel, *The Floating Light of the Goodwin Sands*: 'Of shoals there are the East and West Barrows, the Nob, the Knock, the John, the Sunk, the Girdler, and the Long sands, all lying like so many ground-sharks, quiet, unobtrusive, but very deadly, waiting for ships to devour.'

In addition to the natural movement of silt and sand in the estuary, there are artificial channel management and deposition. The Port of London Authority maintains the depth of some channels with extensive dredging so that the big commercial ships that enter the estuary heading for one of the ports don't have to wait for a high tide to proceed upriver safely. The material that is sucked from the bottom in the Princes Channel or the Queens Channel has to go somewhere, and there are designated disposal and placement sites further out to sea where the dredging vessels can safely discharge their loads without the sand floating back, suspended in the sea water, to build up in the channels again. To make sure it stays put, the dredged material is shot out of the hull of the boat in 'a well-defined turbulent jet' so that it reaches the seabed before it can drift away.

It's easy to think of the sea as endlessly deep, but I know from experience that – here at least – it is not. Especially when using one of the narrow channels between the estuary sandbanks, like Fisherman's Gat or the Swin, it is vital not to stray beyond the slender strip of deeper water through the sand marked by buoys. Otherwise, the numbers displayed on the depth sounder on the instrument panel will start tumbling: from eight or nine metres down to less than one in a matter of seconds. I will never forget the few times this has happened when I have been on board *Cantilena*; the sudden scramble into frantic motion, the wheel flung over, the sails loosed so they spill their wind and flap uselessly. The sands shift and the tide can pull the boat imperceptibly, gradually off course so that, even though she is still pointing the same way according to the compass, the edge of the channel is much nearer than is comfortable. Coastal sailing, especially in a busy commercial shipping lane full of unpredictable hazards like the Thames estuary, requires constant vigilance.

The UK Hydrographic Office was set up in 1795. Proper mapping of coastal waters was vital to prevent disasters, so the charts then in existence were swiftly collated and others commissioned, as well as arrangements set up with official chart-issuing organizations in other countries to share navigational information. The Admiralty charts are still, 200 years on, an industry standard – something like 70 per cent of all commercial shipping in British waters use them, as well as many amateur sailors like my family. Today, they are printed in colour, and have a distinctive palette and gradient instantly comprehensible to those accustomed to using them. I remember being gradually initiated into the trick of reading them when I was a child, squeezing onto the padded seat at the chart table next to my father and fiddling with the calipers, dividers and compass he used to plot our course. Everything familiar from a map of the land is inverted: the shore is filled in with an ochre-yellow colour and mostly left blank, with just a few markings to sketch in the location of villages and towns or landmarks visible from the water. All of the detail is in the water, where hundreds of tiny figures denote the depth at each point. Contour lines show how the seabed shelves, just as they indicate the rising slopes of a hill on land. Areas of different depth are coloured accordingly, the darker the blue meaning the shallower the water. At ten metres deep, a channel is completely white. These blank areas are safe; in the estuary, almost everything except from a narrow dredged strip down the middle is shaded in darkening blues.

Boats that are purpose-built for these conditions, like the Thames barge or the Dutch *schuyt*, have flat-bottomed hulls that can skim through the shallowest water and even ride up the foreshore at high tide to dry out there. Some barges, particularly the Dutch ones, have leeboards, which are movable panels that can be folded against the side of the boat's hull in shallow water or pivoted down into the water to provide extra stability in deeper areas. Smaller vessels and sailing dinghies sometimes have centreboards too, essentially a keel that can be pulled up through the hull from inside and secured to prevent it from touching the bottom. One of the book series that I read over and over as a child, Arthur Ransome's Swallows and Amazons, features this quirk of boat design as a plot point – the heavier, fixed-keeled *Swallow* beats the lighter *Amazon* in a thrilling race when the crew take a short cut through shallow water but avoid running aground by throwing their weight over to one side, temporarily lifting the keel sideways out of the water. I adored this passage and longed to try the trick for myself, but my parents' boats have always been heavy and deep-draughted – sadly unsuitable for such antics. *Cantilena* can sail close to the wind and make long-distance ocean passages with ease (my parents have competed, separately and together, in races across the Atlantic and to the Azores, and sailed to the Arctic Circle and around the Baltic Sea). But we have always had to take extra precautions in these waters, because while a heavy two-metre keel on the bottom of the boat might help her keep a better course when sailing against the wind, it also increases the chances of running aground.

I learned early to regard open water beyond the marked channel with deep suspicion, knowing that however innocuous it looked, the riverbed could well be less than a metre beneath the surface. I knew never to go exploring up narrow creeks when the tide was falling, lest I get stuck and have to wait for it to ebb and then flood again before the boat could be floated free of the obstruction. Occasionally we would hear other sailors reporting such incidents over the VHF radio that is always buzzing away quietly in its cradle in the cockpit, telling the coastguard that they were quite safe, but that their boat was stuck fast in the side of a sandbank and the tide had fallen away. Sometimes a yacht with a long, narrow keel like *Cantilena* will even float gently down on her side in such a situation rather than remaining vertical – I saw this happen once on the long sandbank that blocks the entrance to the River Ore in Suffolk – and those aboard will have to use the wall of the cabin as the floor until the water floods back in and rights them.

Mud is commonly defined as a viscous mixture of earth and water, a mingling of the elements that sits on the boundary between one thing and another. It is a material in transition, and it is everywhere here where the land and sea meet. It is impossible to think of the estuary without thinking of all its different varieties of mud, from the silky ochre liquid that holds rills and ripples like frozen water to the gleaming, thick, caramel-brown texture exposed on the shore at low tide.

For all that it is the great watery flatness of the estuary that lingers in the mind, here the movement of mud is constant, dramatic and contested. For birds, it is a vital source of nutrients – each square metre can contain as much energy as eight Mars bars, in the form of worms, invertebrates and bacteria, and migrating species flock to the exposed foreshore every year to fuel up for the long flight south. In recent years, there has been some recognition of the mud's part in the ecosystem, and steps have been taken to preserve it in nature reserves and protected areas. But for centuries, the Thames mud was a source of shame, associated with dilapidation, backwardness and moral impurity. There was little recognition that the mud was as natural a phenomenon as the much-admired peaks in the Lake District, or the sparkling waters of rivers like the Avon and the Severn. The nineteenth-century journalist James Penderel-Brodhurst decried 'the nude expanse of festering mud' to be found by the Thames. After London's struggles with sanitation, the estuary's mud was too strongly associated with filth and poor health to be viewed with anything other than disgust; it had to be pushed back so that civilization could flourish. Great engineering works like Bazalgette's embankments in central London or Marc Isambard Brunel's tunnel beneath the Thames at Rotherhithe were celebrated for the great movements of mud they required.

Today, as well as the channel-dredging operations, there

are bigger, more contentious excavations going on. Just downstream of Mucking, the entire northern bank of the Thames has recently been altered by the biggest mud transplantation ever to happen in the estuary. Beginning in 2010, a Dubai infrastructure conglomerate began sucking up tonnes of material from the seabed at a time and dumping it on the shore to create new land on which to build a vast new port, now known as London Gateway. The vessels that do this are like incredibly high-tech maritime Hoovers: they trail a great pipe below them which pulls up the mud and gravel at great speed. The soggy mud was then added to the site of the old Shell Haven oil refinery on the north bank, which had closed in 1999, and any excess water was spewed frothily back into the river. Over 30 million tonnes of silt were transported in this way, in a great land-reclamation project that added an extra 400 metres of solid earth beyond the original riverbank. The British coastline was moved and maps were redrawn, the naturally wiggly line of the shore replaced by an artificially straight edge.

The dredging continues even now that the port is open for business, because the channel that leads to it is not naturally deep enough for the enormous container ships which arrive on every tide. The writer Rachel Lichtenstein has extensively investigated the possible impact of this vast, continual movement of mud. She has exposed fears that toxins and heavy metals that had been trapped in the seabed for centuries will be stirred up by the activity, harming wildlife and damaging the nearby mussel and oyster beds. An Essex fisherman told her that stocks of white weed, the bushy aquatic sea plant *Sertularia argentea* that had long flourished in the estuary, were almost completely depleted during the land-reclamation process, resulting in a huge loss of habitat for creatures including crabs and other crustaceans – a vital part of the food chain in the outer Thames, where fish such as the cold-water smelt breed and are in turn eaten by bigger species such as seals, salmon and cormorants.

The water quality in the estuary is continually monitored for environmental problems by a series of buoys loaded with specialist equipment and there is yet to be a firm conclusion about whether the dredging at London Gateway has done the estuary long-term harm. An environment officer told Lichtenstein, 'I can't look you in the eye and say that the dredging work has not had an impact on the river, but it will recover.' Britain's destructive industries, like mining and quarrying, are much reduced these days, so there is little else comparable to this mud-moving . I can't help wondering whether such potentially harmful activity would be permitted in a more highly regarded landscape, or if there was less money at stake.

The Mucking No. 5 buoy was almost upon us, suddenly shockingly close over *Cantilena*'s starboard bow. I could see by the way that the eddies were pulling at the water around its base that the tide was still flooding out of the Thames. We were just beyond the main channel, the depth sounder showing about four metres beneath the keel, yet a few hundred metres away on the other side of the boat I could see the uncovered grey mud spreading out from the Essex shore. The marshy flats here are protected habitats for wading birds and other rare creatures, but although I know that more than enough mud has been dredged around their fringes to give us safe passage past, I still find it eerie that the boat can slide so close by without encountering obstacles. This time, I could even see the weed-covered rocks and spiky grasses where saltmarsh gave way to mudflat, and the shining silver rivulets of water drained across the mirrored, liquid surface of the silt, back into the river. The river was curving now; the horizon was opening up with every slight eastwards turn of the boat. Finally, it felt as if the sea was within reach, even though the south bank of the river was still barely more than 750 metres away.

The name 'Mucking' is curious, given the amount of mud and sludge and slime in the estuary. More than once, when trying to explain to people about the place, I heard questions like, 'But what about all the muck out there?' The river's reputation for dirt and grime is pervasive. All through my planning for this journey, I kept coming back to this one word, circling it on the charts and scouring the almanacs for more details. Then one day, when killing time in central London waiting to meet a friend, I got caught without an umbrella in one of those out-of-nowhere deluges so strong that the drops bounce a foot back up off the pavements and for hours after it is over you catch whiffs of the coppery, dusty scent of rain. I ducked into the nearby British Museum for shelter and wandered aimlessly through the galleries, heading for the relative solitude of the less populated exhibits on the upper floor that deal with early British history – away from the crowds taking pictures of the Parthenon marbles and the Rosetta Stone.

Eventually I ended up in Room 41, where objects spanning the demise of the Roman Empire and the emergence of pre-medieval European culture are displayed. I spent a few minutes in front of the glass cases holding the treasures from the Anglo-Saxon ship burial discovered at Sutton Hoo on the Suffolk coast in 1939 – including the famous ornate iron helmet and a gloriously intricate golden belt buckle formed from writhing snakes – and then idly looked over some of the less familiar exhibits before moving on. Just before I left the room, a strange green goblet in the corner near the door caught my eye. It was about twenty centimetres high and covered all the way round by what looked like protruding tentacles, sculpted from

the same transparent, jade-coloured glass as the main vessel. Each one dangled down towards the base and featured a line of textured bubbles on the outside, which looked to me a little like an octopus's suckers. I had never seen anything like it – it was so fantastically weird-looking – and I stopped to stare. In its way, it was as ornate and intricately wrought as the shining gold of the buckle, but utterly otherworldly and almost eerie. My eyes flicked down to the label, which explained that it was a claw beaker, probably made around AD 400 by a glassworker still working in a style informed by Roman craftsmanship. Then I saw that word again. *Mucking.* This brilliant, weird glass creation had been found in the grave of an Anglo-Saxon woman buried in the first half of the sixth century just to the north of where the Thames estuary takes its final turn towards the sea. I scoured the gallery after that, looking for any other artefacts from the same place, but found none. Eventually, I left the museum, but now I was determined to find out more about how the green goblet had got here from the Essex mud.

In the following weeks and months, I began to piece together the story of what had happened at Mucking. In 1965 there had been an eighteen-hectare excavation on the north bank of the Thames. The earliest aerial photographs of Mucking had been taken by the Luftwaffe in 1943 as part of German bombing reconnaissance; in 1964, an RAF veteran and Cambridge University professor named Kenneth St Joseph repeated the exercise (it was a burgeoning strand of archeological research at the time) and spotted a pattern of distinctive crop marks in one of his own photographs. They were some of the clearest ever recorded and indicated the need for substantial excavation down below. An eight-week exploratory dig took place in 1965 with an experienced freelance archaeologist called Margaret Ursula Jones in charge. The Mucking site was earmarked for gravel extraction and she knew all about 'rescue archeology', working at speed to recover as much as possible from the ground before the bulldozers arrived. With her husband, Tom, acting as her assistant and photographer, Jones worked at Mucking almost continuously for the next thirteen years, keeping ahead of the gravel extraction and recovering more than a million finds (including six tonnes of ceramics), with 1,145 burials and 400 structures identified. It became Britain's largest-ever archaeological excavation. The objects she recovered spanned a period of over 3,000 years, from the Neolithic era through to the Middle Ages, including particular treasures like the claw beaker in the museum from the early Anglo-Saxon period in the middle of the first millennium AD.

Many of the accounts of the dig wax lyrical about how extraordinary it was to find settlements of so many different periods in the same place, suggesting that this slightly raised area on the north bank of the Thames had been occupied for thousands of years. Mucking was described as a 'multiperiod palimpsest' of lives layered into the earth. Jones herself explained why this might be: the strategic advantage that the settlements would have enjoyed, positioned so that they commanded one of the lowest crossing points on the Thames and looked straight out through the remainder of the estuary to the North Sea, was sufficient to ensure continued occupation. The site itself was remote and relatively featureless – certainly not a beauty spot, being fringed by marshes and mudflats and adjacent to active gravel pits and quarries – and Jones wrote later of how difficult it was early on to create a precise grid system for documenting finds because there were almost no landmarks from which to take references. The photographs

I saw that were taken during the dig bear this out, showing a huge area of dusty grey earth stretching off into the distance, with the cranes and buildings further along the river at Tilbury faint shadows on the horizon.

As well as the extraordinary finds at Mucking, Jones's dig was remarkable for the sheer amount of manpower and organization it required. Unusually, the archaeologists worked on the site all year round, rather than just in the summer. Thousands of student volunteers from all over the world came to assist, with more than 5,000 people involved in total by the time the excavation wound down in 1978. Many went on to excel in their field; the *Independent*'s obituary of Jones, who died in 2001 at the age of eighty-four, said that 'for a generation of respectable middle-aged archaeologists ... to have dug with Margaret Jones at Mucking remains a badge of honour'. They moved from tents into caravans and other vehicles when the winter became too cold for them to sleep under canvas. This makeshift camp relied partly on donations to keep going: water was piped over from a nearby farm, many slept under deck blankets from discontinued cruise liners, and some even dossed down in a worn-out lorry (it made 'a splendid dormitory', Jones wrote later). Initially, there was no electricity, and all food had to be stored and cooked on site because the nearest shops were miles away. It came in bulk crates – heaps of bananas and endless tins of cod's roe, acquired by Tom Jones wholesale down at the docks. Yet the diggers were devoted to their work and believed in the importance of rescuing the evidence of the past lives lived here. If it felt isolated and disregarded on this unglamorous stretch of the river, they didn't care.

The atmosphere at Mucking during the years of excavation was jolly, bohemian and earnest. The journalist Tina Brown, who spent a night in the camp in 1976 and wrote about it in her column in *Punch*, described the diggers as 'a cross between the Desert Rats and the Bloomsbury Group on a walking tour'. The hippy atmosphere was strong: a 'genial, shaggy-haired young woman' showed Brown around the site while glibly comparing the set-up to the murderous cults then grabbing headlines in America – 'you can understand how the Manson club got the way they did,' she said. 'Apart from Heavy Rock in Mucking on Thursdays there's not much in the way of night life.' Another archaeologist who spent many years in the camp, Warwick Rodwell, later described how difficult the conditions were for digging. While trying to uncover some Roman pottery kilns on Christmas Eve in 1968, he recalled that 'we burnt bales of straw on the kilns to thaw the ground; otherwise trowels would not scratch the surface, and pick-axes simply bounced off'. The extreme cold they experienced crops up again and again in the accounts written afterwards by those remembering their experiences at Mucking. Overlooking the outer Thames estuary may have had strategic advantages for the Romans and the Anglo-Saxons, but in the twentieth century there was 'the ever-present arctic wind driving up the Thames estuary along the gravel terrace, blasting the site with a ferocity that had to be experienced to be believed' to contend with. From my reading a picture emerged of an eccentric, hardy, peculiar little community perched above the estuary. Rats ate the soap and mice lived in the sacks of rice. A local vicar was persuaded to hold a service 'to expel the ghost of an Anglo-Saxon woman, lost amongst the extra-large tins of spam'. Day after day, the painstaking work of digging, sifting and recording continued.

The more I read about Mucking, the more Jones intrigued me. For all the thousands of people who wielded trowels there, it was her character that shaped the work. Brown described her as 'a brisk figure with a windburnt face and peppery blonde hair'.

Photographs taken during the dig show her working on the great grey expanse of the excavation site, kneeling over a trench with a trowel or making notes. It was unusual but not unheard of at the time for a woman to be in charge of a major excavation; there were other husband-and-wife teams in archaeology, but few others like the Joneses in which the woman was the leader and the man the assistant. The same words come up again and again in the descriptions of her written by colleagues and volunteers at Mucking: she was 'formidable' and 'a hard taskmaster'. At the Ministry of Works, which provided her meagre budget, her nickname was 'Boadicea' – and, like the ancient warrior queen, Jones fought passionately for the rights of this patch of Thames-side Essex. Her method of excavating as much as possible in the shortest period without taking time out for analysing or writing about the finds was criticized by some academic archaeologists, who argued that such 'excavation without publication' contributed little to the field, but Jones felt that her primary job was to preserve the objects from destruction, and that good work in the field and properly organized site records would lay the foundations for subsequent academic study. Mucking always struggled to attract funding (hence the strange food provided to the volunteers) and some of the published analysis of the finds only began to appear after Jones's death in 2001. Histories of archeology have always tended to ignore the substantial contribution of women and to place less weight on those who primarily worked in the field rather than in universities, and as such Jones has been doubly overlooked. But thanks to her, the idea of 'rescue archaeology' is now firmly established in Britain, and planning laws often require that developers give access for excavation before buildings can be demolished or land disturbed.

Perhaps the most vital thing that Jones did, though, was to make the case for the preservation and study of the erstwhile inhabitants of Mucking, despite the fact that they were not royal or noble. In her obituary in the *Guardian*, Mike Pitts wrote, 'Thanks to her, the history of forgotten lives can one day be written', and I found myself thinking of this again and again as I paged through the extensive literature describing the Anglo-Saxon cemetery, the Bronze Age hill fort and the Iron Age roundhouses that were discovered there. The burials were of craftsmen, soldiers and labourers, who lived and worked by the estuary thousands of years ago. Their stories deserved to be told. Unlike more famous royal burial sites such as Sutton Hoo, which now has a visitor centre and attracts thousands of tourists every year, what Jones found at Mucking revealed how ordinary people lived. She enlarged the understanding of multiple periods of history, but outside of a fairly narrow circle of enthusiasts and academics, her contributions are unknown. The site at Mucking has now vanished beneath further gravel extraction. When I visited on foot, I found nothing but a sleepy Essex village and a great expanse of stony scrub beyond. There was nothing to suggest that a major settlement had existed here thousands of years before, or that a glowing green glass beaker had once been tenderly lifted from the ground and wiped clear of mud.

The banks were receding rapidly now as the river widened. Looking out over *Cantilena*'s bow to the north, I could just make out more cranes on the shore reaching up into a bank of heavy cloud, and a huge ship beneath partially stacked with multicoloured containers. I climbed down the steps into the cabin to look at the chart. The Blyth Sands, which shelve away from Hoo to the south, lie opposite the unnaturally straight north bank. The computer showed a cluster of luminous dots along this stretch, indicating that a number of large ships were moored along the edge. We had arrived at London Gateway: the final port on the Thames, over thirty miles from central London.

As the dredging operation that created it would suggest, this port is enormous: it covers an area twice the size of the City of London and cost £1.5 billion to build. The cranes that I spotted in the distance tower over everything and are the largest on any quay in the world, standing 138 metres high. They were assembled in China and brought over intact on ships to be stood up on the dockside in Essex. The ships that this dock is designed for are gargantuan – often 400 metres in length, with up to 18,000 containers stacked eleven storeys high on their decks. For all that the port upriver at Tilbury has been expanded since it opened in 1886, there is no way that a Victorian dock could ever hope to handle these monsters; London Gateway has brought the Thames back into competition as a modern, global port. Indeed, it is the location, so near London yet still completely accessible from the sea, that has made this site attractive for yet another downstream dock.

Goods unloaded here can be processed in the enormous

230-acre logistics park behind the quays and then sent by lorry or train straight to the city. Competitor ports like Felixstowe on the east coast or Southampton on the south are much further away from the goods' final destinations in London or the south-east, necessitating longer delivery times. The same logic that led the Romans to create the first trading port on the Thames two millennia ago applies today. Those in the industry argue that having a mega port that can also serve as a major distribution centre in the Thames estuary is better for the environment, because goods don't have to be trucked from the port to a distribution centre in the Midlands, say, and then back south to their final destination. Fewer lorries on the motorways and lower mileage for what we consume are undeniably a good thing.

It isn't just in the water that there are environmental consequences for the estuary from the construction of this vast industrial structure. The refinery site upon which the land reclamation for its base took place had been derelict for over ten years before construction began, and very efficiently colonized by a range of species, including avocets, water voles, adders and newts. To compensate for the damage done to this wildlife by the dredging and the building of the port, over 320,000 creatures were captured and relocated to a new nature reserve created to the west of the port – a move criticized by some as merely an attempt to foster good PR for the development rather than actually protect wildlife. There are fears that the continuous movement of mud from the riverbed could speed up coastal erosion elsewhere along the banks, and that the ships' fuel will pollute the water. Meanwhile, the great container ships arrive on every tide.

London Gateway is one of the most highly automated ports in the world; the cranes, which would dwarf the London Eye, appear to bend and lift of their own volition. Yet seen from the water, it is difficult to appreciate its vast scale, so on a bright, blustery spring afternoon my mother and I parked at the entrance to the recently created Essex Wildlife Trust site on the other side of the wetlands to the port, and walked the two miles through undulating grassy hummocks and stagnant boggy puddles to the Thames. The wind was bending the grass towards the sea, making it flow like water. There is a visitor centre on the headland, a round building made from vertical wooden slats that looks like a beacon from a distance, which houses a shop that sells birdwatching guides and local honey. It was only when I stood outside and looked east that I fully appreciated how massive the new port development is: it stretches back from the river for miles, in a vast paved-over area covered in warehouses, distribution centres and lorry parks. 90 per cent of the world's cargo is moved in containers stacked on ships and now the majority of Britain's imported goods come through the Thames estuary again. London can still claim to be a port city, even if the docks in the city itself have long been silent. The labour has been outsourced to robots and the site to the estuary.

The bow is pointing due east now. *Cantilena* has rounded Lower Hope Point, the north-eastern edge of the Hoo Peninsula, and left the Mucking No. 1 buoy behind to port. We are in Sea Reach, the last named stretch of the Thames. The wind is coming over the stern quarter, the perfect direction for a swift run out to sea with the remainder of the tide. My father makes one last careful trip from the cockpit to the deck to check that all is ready to hoist the sail, while my mother and I clear the mugs away and move into position. Without looking, I reach down the side of the wheel and grab the straight metal shaft of the winch handle that is stored there. I am going to unfurl the genoa, the large sail attached to a cable stay running from the top of the mast to the end of the bow. This particular style of sail can be wound tightly round a long rotating drum on the cable, making it easy to roll up in situ when not wanted. There is no need to hoist it, therefore; all I have to do to bring it out is pull on the rope that unwinds it, carefully paying out the sheet with the other hand to make sure that the sail doesn't catch the wind while still partially wrapped and cause damage. My father jumps back down into the cockpit and slackens off the engine. I begin to yank hard on the rope, trying to pull as much of the sail out quickly before it becomes too taut to control. I make it most of the way there before the wind bellies the genoa out and I have to wrap the sheet around the winch and slot in the handle to wind it the rest of the way.

Meanwhile, my parents have loosed the much larger mainsail from its fastenings. My father climbs onto the foredeck and heaves downwards on the halyard, while my mother pulls from the other side of the cockpit. I instinctively duck down to look out underneath the mass of slippery white canvas that is gradually ascending the mast from its resting place along the boom, to make sure that there are no other vessels on a course to hit us – it's when hoisting or trimming sails and the crew is distracted that accidents can happen. By the time I have completed my careful scan of the horizon, the sails are both up and my parents are busy tidying away the ropes that we had used to hoist them. After a couple of careful adjustments – the genoa has slackened off slightly, the boom has moved across to the left to expose a larger area of the mainsail to the wind – I begin to feel the difference in *Cantilena*'s motion. She dips more purposefully into every wave now that she is under sail and heaves over slightly from the force the sails are channelling from the wind. My father moves the throttle lever into neutral and then leans down the side of the cockpit to press the button that cuts the engine. It makes a long, high beep and then there is silence, except for the rushing of the water against the hull and the creaking of the ropes straining to hold the sails in place. Our speed is picking up, from five knots to six and a half, sometimes seven when the boat accelerates before larger gusts of wind.

Once we have all sat down again, the course set and the sudden burst of activity over for now, I realize that I am grinning. My stomach lifts with the thrill of the speed and the vast expanse of water before me. Conrad captured this feeling when he wrote in *The Mirror of the Sea* that 'the estuaries of great rivers have their fascination, the attractiveness of an open portal ... That road open to enterprise and courage invites the explorer of coasts to new efforts towards the fulfilment of great expectations.' The open water ahead, shifting in colour between pewter grey and mustard brown as the scattered clouds are blown across the sky, holds vast potential; all journeys can begin here. It provokes a feeling of almost euphoric expectation which I have experienced only once anywhere else: on the long, straight, bleached concrete highway that runs through the desert from Las Vegas to Los Angeles, late on a baking summer afternoon. That frontier-pushing, optimistic feeling I had as I drove west towards the setting sun felt oddly familiar – the landscapes could not be less alike, but they share the same sense of adventurous optimism, of a freedom yet to be fulfilled. As a teenager, I used to rage against my parents' obsession with sailing to nowhere and could not understand why the journey itself was the part they enjoyed. Now, finally, I understand.

7

Cliffe Fleet to the Medway

The boat was scudding along now, the sails pulling hard. Occasionally a bigger wave caused the bow to plunge further and smacked the spray back along the deck. The speed made this otherwise quiet journey suddenly loud: the wind was ringing in my ears and booming in the sails, and the river was rushing beneath the hull. Out in the channel, it felt as though we had come sharply into focus, the boat a pinprick of tension between wind and water, and everything else beyond receding into blur. I knelt up on the cockpit seat and put my head above the shelter of the canvas awning that was keeping most of the wind off us. My hair was immediately whipped into an intractable tangle but the smell was extraordinary – now that we were running parallel to the Hoo Peninsula, the brisk south-westerly breeze was bringing the tang of the marshes out to me. I took a big gulp of it, the brackish, salty and slightly rotten notes in the air buzzing on my tongue. The land to the south of us was so low-lying that as the boat rocked along I could barely distinguish it, a mere smudge of mud squashed between the expanses of sea and sky.

This is one of the loneliest stretches of the estuary; from the water, it's a desolate-seeming outlook that forces the eye to slide away, so determined is it to remain unseen. The disused jetties that have tumbled from many of the banks upstream are absent here, because no one has wanted to land on the slimy green stones that slide beneath the water. More than a third of the peninsula is formed from reclaimed land – a process begun by the Romans, and continued down the centuries as more pasture for 'marsh mutton' and space for industry were required – and it still holds memories of its watery origins. A spine of London clay runs through the low hills in the centre, giving way to chalk, gravel, sand and silt on either side. To the south, it rolls away gradually to the Medway, but on the northern side it shelves in a dramatic escarpment down to the flats that run next to the Thames. Few trees grow in the shallow marshy soil and so the flat land extends as far as the eye can see, punctuated only by the pylons and chimneys of the Isle of Grain, which lies off the eastern end of the peninsula, in the distance. More than anywhere else I have been, Hoo feels remote, as if this narrow spur of land between the Thames and the Medway has all but drifted off into another world. Peter Ackroyd writes that 'it has been said that "it is the last place God made – and never finished"'. There is a sense of abandonment, of a place forgotten by all but the few who have made their homes here.

For a place that so few outsiders down the years have visited, the way it is portrayed in the accounts that do exist can have a disproportionate influence. Daniel Defoe was one of several prominent eighteenth-century writers to suggest that the place was unhealthy – partly because of the persistent prevalence of the malarial 'ague' – and that nobody of any status would choose to live there. Hoo and the Medway islands became known as

unsophisticated, ill-favoured outposts, contrasting unfavour-
ably with the civilized metropolis upriver. In 1732, William
Hogarth cemented this opinion when he visited the churchyard
in the village of Hoo St Werburgh briefly and documented
it in a slim volume entitled *Five Days' Peregrination Around the
Isle of Sheppey* – a kind of Georgian 'lads' tour' of the estuary
he had taken with four friends. In the churchyard, Hogarth
'having a motion, untruss'd upon a grave rail in an unseemly
manner' – that is, he defecated on a tombstone – and then
his friend 'administered penance to ye offending part with a
bunch of nettles'. He was thirty-four and flush with the success
of *A Harlot's Progress* the previous year; the whole thing reeks
of arrogant young men having a good time at the expense of
others. The book is a parody of the 'grand tour' travelogues
commonly written at the time about Continental adventures,
full of doggerel and amusing sketches of waterside characters:
applying this mode of writing to the unlovely, lowly location
out in the estuary was the basis of Hogarth's satire. Later, when
Londoners began to outsource their refuse and waste, a place
so famously undesirable as this, where nobody of consequence
would complain, seemed like an obvious choice. As I began to
dig deeper into the stories of this place, though, it was the casual
way in which people – often destitute and unwell – had been
condemned to this place as a punishment that shocked me.

For a long time Hoo made no impression on me; I must have
sailed past dozens of times without troubling to look at it. That
changed after I saw a television adaptation of Dickens's 1861
novel *Great Expectations* in my early teens. Part of it was filmed
at Stangate Creek, a muddy inlet running into the Medway
where we often anchored for the night on weekend sailing trips.
I remember sitting on the edge of the sofa, open-mouthed with
surprise at seeing it on screen. My father, wisely, took the book

down from the shelf and put it in my hands, and I devoured it over the next few days. It begins in a gloomy churchyard, perched on the ridge of the peninsula above the estuary, with the description, 'Ours was the marsh country, down by the river, within, as the river wound, twenty miles of the sea.' Pip, the narrator, observes 'the dark flat wilderness beyond the churchyard, intersected with dikes and mounds and gates, with scattered cattle feeding on it, was the marshes; and that the low leaden line beyond was the river; and that the distant savage lair from which the wind was rushing was the sea.' I was bewitched by these lines, which described a landscape so similar to the familiar shores of the Medway on the other side of the peninsula, where I had sailed so often. The more I learned about Hoo's unlovely reputation, the more striking it was to find it here, in a novel by a famous author. That it had been characterized as 'a dark flat wilderness' inhabited by desperately poor people and roving escaped convicts mostly passed me by, as did the fact that Dickens was using the estuary and Hoo as a metaphorical space, so near and yet so far from the modern metropolis of London, to show the extent to which the nineteenth century's social evils proliferated under that supposedly progressive society's very nose. I was just thrilled to see it on the page at all.

The plot of *Great Expectations* is superbly bleak, as befits the estuary of Dickens's imagination. It turns on the appearance of Magwitch, a convicted felon escaped from captivity, in the graveyard where a young boy called Pip is paying his respects to his dead parents and siblings on Christmas Eve. The setting for this scene is believed to be based on St James's Church in Cooling, a tiny village of around 200 people towards the western end of the Hoo Peninsula, overlooking the marshes and the Thames to the north. In this graveyard there are rows of tiny 'stone lozenges' marking children's graves, just as there are in the novel, almost certainly victims of the local ague. There is so little high ground in the estuary that this point on Hoo feels like the top of the world. When I visited on a bright March morning, the grass glowing into life under the first spring rays, I could see the whole estuary laid out before me. From the lane that runs past the church, I stared at the marshes spreading out towards the horizon, the river unseen beyond. This is a rare tourist spot in the estuary – the church is no longer in regular use, but is kept open for its connection with Magwitch and Pip. Dickens's story means that those little graves, crammed so close together, have thousands of visitors every year.

Dickens had spent part of his childhood in this area while his father worked at the nearby naval dockyards at Chatham on the Medway. In 1857, already a hugely successful author, he bought a manor house at Gads Hill, about five miles south of Cooling. For decades, the foreshore on both sides of the peninsula had been a regular mooring spot for notorious prison hulks, and just before Dickens took possession of his new country retreat, the last one was abandoned. It was ideal terrain for these floating prisons. Driving around the peninsula, the windows down and the hedgerows on either side of the narrow lanes reaching into the car, I experienced first-hand how acutely remote this place can feel. Where better to park rotting hulks full of convicts? If, like Magwitch, somebody did manage to escape, there was nowhere for them to go but miles of saltmarsh or into the river. Squinting across the fields, I wondered how many actual flesh-and-blood bodies had rotted into the earth here, the victims of a particularly cruel passage of British history.

Until the American colonies declared independence in 1776,

the British authorities had habitually transported criminals to America to relieve overcrowding in domestic prisons; once cut off from that option, they deported them downriver to the estuary instead. Many of the hulks were former naval vessels, some of which had been used to more glorious purpose in the sea battles of the Napoleonic Wars, and in fact the use of ships as temporary housing for prisoners of war had begun during the Continental conflicts of the early nineteenth century. With their masts and rigging removed and their portholes barred with iron, these old ships were beached in marshy areas of the estuary where few people lived and filled to the gunwales with prisoners. In *Great Expectations*, Dickens describes the hulk from which Magwitch has escaped as 'a wicked Noah's ark, cribbed and barred and moored by massive rusty chains'. The guards, upon realizing that he has absconded, fire 'great guns' into the air to warn the locals that a criminal is at large and to stay indoors. Even now, there are few lanes across the peninsula, and great open spaces everywhere with no way of accessing them apart from on foot. It isn't hard to imagine how a gunshot on a foggy night would reverberate, booming across the marshes again and again.

Some of those incarcerated in the prison fleet were facing deportation to Australia, Britain's new penal colony of choice, waiting for a berth on a ship. Others were more or less permanently 'employed in hard Labour in the raising Sand, Soil and Gravel from, and cleansing, the River Thames', as the law put it. Those who were not deemed healthy or strong enough to survive the sea voyage to the Antipodes were kept in the hulks for the duration of their sentence, sometimes for as long as ten years. By 1828, 4,446 people were imprisoned on the river in this way, in ten different vessels. They were kept in chains (Magwitch still has an iron hoop on his leg when he enters the graveyard and terrifies Pip into stealing a file from his uncle's forge so that he can remove it) and put to work clearing mud for riverside construction and driving piles for jetties. The guards carried sticks, and used them liberally to enforce this regime.

James Hardy Vaux, a serial criminal who was deported to Australia three times in his life, left a first-hand record of life aboard the hulks in his memoirs, published in 1819. He called them 'receptacles of human misery' and described his first sight of life aboard the prison ship *Retribution*, then moored on the marshes at Woolwich: 'Of all the shocking scenes I had ever beheld, this was the most distressing. There were confined in this floating dungeon nearly six hundred men, most of them double-ironed; and the reader may conceive the horrible effects arising from the continual rattling of chains, the filth and vermin naturally produced by such a crowd of miserable

inhabitants, the oaths and execrations constantly heard among them; and above all, from the shocking necessity of associating and communicating more or less with so depraved a set of beings.'

These vessels were infamous for the filth, cruelty and horror of life aboard. Such was the climate of fear surrounding them that many prisoners were said to prefer hanging to this floating hell. The hulks were supposed to be a solution to overcrowding in conventional prisons – with over 200 capital crimes on the statute book in the early 1800s, there were a lot of prisoners, some of them teenagers or even young children – but were so full that in some cases each man had only a few inches of bunk to lie in at night. Many prisoners were in poor health when they arrived on board and the cramped conditions meant that infections were rife. On some vessels, the death rate was almost one in three. The same waterborne diseases that were spreading rampantly through the poorer neighbourhoods of the Thames in the first half of the nineteenth century stalked the hulks to deadly effect. Many prisoners died of cholera and typhoid and were buried in unmarked graves in the marshes. One account from during the cholera epidemic of 1832 reveals that the hulks' chaplain was too afraid to go ashore onto the festering marshes to read the burial service for his dead charges; instead he conducted a kind of long-distance funeral on the deck of a ship a mile away and dropped a handkerchief when it was time for the diggers ashore to lower the corpses into their shallow graves. It was said that, on approaching, you would smell a hulk before you saw it, and that overnight when the prisoners were confined to the cabin and the hatches locked, the miasma would grow so thick that a candle would not burn in the foul air.

Initially planned as a temporary stopgap, to be used for two years while a more permanent prison solution was found, the hulks remained a regular feature of the estuary for eighty years. The majority of the people imprisoned in them were young men under the age of thirty-five who had been convicted of some kind of theft, but there were boys as young as eight. Social reformers like John Howard and Patrick Colquhoun had been campaigning to get rid of the hulks ever since they were first used (the latter called them 'seminaries of vice and wickedness', arguing that reoffending rates among those released from the prison ships were so high that they served little purpose other than to hurt their inmates). Dickens was part of this dogged movement: he had spent six months in a debtors' prison on the south bank of the Thames in London with the rest of his family when he was a child and he retained a lifelong interest in penal reform. In both his journalism and his fiction he returned to the subject again and again, writing accounts of the hideous conditions and terrible lack of justice that those caught up in Britain's prison system experienced. *Great Expectations* was published four years after one of the last hulks, the *Defence*, burned to smouldering ruins off Woolwich in 1857, but his depiction of Magwitch's terrifying escape across the marshes of the Thames estuary became one of the best-known passages of nineteenth-century fiction. It brought a measure of fame to this lonely part of the river – albeit of a grim, dark kind. When people come here, they are more likely to be visiting Dickens's imagined terrain than the landscape of today.

As well as its reputation for isolation and misery, the Hoo Peninsula is known for being geographically inconvenient. It divides the Medway from the Thames, its east–west orientation postponing the moment when the two rivers come together as one estuary before they meet the sea. Even with the wind building and the sails briskly pulling *Cantilena* forward, the land was only sliding slowly past. I was undertaking this journey to observe the estuary, rather than to reach a particular destination, but I still felt a prickle of frustration at our apparent lack of progress towards the entrance to the Medway. Over the centuries, the two rivers have become closely connected, through trade, industry and military concerns, and the delays caused by waiting for the right tides to carry goods or ships all the way around the end of the peninsula to move from one into the other felt wasteful and irksome.

The need for a short cut for boats through the neck of the Hoo Peninsula became more pressing in the late eighteenth century, when war with France resulted in a naval struggle for control of the English Channel. French privateers were operating in the outer estuary, seeking supply ships to attack or capture, and the flow of barges carrying stores and weapons from the Thames base at Deptford to the fleet at Chatham in the Medway was interrupted. A canal was proposed that would shorten the distance between the two rivers from nearly fifty miles to around seven, and ensure that all the supply ships arrived at their destination. Work eventually began on cutting a channel between Gravesend on the Thames side and Strood on the Medway in 1800, but ran into difficulty after the first year of construction because of the hill at Higham, roughly halfway across the place where Hoo joins the mainland. Digging a tunnel through the chalk was costly and time-consuming, and the Thames and Medway Canal didn't open to shipping until 1824, by which time Britain and France were at peace again and the military need for it was much diminished. A couple of decades later, the route was resurrected as a railway line, initially with a single track laid on the canal's towpath and later with the canal filled in and sleepers laid over where the water had been. This formed the first railway connection to the Medway towns. Other parts of Kent already had train services to London by the 1840s, but the riverside areas lagged behind because, although legislators agreed on the advantages of a fast link to the Medway, nobody wanted to bear the costs of building a safe train line over marshes and through escarpments.

Even though the canal was not a commercial success – it cost so much to build that the tolls were set too high to attract much traffic – I always liked the idea of a watery connection between the two rivers, which have long been closely linked in my own understanding of the estuary landscape. It was said that the two-mile Higham tunnel was so straight that it was possible to see a ship's light at one end all the way from the other through the darkness, as if it was a secret smugglers' passage rather than a well-used thoroughfare. The train line follows its route today, and parts of the canal survived the infilling, mostly overgrown by the brambles and scrub that cover the adjacent railway embankments. For me, these little patches of weed-choked water, which can sometimes be glimpsed from the train, are a lingering reminder in the landscape of a period when engineers and investors had a mania for connecting rivers together, for digging canals between them so that the water could flow uninterrupted through the land. As well as this short-lived channel, a much more ambitious project was constructed at the other end of the Thames, where in 1789 a canal that was intended to allow inland passage from London to Bristol was opened. The Thames and Severn Canal connected an existing artificial channel from the Severn to Stroud in Gloucestershire to Inglesham Lock at Lechlade in the Cotswolds, the highest navigable point for vessels on the upper Thames. This brought together the two longest rivers in the United Kingdom, making it possible for a boat to travel from the east coast to the west through the heart of England and linking two great cities of Empire together. The craze for connective canals was short-lived. The Thames and Severn was abandoned in the early twentieth century, having been plagued for decades by a lack of water that made it unreliable for navigation. The impracticalities of these waterways were soon solved by the advent of the railways, but there is still something alluring about how they expanded and augmented the existing mythology of the rivers they connected. Both of these Thames canals are now part of restoration efforts, with volunteers and devotees working to reopen stretches of them for leisure use and as a way of preserving a ribbon of natural habitat in otherwise built-up areas. More than a century on, they still inspire passion, and I think I understand why. A river naturally has a beginning and an end; this way, it runs on forever, from sea to sea.

The road that leads across the Hoo Peninsula to the Isle of Grain feels disproportionately wide, given how little traffic there is. On the day that I drove with my mother through the tunnel under the Medway at Upnor and on north-east through the villages of the old Hundred of Hoo, we were the only car heading out towards the water. Every few hundred metres, we passed a sign reminding us of the speed limit or saw a speed camera pointed at the road. At first, I couldn't make sense of this – was there an epidemic of road rage among the lorry drivers taking goods away from the container terminal on the Isle of Grain, at the very end of the peninsula? But as we crested the ridge and the road descended again towards the marshes, I realized why all these precautions were necessary. If I had been driving this smooth, wide road at night, with only the distant lights of the ships out in the Knock John and Black

Deep channels twinkling at me in the far distance, I would be tempted to step on the gas. To streak down this road towards the river must feel like flying, as if the wheels could keep spinning and shoot you out across the North Sea.

Before the end of the main road, we turned off north up the lane that leads straight to the Thames. On the coast here is the hamlet of Allhallows, the houses mostly small and clustered around the twelfth-century flint church. This is one of the few historic buildings on the Hoo Peninsula. A sign inside explaining that it was 'previously scheduled for demolition under proposals for a London orbital international airport' is a reminder of the vocal local opposition to the successive airport schemes proposed in this vicinity during the last two decades. The estuary has long been considered a potential solution for London's air-capacity problems, with the planes, their pollution and noise to be outsourced downriver much as the container ships have been. One proposal from 1973 for an airport on the Maplin Sands off Foulness Island in Essex, the site of the famous Broomway walk, even received planning permission, although nothing was built there. It wasn't until the early 2000s, though, that this side of the estuary was threatened with such a development, when a number of schemes for an airport on reclaimed land on the Cliffe Marshes or further out at the Shivering Sands were suggested. The press gleefully dubbed the latter 'Boris Island' because the then Mayor of London, Boris Johnson, was so keen on the proposal, and discussions dragged on for years. There were many disadvantages: Met Office research found that an estuary airport would be plagued by fog delays, the RSPB produced a long report detailing the irreversible damage it would do to numerous unique habitats for wading birds and other estuary-dwelling creatures, the shipping industry pointed out the dangers of low-flying planes so near to channels used by huge container ships, residents raised objections to the pollution and noise it would cause. For all that, the politicians upriver in central London refused to abandon the scheme until it was formally rejected by the Airport Commission in 2014.

Beyond the church, the lane curves around and ends abruptly outside a large, art deco-style pub which looks too big for the tiny community it serves. We parked outside and walked into its beautiful tiled saloon, where a couple of weekday patrons sat scrolling through their phones or chatting in undertones. It was almost like walking into a cathedral, that same rush of cool stillness enveloping me. My mother ordered two ham doorstop sandwiches and we sat by the huge empty fireplace (decorated over the mantel with the dried hops obligatory everywhere in Kent) to devour them. We were only two at a table that could hold twelve, so I spread the map out next to our places to trace our route from here through the marshy land behind the sea wall and back to the Thames.

The little cluster of buildings around the pub is called Allhallows-on-Sea, even though no water is visible from here. Its name was part of an attempted rebranding exercise in the 1930s, when the Southern Railway company tried to create a seaside resort on the north coast of the Hoo Peninsula, accessible via a new branch line from the existing railway that ran east from Gravesend. In books about disused railway lines I found images of the posters, which called it 'a new seaside resort in the making!', with the qualifier that it was 'facing Southend' and the offer of specially discounted tickets and express services from Charing Cross. The posters even tried to lure people into moving here permanently, with a cheerful orange illustration of the 'healthy homes' available just '37 miles from London'. There are similar advertisements from this period for other coastal places in the estuary too, including Southend, Clacton, Margate and Broadstairs, all in bright, saturated colours and showing healthy-looking people stretched out on beaches or striding vigorously across rolling fields. Nothing could be further from the Dickensian vision of life here when the prison hulks were beached nearby. Expectations were high for the new development at Allhallows, which is why such a large pub was built, but the Second World War put paid to the idea that this would become the new bank holiday destination of choice for East Enders desperate for a break from the slums and a day out by the sea. The branch line closed in 1961 and at the same time the main Hoo railway became a goods-only line serving the port on the Isle of Grain.

After a brief chat with the woman serving behind the bar – whose north Kentish accent sounded so familiar to me from my childhood growing up just south of here in Sittingbourne that I was half convinced I knew her – I gathered up the map and we set off towards the dusty track that leads out onto the marshes. A tangled thicket of blackthorn bushes marked the transition from suburban street out onto the flat wildness ahead, the profusion of white blossom contrasting starkly with the dark stems. On the way, we passed the entrances to two holiday parks facing each other across the stile. These are the latter-day answer to the dream of the Allhallows seaside resort, long rows of prefabricated bungalows and caravans lined up like a child's toy village. The atmosphere of the seaside resort long past its prime is familiar these days, but this was something different – a more temporary, transitory affair, because the traditional promenade, amusement park and four-storey sea-view hotels were never built.

Our way led out east, towards the distant chimneys, warehouses and pylons of the industrial complex on the Isle of

Grain. The concrete sea wall to the north is high here, because this is reclaimed land, with a grassy slope leading down from it. The path towards it was raised slightly to keep it dry, but on either side the navy-blue, wind-ruffled water was visible between the lime-green stems of the grasses and reeds. Strangely, it reminded me of the Thames in Gloucestershire, that shade-dappled stream that I, and the river, had left behind so long ago. If I looked straight down, I could believe that this was the same river I had sought at Kemble. It was only when I raised my head and saw the grey industrial smudges to the east and took in the great flatness of the treeless lands around me that it was clear how far I had travelled. A heavily laden container ship heading for the port at London Gateway was moving swiftly upriver. From my perspective, with the river still hidden behind the sea wall, the ship seemed to be gliding along the surface of the marsh itself.

As we walked, the water in the drainage dykes was being pushed to and fro by a strengthening wind blowing strongly downriver. During the heave up the slope to the top of the sea wall the throbbing in the air increased until it was almost deafening, pushing against my ears and whipping my voice away unheard when I tried to shout something across to my mother. We walked east along the top of the wall with it pushing at our backs, as if it were hurrying us towards the sea. To the left of the path, the cemented side of the wall sloped down, joining seamlessly with the foreshore. There were distinct stripes of colour marking the reach of the tide, the speckled grey of the wall suddenly giving way to a leafy green stretch of lichens, followed by a darker, almost purple, longer weed where the stones smooth into the golden-tinged brown of the mud. The tide was about halfway up, so the rest was obscured under the water, which that day was a gunmetal grey with a sly azure sheen that showed with the movement of the waves. Conrad wrote in *The Mirror of the Sea* of his brief glimpse of Grain on the way up the Thames that he saw only 'a few low buildings like the beginning of a hasty settlement upon a wild and unexplored shore', and there is something of that feeling of an untouched world about it.

Soon, we came to a break in the wall, where what is left of Yantlet Creek flows out from the south to enter the Thames. The creek used to wind its way across the whole peninsula and join up with Colemouth Creek, which flows from a point further south down into the Medway. This is what once made the Isle of Grain an island, cutting it off from the rest of Hoo. Joined, the two waterways were sometimes known as 'the Stray' and in medieval times were an important navigation channel. In a 1798 edition of Edward Hasted's landmark four-volume study *The History and Topographical Survey of the County of Kent*, it is recorded that this was 'the usual passage for all vessels to and from London, which thereby avoided the more exposed and longer navigation round the outside of this island'. The creeks silted up in the post-medieval period, as the rivers on either side deposited sand and mud in the channel, so now it trickles slowly across the marshes, in some places indistinguishable from the standing water that permanently laps among the grasses. On the map, or seen from above in aerial photographs, the creek makes a tight S-shaped curve through the marshy paddocks, waxing and waning in width as it goes, at some points looking like a miniature Thames, at others barely visible at all. At its mouth is a silty beach, small now because the tide was almost at its highest point, but which would extend much further at low water.

Yantlet Creek is not just the nominal boundary between Hoo and Grain. There is another dividing line here, marked by a granite obelisk that stands out on the Thames foreshore. I could see it almost exactly due east of where I was standing on the curve of the creek's west bank, the Thames lapping around its plinth. This is the latest incarnation of the London Stone, erected in 1856 to mark a very old line drawn across the estuary. The stone itself stands about eight metres high, with a shallow pyramid-shaped point at the top. It has a counterpart, the Crow Stone, almost due north on the other side of the Thames at Chalkwell in Southend. Between them runs what is known as the Yantlet line, an invisible border denoting the outer limit of the City of London's control over fishing rights and tolls on the Thames. There is also a stone at Upnor, around the other side of the Isle of Grain in the Medway, showing that the rights extended to this last tributary river. The City purchased this jurisdiction over the river and estuary from Richard I in 1197 – he supposedly put the 1,500 marks paid towards his crusades

in the Middle East – and it is thought that there have been boundary markers of some kind at these points since Edward I confirmed the rights by charter in 1285. In the 1800s, they became the focus of celebration. Every seven years the Lord Mayor of London and his aldermen in full ceremonial dress would process out to the line in a fleet of barges to check their boundary. At the Crow Stone, crowds would gather to watch the officials raise glasses of wine in a toast: 'God preserve the City of London.' For a long time, this was considered to be the limit of 'London's river' and the end of the Thames; the other side was the wild unknown. In 1857, the City of London finally lost its claim on the Thames after years of legal wrangles with the Crown about which body was responsible for the costs of building and maintaining the new embankments and bridges. The Thames Conservancy Board was created to oversee the river as a whole, from Cricklade all the way out to the Yantlet line, and then in the early twentieth century the responsibility was passed to the Port of London Authority. The stones remain, though, as a reminder of how far the City's control once extended, and in remembrance of the celebrations that took place here.

The tide had risen almost all the way up the obelisk's plinth and the wind was starting to make my mother's ears ache. From where we were standing, we could see across the marsh on the other side of the creek all the way to the small village of Grain, on the very eastern tip of the island. Although still one of the least accessible places in the estuary, Grain can today be reached relatively easily via the main road that runs along the southern side of the Hoo Peninsula to the industrial buildings on the Isle. This wasn't always so, though: in 1824, a major court case at Guildford found seven men guilty of cutting through the causeway and bridge that had carried traffic across the silted-up

Yantlet Creek for decades. Residents testified to their need to access their salt pans, oyster beds and lobster pots in the creek and on the Grain Marshes beyond. Finally, the court ruled that, despite the presence of the London Stone at the mouth of the creek, the City of London had no right to redredge a seaworthy channel and cut off the inhabitants of Grain from the mainland. The land didn't remain in public hands, though, because in 1917 it was requisitioned by the Admiralty and used as an artillery firing range – a counterpart to the existing battery testing site on Shoeburyness opposite, on the Essex side of the Thames. Although no longer active, the marsh is still used occasionally for military demolition exercises. A manned guard post on the only road into the site prevents entrance and all the footpaths in the area terminate in 'danger' signs. The estuary has always been a favoured place for military exercises, because of both its proximity to major bases and its relatively remote and uninhabited character. These areas are like a secret within a secret: unmapped and inaccessible.

After a last look at the London Stone, we turned and walked back along the sea wall, bending forward so we weren't blown off our feet. Ahead, I could see the caravan park at Allhallows-on-Sea, and beyond the cranes of London Gateway on the horizon. The container ship that had glided past was manoeuvring into its berth alongside the quay, several tug boats buzzing about the vast sheer sides of the massive hull like waterborne bees. On one side of the sea wall, the silty grey water of the estuary lapped ceaselessly at the weeds, while on the other the almost indigo surface of the drainage dyke was calm. I had reached the defined edge of the river. It was time to cross the line and see what lay beyond.

During the planning of my trip with my parents into the estuary again, I had been prepared to find that plenty had changed since I was last on these waters. I knew that the river was cleaner and that there were now wind turbines both on its banks and out on the shallows and sandbanks. I had read about the new port at London Gateway; I was used to the fact that huge container ships and tankers still used the river in its outer reaches, far out of sight of London. I was ready for new sights and experiences. But I was not expecting to find that old familiar landmarks would have disappeared, or how disorientating their absence would be.

The eastern tip of the Isle of Grain is the site of several major industrial plants: a former BP oil refinery, a liquefied natural gas import and storage facility, and London Thamesport, one of the UK's largest container terminals. Together, their warehouses and silos and chimneys form a familiar skyline, which I have spent many hours staring at on long, slow sails past this shore. Thrusting upwards from the flat marshland, these great man-made structures make the sky look even larger. There were two in particular I was especially fond of, because the sight of them always indicated that we were nearly home: the tall, cigarette-shaped chimneys of the two power stations on Grain. For much of my childhood, my parents kept their boat in the River Medway. These two chimneys were my leading lights, and part of the system of landmarks that my father used to teach me how to steer out of the river and into the estuary safely. Both the oil-fired power station at the very eastern tip of Grain and the combination oil and gas plant at Kingsnorth further around into the Medway itself, on the south side of the Hoo Peninsula, feature prominently in my memories of growing up. They were always on the edge of my vision, helping me to get my bearings in this flat, seemingly featureless landscape.

As *Cantilena* surged east through the channel between the shallows of the Nore sands and Grain Spit, it was with an unpleasant jolt that I realized that the chimneys had gone. To safely avoid these sands, boats must go a long way past the peninsula before turning into the Medway; although it looks like perfectly innocent water, the riverbed is often only a foot or so beneath the surface in places. I remember finding this part of a journey tortuous as a child – I could *see* the chimneys, so why couldn't we head straight for them? It took many patient tutorials from my father, drawing lines on the chart with a ruler through the dark blue shallows shaded beyond the end of the peninsula, for me to understand why we had to stay in the white or pale blue parts if we wanted to avoid running aground. This time, I found it difficult to tell how far past the sandbanks we had travelled without the chimneys for reference. I felt unmoored, adrift from the map of this place that I carry in my head.

Neither power station had been operating at full capacity for a long time. As the UK became more conscious of pollution and the cleanness of our energy, both were found wanting. Grain was mothballed in 2002, only returning to production at moments of high demand, and Kingsnorth closed in 2012 once it no longer met EU standards on air pollution. The wind farms sprouting in the estuary, on the Kentish Flats, at Gunfleet Sands, off Thanet and London Array further out off North Foreland, were taking the place of these outdated fossil-fuel plants. Kingsnorth in particular had long been the focus of protests about the British government's slow adoption of renewable energy sources. In 2007, a group of six Greenpeace activists broke in, climbed the chimney and wrote the word 'Gordon' vertically down from the top (they were planning to write 'Gordon, bin it' as an instruction to the then prime minister, Gordon Brown, to abandon coal, but were arrested partway through). The subsequent court case produced a landmark judgement, in which it was recognized for the first time that activists had a 'lawful excuse' for damaging property while acting to try and prevent climate change.

I spent some time in the cabin studying the chart on the computer in an attempt to reorientate myself; when I came back on deck, *Cantilena* had made it past the shallows off Grain. The wind that had pushed her from behind all the way out of the Thames was now going to be coming straight over the bow, but since it had dropped significantly in strength, my parents decided it would be more fun to tack into the Medway ('like the old days!') than drop the sails and switch the engine on. As soon as we reached the red buoy named Nore Swatch, which along with another called Grain Edge marks the extent of the dangerously shallow water, my father switched the autopilot off and took the helm. Gradually, he eased the boat round to point south, while my mother and I hauled in the sails to suit the new course. Soon, we were speeding towards the fort at Garrison Point, the northernmost tip of the Isle of Sheppey.

In the last few years, both power stations on the Medway have been demolished, piece by piece. The chimneys were left until the very end, but eventually, in March 2018, the last one came down too. I found footage of the demolition afterwards and in slow motion watched the charges explode all the way up the 650-foot tower; and then the whole thing crumpled and descended in on itself, subsumed by the cloud of smoke and dust that boiled up to obscure the rubble. Looking online, I found a 'Save Kingsnorth Chimney' group on Facebook, with people commenting sadly about the demise of a 'Medway icon' and posting nostalgic pictures of the chimney at sunset. I felt reassured that I wasn't alone in thinking that the disused industrial architecture of the estuary was beautiful. People love the place as it is, not an idealized version of what it could be.

The tide had turned. At Garrison Point, the water was beginning to flood back into the Medway. The eddy around the green buoy marking the edge of the channel was now upstream and I could feel the change in *Cantilena*'s movement too – she was once again being pulled along by more than just the wind. This is the Thames's final tributary and a substantial river in its own right. It rises in Sussex and runs for ninety miles east and north across Kent before joining the Thames here, at the point when neither stream looks much like a river any more. It is more like the confluence of two estuaries, one large, one smaller, water spreading as far as the eye can see. It's the final act, the last piece of action before the sea takes over. The Tudor poet Edmund Spenser was infatuated with this joining point and all that it symbolized: in 1580, he wrote to a university friend that he wanted to pen an 'Epithalamion Thamesis' which would describe 'the marriage of the Thames'. His project was not that different from mine: he aimed to 'shewe [the Thames's] first beginning, and offspring, and all the Countrey, that he passeth thorough, and also describe all the Riuers throughout Englande, whyche came to this Wedding'. The poem was never written, but Spenser returned to the idea of a marriage between rivers in his 1590 allegorical epic about myths and Elizabethan nationhood, *The Faerie Queene.*

A section of the poem is devoted to 'the spousalls, which then were/Betwixt the *Medway* and the *Thames* agreed'. The wedding was attended by sea gods and nymphs, the mythical founders of nations, and other rivers of Britain and Ireland; the Ouse, the Humber, the Liffey and the Boyne were all there. In these passages, Spenser is refashioning existing mythologies for a new purpose, bringing the classical grandeur of Homer and Ovid to the muddy waters of the estuary. When I first came across these passages while studying in Oxford, the Thames just a few hundred yards from my window across the water meadows, I was astonished to find that this place had been given such significance and grandeur by an Elizabethan courtly poet. The harmony and concord represented by the solemnizing of a marriage between the two rivers are a metaphor for the unity to be found under the rule of Elizabeth I. Two years before, with the threat of invasion from the sea by the Spanish Armada, she had committed herself to her kingdom body and soul by the Thames at Tilbury; in his poem, Spenser is celebrating her 'marriage' to England by writing about the nuptials of England's greatest river. Elizabeth's life was bookended by the Thames: she was born in a palace at Greenwich and died upstream at Richmond. Her body was transported by barge in a torchlit procession to Whitehall before her burial in Westminster Abbey, but the symbolic joining of the river and the nation was formalized long before that, out here where the Medway and the Thames join together and flow towards the sea.

The sails began to flap as we moved into the shelter of the river, the docks at Sheerness on our left. It was time to drop the mainsail: a few minutes of flurrying and billowing as it descended, helped by my father on the foredeck hauling hunks of canvas into their proper places. For a moment it looked far too large to fit back between the network of strings ('lazy jacks', they are called) that are supposed to stop it from flopping all over the deck and into the water. But, as always, everything suddenly slipped into place, the sail neatly stacked on top of the boom and the engine started again to help the genoa propel us along. My father changed sides in the cockpit and reached for the binoculars so that he could study the docks slipping by. He worked here for the best part of two decades, some of the time in the chief executive's office that overlooks the whole operation. It's been a few years since he left, but he still has friends in the ports business and he was curious to know what they had been doing in his absence.

The cranes and the quay soon gave way to a vast car park, built in the 1990s on land reclaimed from a mudflat called Lappel Bank. This used to be a huge area of intertidal habitat, and became the subject of a landmark European Court decision in 1996 after it was found that the government had acted illegally in not protecting the habitat of the over 50,000 wading birds that used to overwinter here. Eventually, part of Wallasea Island on the Essex side of the estuary was transformed into a nature reserve to compensate for the loss. The light bounces off the tens of thousands of brand-new vehicles parked on the low-lying concrete, shooting rogue beams back up towards the clouds. I remember visiting my father at work in the late 1990s and seeing a car ship being unloaded – dozens of specialist drivers carefully piloting the vehicles one by one down a narrow ramp and off to be parked until sold. It had been explained to me that this was much the safest way of getting the cars off the ship, since it resulted in less damage than swinging them ashore with a crane. Still, aged eight or nine, I watched with baited breath from the window of my father's office as each one crept slowly forward onto the ramp, convinced that this would be the car that slipped and fell into the river beneath.

I was born in the hospital at Chatham, four years after my parents arrived in Britain. They kept their boat in the Medway until I was in my teens, and so perhaps of everywhere on the estuary this is the place that I am really from. I learned to sail here, studying the diagrams of sail shapes and wind directions my father drew for me at the chart table before taking the tiller for the first time to steer the boat between the buoys that mark the channel. Gaps in the shore are everywhere here, leading to tiny inlets and muddy creeks that wind for hundreds of yards through the marshes, and I know them all. The entrance to one in particular, marked by the end of a procession of electricity pylons where the thick cables plunge down from the great metal structure in the sky to the earth, makes my heart jump in my chest. This is the way into Stangate Creek, which reaches deep into the land and even has its own smaller branches: Halstow Creek, Twinney Creek, Milfordhope Creek, Sharfleet Creek. It's been a popular anchorage for ships waiting for the tide to take them in or out of the Medway for centuries – Turner even painted it in watercolours, showing the water glassy smooth and the sun burning through the clouds above. On weekend sailing trips, when there wasn't time to go further afield because of the need to be back for school and work on Monday morning, Stangate was often where we stopped overnight. My father would lovingly clean out the old hurricane lamp, a relic from their ocean-going days, and fill it with paraffin before hanging it from a hook in the ceiling of the cabin. The electric lights would be switched off and we would settle down to listen to the radio or read in silence, the only sound the slapping of the water against the hull and the cawing of the birds on the marshes on both sides of the creek. I had teenage tantrums here, brooding and sulking on deck in the dark while the halyards clattered against the mast in the breeze and the anchor warp creaked, straining against the tide.

In the morning, it was my job to crouch on the foredeck behind my father while he hauled up the anchor from the muddy creek bed so that we could get under way. The boat my parents had built in Cape Town, *Scherzo*, had no electric windlass so the hooked metal anchor and heavy chain had to be pulled up by hand. My mother would start the engine and keep the boat hovering over the anchor while my father, shirt-sleeves rolled up and thick yellow gloves on his hands, would heave the salty chain aboard. I held the home-made canvas bag ready behind him, feeding the chain into it in a figure-of-eight pattern as it was passed back to me through his legs. It was a deep tawny brown colour, oxidized from years of immersion in salt water, and rough to the touch. The lower stretches had strands of wispy green weed caught between the links of the chain. I found the process stressful and unpleasant – I had to keep pace with my father, who couldn't afford to let the chain slip through his hands at all, in case the anchor swung in the water and hit the hull. In early spring or late autumn the water and metal would be so cold that my hands would start to go numb. Trickles of river water and mud ran down inside my sleeves, turning my wrists grey. Clumps of bluish-brown clay splattered onto the deck, and when the anchor finally emerged and was locked in place over the bow, great hunks of riverbed would still be attached to it.

We had taken just a brief diversion into the Medway; the way out to sea still awaited us in the wider estuary. Beyond the entrance to the creek, *Cantilena* made a great arc across the channel and we turned back the way we had come. I went and sat in one of the seats cut into the railing over the stern so I could still see the marshes around Burntwick Island, a small patch of firm ground amid the marshes. I left a version of myself here when I stopped coming in my mid-teens. She's still wandering among the reeds on the silky mud of the foreshore and it was strange to re-encounter her, albeit briefly. I never thought this place was ugly – I don't remember ever having any idea that a place shouldn't look like this – but I grew to resent it, all the same. Spending every weekend and holiday sailing here seemed completely normal to me when I was a child, but as I grew older I came to realize that other families went on holiday to places with sandy beaches and sunshine, and that perhaps there was more to the world than these muddy marshes. Like every teenager, I chafed against what I thought was the unfairness of this – why did *I* have to have parents who liked sailing out into the North Sea in the dark? It was only later, when I was in Oxford and then in London, that I appreciated the spoilt ridiculousness of my behaviour, of how I had resolutely sat in the cabin reading a book even when it made me seasick, just to make the point that I wasn't enjoying looking at the view. And of course, once I had escaped the Medway, all I wanted to do was return to the estuary. The tide washes out the patterns left on the mud every day, leaving a pristine, glossy surface for a new day. My parents were right all along.

8

Deadman's Island to the Nore

The wind had died almost to nothing. Without it, I was suddenly aware of the layers of clothing I was wearing; a muggy warmth to the air now suggested that a storm was brewing out to sea. The tide was flooding into the Medway at speed now. As *Cantilena* glided back out of Stangate Creek, I leaned over the cockpit rail to look at the long ripples pulling at the mooring ropes of the boats anchored at the edge of the narrow channel. The water was opaque, a thick yellow-brown full of suspended silt and grit. Even in the time it took for the boat to reach the main channel again, the expanse of exposed mud on either side shrank, disappearing under the oncoming tide.

My father was at the helm, keeping the engine ticking over slowly. I wanted to get a good look at the spit of land immediately to the right of the channel as we turned out of the creek and back into the Medway itself. I knew that this peninsula, which juts out all the way from the bank to the south and runs the length of Stangate Creek, was mostly covered by the Chetney Marshes. This is a major habitat for migratory and wading birds, and like much of the land in this vicinity is part of a Site of Special Scientific Interest because of the diversity and rarity of the birds that visit or breed here. At the very end, though, is a narrow stream known as Shepherds Creek, which separates the end of the peninsula from the rest. This small section, less than a kilometre long and only about 200 metres wide, is Deadman's Island. Access on foot is prohibited – partly because of the risk to the wildlife and partly because it is let by Natural England to private tenants – so the only way to see it is from the water.

I rested my elbows on the firm fibreglass rim of the cockpit so I could balance the binoculars better. At first sight, it looked like any of the other areas of intertidal land I had seen on this journey in the estuary. As I looked, the clouds shifted overhead so that the light hit the sheen of the mud sloping away from the water, cut through by rivulets and spiked with grasses that became denser on the island itself. This land is mostly formed of London clay, giving the mud a reddish-orange tinge not seen quite so much upstream. This part of north Kent was, in the eighteenth and nineteenth centuries, famed for its brick making: the brickworks exploited the clay deposits by the water and could load their bricks straight onto the flat-bottomed Thames barges to be sailed up to London on the tide. The classic yellow 'London stock' bricks, which can be seen everywhere in the nineteenth-century houses in areas such as Islington and Clapham, were made in places like this. The mud of the estuary built the city upstream; even Downing Street is built from these yellow bricks, which were then painted black and subsequently discoloured by pollution to give them their familiar dark, sooty patina.

I have heard rumours about Deadman's Island for years, about whole corpses washing free of the mud at high tide and floating away into the Medway, about human bones littering the tideline like pebbles. Local horror stories cluster around this place: it is supposedly haunted by the Devil and riddled with the ghosts of the damned; the very furthest, shallowest part of the creek is known as Bedlam's Bottom. Like many such legends, there is a hard kernel of truth: from the early eighteenth century, Stangate Creek was used as a quarantine anchorage for vessels that arrived in the estuary and were suspected of carrying the plague or other diseases, and anyone who died during the isolation period would be buried in an unmarked grave on this isolated, muddy island. In Turner's idyllic-seeming painting of Stangate Creek from 1823 there are dark shadows near the horizon beneath the luminescent sky – mastless hulks crouching near the shore.

Over the centuries since the burials, the tide has been slowly peeling the mud away and sheering off whole sections of shore, so that in recent years the graves have been exposed again. The film-maker Adam Curtis, who was born in Dartford, further up the Thames, managed to get onto the island in 2013 and posted a short film clip to his BBC blog. He captured images of ruptured coffins sticking out of the mud, the planks ripped apart by the tide and the remains inside scattered along the foreshore. The wind roars in the camera's microphone as he keeps it pointed at his feet, stepping carefully over several pelvic bones and what look like a few leg bones. 'Pretty horrible, really, isn't it?' his guide says to the camera, matter-of-factly. The constant grinding erosion echoes the wretchedness of the lives that ended here, in another manifestation of the 'the turbid ebb and flow of human misery' that Matthew Arnold observed on Dover beach. There are hundreds of graves on the island and gradually, as the mud shifts, they are all being washed out to sea. With the binoculars I could see the hollows in the shore where the rough plank coffins had once lain. The island dwindled quickly from view as *Cantilena* moved eastwards through the flooding tide: a dismal, sombre, abandoned place.

The Isle of Sheppey was directly ahead of us now, the low marshy island off the north Kent coast that faces the Isle of Grain across the mouth of the Medway. The narrow muddy channel leading off to our right past Deadman's Island that divides Sheppey from the mainland is known as the Swale. Although the name is thought to derive from a combination of the Anglo-Saxon *swalm*, meaning a whirlpool, and the Old English *swillan*, meaning to wash, it is no longer a whirling, rushing river. The tide creeps in from either side of the island and marshland has gradually encroached upon it. Slow-moving, winding creeks meander inland through the marshes to villages and market towns like Oare and Faversham, waterways which were once used by smugglers and bargemen alike to transport goods between Kent and the wider estuary. The port at Sheerness, where my father used to work, dominates the main town on Sheppey; the steelworks where he had his first job in the UK has long since closed, as has much of the other heavy industry on the island. In a strange echo of the bygone age of the hulks, there are also three medium-level-security prisons here, all in a row on the higher land to the south, near the marshy flats running alongside the Swale.

Sheppey was the first land-based home my parents had when they came to Britain. After their winter spent living on the boat in St Katharine Docks, they made this journey out of London towards the sea. The steelworks provided a house for them in the village of Minster, which occupies the highest point on the island, and they moved ashore to begin their new lives. Every day, my mother took the train from the tiny station of

Sheerness-on-Sea all the way back up the Thames to her job at Shell, on the south bank of the river in central London, tracing and retracing the journey they had first made by water. The island – for it is always *the* island to those who live on or near it – has a reputation for peculiarity. An easily accessible road bridge runs over the Swale and the train to the mainland takes less than ten minutes to reach the next town, but for as long as I've been aware of it Sheppey has been an insular, inward-looking place (inbred, some unkind people say). Quite soon after he had started work, my father met an eighteen-year-old lad at the steelworks who had been born and brought up on Sheppey and who had yet to leave the island to go to mainland Britain. He just didn't see the point. My parents, emigrants from another hemisphere, found this so extraordinary that it became a family legend, repeated whenever they talked about the island. They had spent years plotting their departure from where they were from; that someone would just *stay* seemed extraordinary.

By the time I was born, my mother had moved job to a research site in north Kent, and so my parents had moved across the Swale to the mainland. Sheppey still loomed large in our lives, though – my father drove across the bridge every day to go to work, and as he moved up the rungs at the steelworks and then the port, he became moderately well known in the tight-knit community. In 1993, he and hundreds of others lost their jobs at the port after a botched management buyout, and he ended up leading a class action on behalf of the dockers who had been shortchanged by the deal. Stuffing envelopes with the letters that kept the other 300 complainants informed about the progress of the case became a regular father–daughter Sunday afternoon activity, and as a result I probably knew more about share valuations and sharp accountancy practices than most eight-year-olds. It took years, but the case was eventually settled in their favour, and after that my father was a popular person on the island – my mother and I used to tease him that people would soon be asking him to kiss their babies like a politician on the campaign trail, but I did witness people crossing the street to shake his hand a couple of times. He may not have been a native 'swampie' – the affectionate local nickname for the islanders – but he had earned their respect.

Throughout my childhood, we would go back to Sheppey for his old colleagues' retirement and birthday parties. I would whinge and complain all the way there, having already imbibed the rest of Kent's disdain for this isolated, marshy place, but my normally easy-going father would absolutely insist that we all attend. Once we arrived at the working men's club or village hall where the bash was taking place it would all make sense. People appreciated that although he was an outsider and had been promoted to management, my father bothered to come back to the island to celebrate with them. I remember on one occasion having a memorably incoherent conversation next to the portable DJ set-up with somebody's drunk uncle, who wept a bit and told me how good it was of my dad to bring his family down for the do. I must have been about nine, old enough to understand; I complained a lot less about going back to Sheppey after that.

The day that my mother and I drove out to the island the sky was absolutely clear, the visibility perfect and sharp. As the car accelerated over the new road bridge – a perfect arc of steel and tarmac that alleviated the pressure of traffic on the squat 1950s concrete structure that I used to doodle everywhere on my homework – it felt like we were flying over the Swale, weightless and floating. On the descent, the car park at Lappel

Bank was laid out beneath us, perfect serried rows of identical cars as far as the eye could see. I couldn't imagine there were enough people in Britain wanting a shiny white pickup truck to find a use for these thousands of immaculate vehicles. They looked clinical in their faultless regimental formation. Once off the bridge, both of us exclaimed every few seconds at the new road layouts and buildings we saw ('There's an Asda here now?'; 'Since when has there been a proper roundabout on Sheppey?') as we followed the signs round the edge of the island. I wanted to see for myself how this place had changed in the ten years and more since I was last here; my mother was eager to visit her first British place of residence. Since I moved away from Kent, the only time I have heard news of Sheppey was in 2016, when a parody 'Vote Shepxit' campaign proposing that the island secede from the rest of Britain, as well as the European Union, was included in a TV round-up I happened to see of amusing political gags.

We stopped first at Queenborough, the tiny port at the western entrance to the Swale, which Daniel Defoe recorded in the 1720s as 'a town memorable for nothing, but that which is rather a dishonour to our country than otherwise . . . a miserable, dirty, decay'd, poor, pitiful, fishing town'. Before Yantlet Creek silted up, this was a major point of embarkation for goods travelling to the Continent, especially the wool from Sheppey and Kentish sheep: boats would head north out of the Medway through the channel between Hoo and Grain, and then cut through the Wantsum Channel, which used to divide the Isle of Thanet on the north-eastern tip of Kent from the mainland, to the English Channel. As this sheltered route for smaller ships fell into disuse, so Queenborough's fortunes faded – although Lord Nelson and Emma Hamilton are reputed to have met for a tryst in a house near the pier. Today, it has a jetty accessible at all points of the tide, so it is still a popular place to put ashore for visiting yachtsmen needing supplies or repairs. As we walked along by the slipway, a group of older men in polo shirts and deck shoes were transferring new radio equipment to a boat rafted up at the end of the pontoon, the static crackling across the water as they tested it. Across the muddy channel, in which lots of smaller sailing boats and dinghies were swinging from buoys and anchors, the crumbling shore of Deadman's Island was just visible.

A great recurved concrete sea wall runs along the shore here and we walked for a couple of miles, trying to adjust to the view without the towering power station chimneys on the north bank of the Medway. On one side of the path, the pebble-dashed slipway sloped down towards the water, striped brown and green and grey by the different phases of the tide. Behind the heavy grey mass on the other, wind turbines had rooted and sprouted into whirring oscillation above our heads. Although the hard surface destroys the marshy ambiguity of the foreshore – what is water and what is not becomes very definite here – the accessible path brings people down to the river. Dog walkers and cyclists were overtaking us at every other step; several of the benches sheltered in alcoves in the wall contained solitary teenagers speaking earnestly into their phones. 'Yeah, I'm by the water, usual place,' one of them yelled as we walked past. 'It's effing windy. Can you hear?'

We drove on, past what remains of the old blue steelworks where my dad used to work, and the Tesco where he used to buy his lunchtime sandwich every day. The road followed the shape of the island, taking us past the wharves and the warehouses and the fort at Garrison Point. We parked in the shadow of the concrete wall on the northern shore. Here the wall was bigger than ever, higher than the top-floor windows of the terraced houses that run along the other side of the road. Steep steps are cut into the side of the wall and there is a steel hand-rail to grasp on either side. I climbed up first, emerging onto the walkway at the top to stand and stare. Despite the brisk wind, the water looked flat and calm, spread in every direction like a sheet of rippled steel. In the far distance, I could just make out the pier and seafront parade at Southend, on the opposite side of the estuary, about seven miles away. I had never seen it on such a bright, clear day before – usually the cloud-dappled grey light and the haze on the water mean it's difficult to see very far. On so many journeys made in a wash of silvery-grey murk, the Essex shore might as well be the edge of the Arctic for all that I could see it. Today, the glowing light and sharp view were a gift: the river and the sea were laid out before us, merging and mingling and overlapping. A container ship was sliding westwards through the main channel, and a tiny pilot boat was bouncing in the opposite direction, no doubt off to help the captain of another giant vessel, hovering out of sight in the deep water to the east, navigate safely into the docks. I thought back to when I had stood on the Wittenham Clumps and imagined having a view all the way down through London to the very end of the Thames. Compared to the wonders of this shining silver flatness, the tamer green slopes in Berkshire seemed to belong to another, more domesticated world. Suddenly, a swallow, the first I had seen that year, swooped in from across the waves and flew in a great circle over our heads, rising on a column of warm air coming from the land. I watched its forked tail whirl round and round above me until I could no longer see it.

The room I lived in during my first year as an undergraduate at Oxford was small and oblong, with a narrow bed and a basin in a cupboard let into the wall. The best thing about it, I thought, was the fact that it had a picture rail all the way around, meaning that, despite the college's prohibition on sticking things to the walls, I could use hooks and string to fill the room with posters. I was far from the only one to make the pilgrimage to the art shop on Broad Street with this object in mind: it was fun to visit other people's rooms for the first time and guess what image of themselves they were trying project through their choice of wall coverings. Band and film posters were most common, of course, followed by the obligatory Che Guevara one and the occasional Rothko or Monet. My own preference was a bit harder to fathom – I had a huge, cheap reproduction of Turner's famous 1839 painting *The Fighting Temeraire*. It hung slightly lopsidedly over the standard-issue plywood coffee table that came with the room and gradually became more dog-eared because it used to fall down a lot at unexpected moments, so I was constantly having to rehang it.

I knew this picture, with its gorgeous orange-blue sky and ghostly white warship, by sight before I left home for university – it's a very popular painting and was voted 'the Greatest Painting in Britain' in a BBC poll in 2005. It was only when I started to feel homesick and turned to the Thames for comfort that I really became interested in it. The landscape it depicts is that of the estuary just off the Isle of Sheppey, broad, flat, silvery water stretching off the edge of the canvas, albeit made to glow with an unfamiliar gleaming light by Turner's brush. A compact dun-coloured steam tug is straining forward towards the viewer, pulling behind it the *Temeraire*, a great ship famed for her part in the naval victory at Trafalgar. It's a melancholy picture, though, which greatly appealed to my teenage angst – the ship is being towed from her berth off the Isle of Sheppey to a shipyard in Rotherhithe, where she will be broken up for scrap. The age of sail, and of heroes, was over, Turner is suggesting. Modernity, in the form of the busily whirring tug, has done for the graceful glory of the old ways. This was a preoccupation for him, especially in relation to the Thames – 1844's *Rain, Steam, and Speed*, which depicts a steam engine roaring across Brunel's new rail bridge at Maidenhead, is another comment on the imposition of new technology on the river.

The twentieth-century art critic Geoffrey Fletcher, in his book *London's River*, argued that in the case of the Thames life imitates art rather than the other way around. 'When Turner had invented burning sunsets over the river, the Thames went on to repeat them,' he declared. I think Fletcher's observation is about what we see in a landscape versus what we choose to value – there were sunsets over the estuary before Turner painted *The Fighting Temeraire*, of course, but by capturing the spirit of the place in oils, he offered those who saw his painting a way to appreciate the beauty of the landscape. The Thames ran through Turner's life as much as through the land, from his boyhood with his uncle at Brentford on the upper Thames, via his sketching expeditions at Weybridge, to his later-life visits to Margate. 'The skies over Thanet are the loveliest in all Europe,' he told the art critic John Ruskin, an early supporter of his blowsy, expansive paintings. For an artist so fixated by the merging of sea and sky, there was no better place to paint. He made repeated trips on the estuary to observe and sketch – a note in the front of a sketchbook from 1805 records that he took 'Varnish/Razor/Blue Black/Bt Sienna/Fishing Rod Flies/Pallet Knife/Shoes' with him on a painting excursion to the Nore. When Admiral Nelson's body arrived at Sheerness before being transported with ceremony up the river to London, Turner was there to sketch the scene for his paintings commemorating the victory at Trafalgar. Tellingly, in the fifth volume of his vast work of criticism *Modern Painters*, Ruskin imagined Turner's boyhood in 'that mysterious forest below London Bridge' as a wholly maritime one, during which he 'floated down there among the ships, round and round the ships, and with the ships, and by the ships, and under the ships ... the only quite beautiful things he can see in all the world, except the sky'.

The more I have learned about Turner and the *Temeraire* over the years, the more I have become attached to the painting. It's not an accurate representation of what the area off the Isle of Sheppey looks like, even on that gloriously bright day I climbed up onto the sea wall at Sheerness with my mother. The passage of the old ship probably looked quite different – there are thought to have been two tugs, not one, and the geography of the picture doesn't work, since the ships are heading west, while the sun appears to set in the east. Rather, it makes a place too often overlooked the centre of everything, just briefly, and captures a feeling of solemnity. What Conrad called the 'throbbing heart of the State' is transplanted to the outer estuary for a moment, and Turner makes it look magnificent.

The writer Nicola Barker once said that the settings for her stories 'have to be quite quiet, sort of almost empty places in terms of literature or, you know, the history of the place'. She found such a place in Sheppey, setting her 1998 novel *Wide Open* here, and peopled it with drifters and eccentrics and wild boars, characters who find themselves 'dead-ended' and dislocated. It was to be the first of three books loosely connected with the estuary; the so-called Thames Gateway trilogy, set in places defined in relation to their elsewheres – Sheppey, Canvey Island and Ashford, the town further south in Kent where I went to school. At the start of *Wide Open*, a man on a bridge is 'always looking outwards, facing away from London, never towards it'. Everyone wants to be somewhere else, but nobody is. Barker's choice of location raised some eyebrows (one critic wrote that the third book, *Darkmans*, was 'phenomenally good' despite its unglamorous setting and lack of plot), but her style, full of half-formed thoughts, dashes and abandoned detours, melds perfectly with this unwritten place. I devoured these books in my late teens, in awe of the way in which Barker pinned this place to the page. 'The sky was massive. Flat land, flat sea, and a great big, dirty, mud-puddle of a sky,' she writes early on in *Wide Open*. Her characters live in run-down farms inland and prefabs by the sea, and frequent the nudist beach on the eastern end of Sheppey at Shellness. A strange collection of knives 'spewed out onto the low dunes' because the sea has no use for them any more; soon it isn't just the landscape that lies wide open. Above all, Barker captures the feeling that abandoned, undiscovered horror can lurk here – unseen only because people choose not to look. The next wave might dislodge another broken skeleton, or bring a bomb halfway up the beach.

From the sea wall east of Sheerness, I could see one of these lurking horrors, lying between the shelving shore and the place where the shipping channel forks between the Medway and the Thames. We had arrived near the bottom of a spring tide, the phenomenon which occurs just after a new or full moon and causes the most drastic movement of water. The level in the estuary was about as low as it ever gets. The tops of three masts were visible above the waves, slanted over on one side, hinting at the ship that lies sunken beneath. Just outside the approach channel for the Medway, they were a regular landmark through-out my childhood and, because they have cross-spars at the top and a bit of rigging sagging down below, I used to think they belonged to a pirate ship. In fact, these are the visible remains of the SS *Richard Montgomery*, an American Liberty ship that was wrecked on a sandbank on 20 August 1944. Heavily laden with munitions destined for the Allied war effort in Europe, she anchored for the night in the deep water to the north of the Sheerness Middle Sand while waiting for other ships to come down the Thames before making her way across to France as part of a convoy. The anchor dragged while the captain was asleep; the *Montgomery* ran aground and then broke apart as the tide went out and bumped her hull down onto the hard surface. A salvage attempt was made immediately after the wreck, but the hull cracked open and part of the hold flooded, so it was abandoned. There were about 1,400 tonnes of explosives – some 13,700 different devices – on board when the *Montgomery* was abandoned to the estuary and they are still there today.

On the island, they call her the Doomsday Ship, although nobody really knows what would happen if she exploded now,

so long after first sinking under the waves. When munitions are transported by sea, different explosives are kept separately in tightly sealed compartments of the ship's hold in an attempt to minimize the chances of spillage or detonation. It's entirely possible that some of these chambers are still dry and the bombs they contain are as potent as when they were loaded in 1944. In addition to the TNT-based devices, the ship also contains smoke bombs, made from a kind of white phosphorus that could combust if it comes into contact with air. In 1970, government research suggested that a full detonation of the *Montgomery* would send a 300-metre-wide column of water and debris almost three kilometres into the air and break every window in Sheerness. That survey also predicted a minor tsunami, perhaps four metres high, after the explosion that would swamp smaller boats and test sea defences along the estuary's shores. An investigation by journalists at the *New Scientist* in 2004 showed that the cargo was indeed still deadly and pointed out that in total it was about one-twelfth the size of the atomic bombs dropped on Hiroshima and Nagasaki in 1945. Their report suggested that there were only two ways to neutralize it for good – remove the explosives or bury the ship entirely in sand and concrete. Both would require residents and businesses on Sheppey and the surrounding shores to evacuate and other ships carrying potentially dangerous cargo to seek other routes – a particularly expensive and impractical demand now that a new gas-fired power station on the Isle of Grain is constantly receiving fresh supplies of liquefied fuel from gigantic tanker ships.

As Sheerness residents had long suspected it would, the news that a shipwreck filled with deadly explosives that could detonate at any minute just over a mile from the British coast caused a minor sensation in the press. Journalists were suddenly visiting this 'rundown and rather unremarkable seaside town', asking passers-by on the high street if they were worried about their conservatories being blown to smithereens. The *Montgomery* has been a feature of conspiracy theory websites for some time – it's not hard to find posts alleging that there are terrorist plots targeting the wreck as a means of razing London to the ground – but mainstream media coverage was new. A government spokesperson patiently told all who asked that there were 'no grounds for increased alarm' and that the wreck was subject to annual sonar monitoring. When I first read this bland-sounding statement, I couldn't help wondering if the double meaning was intentional – did they mean that the newly reported revelations about the still-deadly explosives onboard were no more alarming than the wreck's presence had always been? For over sixty years, the government has pursued a policy of 'leave it alone, it's safer that way' – partly because they believe it to be the least harmful option and partly because of the sheer expense involved in intervening. A precedent supports this: in 1967, when an operation to try and neutralize the explosive cargo of the sunken Polish ship *Kielce* in the English Channel off Folkestone was attempted, it resulted in the wholesale explosion of the munitions on board. A Maritime and Coastguard Agency report from 2000 notes that it caused a disturbance equivalent to an earthquake measuring 4.5 on the Richter scale; although nobody was injured, chimneys and roofs were damaged and the whole episode 'brought panic to Folkestone's town and chaos to the beaches'. It is hoped that the wreck of the *Montgomery* will gradually break up as the sands shift, bringing an end to the threat without a similar detonation.

There are over 600 shipwrecks in the Thames estuary – more per square mile of seabed than anywhere else in Britain's coastal waters. Sailing is hazardous here, especially for the newcomer who ignores warnings about sharply shelving banks and rapid tides, but it has also long been one of the busiest shipping lanes in the world. Some wrecks lie forgotten for centuries, like HMS *London*, a naval gunship that sank off Southend with 300 crew and passengers aboard in 1665 after an explosion (Samuel Pepys recorded in his diary that she 'suddenly blew up', supposedly while a twenty-one-gun salute was being prepared) and was rediscovered by marine archaeologists in 2005. Combustion is a recurrent theme among the tales of estuary wrecks I uncovered. Particularly horrifying is the case of HMS *Bulwark*, a battleship that exploded in November 1914 while anchored in the Medway at Kethole Reach, just west of the entrance to Stangate Creek. Almost the entire crew of 750 perished, with only a dozen survivors – these latter were blown high in the air and clear of the ship at the initial detonation. I first heard of this from my father, who had witnessed the memorial still held there every year. The Mayor of Rochester (who also holds the ceremonial office of Admiral of the Medway) leads an annual procession down the river, reminiscent of the old visits to the boundaries at the Yantlet. At the point where the *Bulwark* sank, now marked by a red buoy, the whole parade pauses while prayers are said and a wreath is dropped into the water. It's a moving ceremony, an echo of the old pagan rituals where an offering must be made to the deity embodied by the water to secure safe passage and a good harvest.

In 2016, the artist Adam Dant created an incredibly detailed map showing some 1,000 wrecks in the Thames estuary. Called *The Museum of the Deep*, it was exhibited as part of a tiny temporary 'Museum of the Thames Estuary' in a shipping container in Southend that year, along with various artefacts recovered from the river itself. The map is a fascinating document to pore over, either in person or zooming in further and further on a screen to see the ships more vividly. Rather than marking them with just dots or lettering as would be the convention on a nautical chart, Dant drew each vessel as it would have appeared prior to sinking, as far as possible to scale. In his vision, the estuary is crowded with hundreds of finely inked ships filling the space from bank to bank. There are trawlers and schooners and steamers and yachts, a profusion of masts and sails and broken hulls. There's even a whale carcass lying near the Isle of Grain, flopped partway out of the water onto the land, abandoned and lifeless like the ships all around it. The map brings what is concealed back to the surface; it's a reminder of what lies hidden.

The wrecks are invisible, most of the time, but that doesn't mean that sailors in the estuary have no idea where they are. The Admiralty charts mark as many of them as is practicable or relevant, and there are also special buoys and lights indicating where they are. Safe passage for bigger, commercial ships is ensured by the use of pilots – a group of highly trained professional navigators who are taken out to incoming vessels in high-speed launches and work with the crew on board to guide them safely into the Thames. This is a centuries-old skill, formalized in 1514 by a royal charter presented to a group of mariners known as 'The Master Wardens and Assistants of the Guild Fraternity or Brotherhood of the Most Glorious and Undivided Trinity and of Saint Clement in the Parish of Deptford Strond in the County of Kent' and designating them the corporation in charge of regulating the pilotage system on the Thames.

Trinity House, as the body is more commonly known today, has endured ever since. In 1566, it acquired additional responsibilities for lighthouses and 'seamarks', and over the years it became the professional organization that manages the navigational marks and lights that keep people safe at sea, as well as continuing to regulate pilot services. It retains its antiquated structure, though: it is presided over by a Master, a ceremonial position currently held by the Princess Royal but previously discharged by the likes of Samuel Pepys and the Duke of Wellington, a Deputy Warden, thirty-one 'Elder Brethren' and a further 400 'Younger Brethren'. The last two groups are drawn from professions with maritime relevance and tend to be naval officers and ships' captains, often retired. The corporation draws its funds partly from the 'light dues' levied on commercial vessels visiting British ports and partly from its property portfolio, which includes the Trinity estate near London Bridge in south London. It pleased me greatly when I first moved into the room from which I departed for my journey back to the estuary and found out that the landlord was, in fact, Trinity House (the land on which the streets I walked every day had been built was gifted to the corporation by one of the Younger Brethren called Christopher Merrick in 1660). Paying rent was far less objectionable once I knew that it was helping to keep those twinkling lights that I knew so well on out in the estuary.

Sailing out of the Medway is still a thrill. The last sight of Garrison Point has always meant the beginning of an adventure, whether we were embarking on a night-time crossing to Holland or just circling around to anchor for the weekend near the old ferry route across the Swale. Once past the western tip of the Isle of Sheppey, the whole of the north Kent coast slides away to the east – a long shore of shoals and groynes leading to Margate and North Foreland, after which there is nothing but clear water. From this point, the estuary opens out like a funnel, the banks angling sharply away as the North Sea rushes in. *Cantilena* was stemming the tide now, bumping against the waves, as I climbed carefully around the stays to sit on the fore-deck again. Ahead, I could see the exclusion zone around the *Montgomery*, its corners shown by four yellow cardinal buoys at each of the compass points, intended to stop boats getting near enough to cause any disturbance in the water that could shift the wreck. I remember when my father was first teaching me to read navigational charts, he used this little quadrant of marks to help me understand what the buoys were signalling to sailors. The same two black cones, orientated in one of four different ways, tell the navigator on which side they can pass safely, away from the obstruction. Here, there is one of each, and the message is clear: go anywhere but near the wreck. Absurdly, the *Montgomery* also has a sign secured to the mast that pokes highest out of the water about the size of a suburban parking-restriction notice. Through the binoculars I read, 'Danger: unexploded ammunition. Do not approach or board this wreck.' It isn't as absurd as I thought, though. Periodically, someone ignores the sign and poses in front of it for a photograph from a canoe or paddleboard. When this happened again in June 2015, Sheerness resident Shaun Fuller told the *Daily Mail* that the wreck had 'become a bit of a tourist attraction for idiots'.

We passed to the south of the *Montgomery*, its mast shrinking again as the tide rose. The channel out of the Medway ran north-east now, taking us back up to join the main dredged route that runs eastwards out of the Thames. The twists and turns of the river itself were all behind us now, and as the deck bobbed and heaved through the waves the only thing I could see ahead was a great panorama of open water, with just the faintest of grey smudges on the distant horizon showing where the Essex shore was curving away to the north at Shoeburyness. This is the point of transition, where the river is at its widest but hasn't quite given up to the sea. It's a no man's land – a place where 'the widening of the shores sinking low in the gray, smoky distances the greatness of the sea receives the mercantile fleet', as Conrad put it. I swept the binoculars across the horizon, tracking the line of green and red buoys marking the channel. It may look like the sea, but these are coastal waters and shifting sands lurk under the water on every side.

Just to the north of us now was the Nore, the sandbank that once marked the end of the Thames and the start of the sea. It remains hidden under the water at all times, but it still looms large in the mythology of this part of the estuary – Joseph Conrad wrote that 'the Nore is a name to conjure with visions of historical events, of battles, of fleets, of mutinies'. For centuries, the Nore was the rallying point for the Royal Navy, with fleets anchoring here in the deep water to the north of the sandbank to wait for the tide to take them to their missions beyond Britain's shores or into the naval dockyards at Chatham and Deptford for resupplying and repairs. In 1732, the world's first lightship was anchored at the Nore, a wooden boat with a small crew that was designed to stay fixed in this one position, perpetually warning oncoming ships of the danger posed by the sandbank beneath. The ship itself was replaced and upgraded many times over the ensuing decades, eventually becoming a red-painted metal-hulled ship, her name painted in white letters six feet high on the side. The lantern rested at the top of her short mast to give it greater reach across the waves. The Nore beacon shines through many, many accounts of sailing here: 'A wonderful ray it sends quivering round the horizon, lighting up for a moment the passing ships, which appear like ghosts and vanish,' the artist William Lionel Wyllie wrote in

1905. The light, and the low boom of the horn that the ship sounded in foggy weather, became a symbol of safety and home for approaching seaman, a projection of British nationhood and a signal that all was well upstream.

The same factors that made the Nore a beloved home-coming beacon also made it the perfect site for sedition. The conditions for a popular uprising in Britain had been bubbling away throughout the latter half of the eighteenth century, as the industrial revolution took hold, common land was enclosed and the ideas of thinkers like Thomas Paine about equality and democracy spread far and wide. In 1765 and 1789, there were revolutions in America and France, and English dissi-dents – especially those in the navy, where men were frequently press-ganged into service against their will and brutally beaten by officers with whips – felt that their moment had arrived. On 12 May 1797, the men of the Channel Fleet, which was anchored off the Nore, let out three great cheers – the signal for the start of a mutiny. They had picked their moment care-fully, when all the officers were aboard one particular ship for a conference, and took control of the ships and locked up the weapons. A general committee was appointed to command the fleet and advance the men's demands, and a sailor named Richard Parker was elected 'President of the Delegates of the Fleet'. Briefly, he became the leader of a floating republic in the estuary, as the sailors tried to rewrite the rules and secure higher wages, better conditions and a pardon from the king for their illegal activities. Their revolutionary intentions were clear: aboard Parker's ship the *Sandwich*, the crew made effigies of the prime minister William Pitt and hung them from the mast so they could take shots at them.

The mutineers used their position at the Nore to blockade the Thames. No vessel could pass through the fleet without

showing a pass signed 'R Parker, President of Delegates'. Any
without authorization were forced to anchor and await developments; ten days in, over 100 commercial vessels were waiting
in this manner. This was the conspirators' greatest hope of
success – by cutting off supply to the London docks, they put
pressure on the government to act. Their long-winded petitions about the arrival of the age of reason and threats of civil
war mattered much less than that they had brought the busiest
shipping lane in the world to a standstill. After three weeks, desperate merchants from the City of London were volunteering
their own services to Pitt as a force to go downriver and clear the
blockade. Their offer was rejected in case the conflict escalated
as a result, but it did spur the government into action. Pitt had
smashed the beacons and buoys that marked the safe passages
through the shoals on the seaward side of the mutinous fleet and
made it clear that any rebel vessel sailing upriver would have to
run the gauntlet of heavy artillery at Tilbury Fort.

Today, the Nore lightship has been replaced with a pair of regular navigation buoys on either side of the channel, romantically named Sea Reach No. 1. As *Cantilena* neared the more southerly of the pair, I tried to imagine how this stretch of water would have looked at the start of June 1797, with dozens of navy frigates defiantly anchored and men shouting words of solidarity across the water to each other from the rigging. They had shifted the seat of power downriver to this lonely reach of the lower Thames; for a moment, it must have felt as if anything was possible. Theirs was a temporary, waterborne Utopia. But in the end, Parker's republic failed for the same reason that it had briefly succeeded. The mutineers were trapped at the Nore, unable to make either a break for the open sea or a dash upstream. By 10 June, the situation was hopeless, morale evaporated and the sailors turned on each other. Some escaped in small boats towards the land, hoping to get a good start before the navy could pursue them; others handed back control to the officers. The surrendered ships vanished from the line of the blockade – flying flags of truce, they slipped upstream to Gravesend, those aboard praying for leniency on shore. On 13 June, Parker's own ship hoisted anchor and sailed into Sheerness to face retribution. The former president received a brief trial and was executed on 30 June, hanged from the yard-arm of the ship that had served as the fleet's parliament. Some fifty others also received death sentences, and hundreds more were punished by whipping and fines. The mutiny had failed. Even some of the ships received a punishment of sorts – the *Sandwich*, the *Nassau* and the *Belliqueux* all ended up as prison hulks eventually, stripped of their rigging and their dignity. But the rebellion did result in some change, for naval historians consider it a turning point in the history of how the navy treated its sailors. Pay increases and better conditions followed, as well as an end to the press gangs. The Nore is a waypoint on the journey towards greater freedom and democracy in Britain, like Runnymede or Peterloo. Out here at the edge of the sea, a few hundred frustrated sailors took on the might of the British Empire and, for a while, they were winning.

If the source of the Thames is elusive, its ending is even more so. There is no definite point at which the estuary finishes and the sea begins. Different lines have been drawn across the map down the centuries to suit one interest or the other: the Yantlet Line between the London and Crow Stones, which once delineated the extent of London's jurisdiction over the estuary; the division marked by the old Nore lightship; the boundary formed between the tip of North Foreland at the eastern extent of Kent and the headland at Felixstowe all the way north into Suffolk. At Tilbury, the professional river pilots hand over to their sea-going colleagues – itself a division of expertise and territory. Just where the Medway disperses into the estuary opposite Southend, boats must switch their VHF radios to a different channel to hear the warnings and signals for the area downstream. And then the Tideway itself, the 100-mile tidal stretch of the river running east from the lock at Teddington, complicates matters. When the tide runs so far inland, it smudges over the differences between river and sea.

Part of the reason that I have been conflicted for so long about this place is that it's so hard to define and describe. Even now, after working on this book for several years, I find it difficult to explain to strangers where I am writing about. Out of my mouth come stuttering half-phrases, to do with power stations, marshes, mud-bound wrecks and enormous ships, until the words stop altogether. People have tried so hard, for so long, to draw lines on maps that hem this place in and make it manageable. Perhaps it's time to accept that the misty horizon is never going to be a sharply defined border between here and there.

I have come to a similar acceptance about my own relationship to the estuary. In my teens, I hated coming here and wished dearly to leave it behind for good. Later, I found that I could not put its wide, watery expanses out of my mind, no matter how hard I tried. There is no boundary I can construct that will keep it out; too many of my memories take place here for that. Returning now has resulted in a layered kind of journey: I have travelled back into my own past and that of my parents, but I have also seen the place as it is now, so changed from what I remember, and caught glimpses of what it might become in the future.

The river is always in motion and so are we upon it. The estuary was Conrad's 'open portal' and it is open still. For him, the Nore was the ideal point, the 'centre of memories' that included both his rapturous first encounter with this place and all of his subsequent arrivals and departures. As the buoy that now marks that hallowed spot grew smaller in our wake, it felt as if something more than just the wind and the tide was propelling the boat onwards. The same sense of narrative, of the river's story that rushes on as the water flows, caught hold of me again. The tale cannot end here, even as the sea mingles with the last vestiges of the ebb tide that has raced all the way down from Teddington Lock, 100 miles inland. There is much more left to discover.

Epilogue

Aboard *Cantilena*, it was time to hoist the sails. The wind was light, coming over the stern quarter, but it felt right to turn the engine off for this last push out to sea. The tide was against us, but it didn't matter; there was no hurry. It had taken me years to make this journey back to the estuary. And time feels fluid on the river – we had locked out of the Limehouse Dock this morning, but it was so remote that it could have been years ago. Only the present moment registered, the first filmy strands of evening light drifting down towards the surface of the water. A grey and white gull swooped out of the sky, a rare bird to have flown this far from the land. It raced us for a while, before descending into a great elegant swoop down to the water. It clawed at the air, hovering for a long moment of neither flying nor falling, before it settled into the waves rippling outwards from our wake.

Everything falls once more into a familiar pattern: my father on the foredeck, swigging away with all his might at the main halyard; my mother at the wheel, squinting ahead; and me on my knees on the cockpit seat, awkwardly hunched over and winching furiously at the sheet that controls the foresail. The great expanses of white canvas were once more taking the strain. The rumble of the engine and the splutter of the exhaust abruptly ceased as my mother turned the key on the side of the instrument panel. Having secured the genoa sheet on a cleat again and checked that the sail was drawing properly, I climbed carefully out of the cockpit and around the cabin top. *Cantilena* was heeling over, the competing demands of wind and adverse tide buffeting her to and fro. I held on to the metal stanchions and cable lifelines that rim the deck. The boat was singing with the tension in her stays, the lines taut as I grabbed them for support in my attempt to reach the bow. The foredeck was partially encased in a cocoon of white canvas, but I could still see around the side of the big-bellied genoa sail to the horizon beyond. I settled down in front of the hatch lid and stared at the wonder all around us. We were heading east, the estuary a great watery drabness stretching off as far as the eye could see.

This is the place I had wanted to return to, more than any other. This last stretch past the Nore is a kind of twilight zone, a blending of start and finish, where everything is still possible. Every particle of sand and fragment of leaf dropped in the Thames finds its way here, to this great flat delta where the tide rushes in at the coast. And more than just the physical flotsam transported by the river, this water is the repository for every silent sorrow and hidden joy ever whispered down by the Thames at twilight and carried away by the stream. I have been many different versions of myself on this river, always returning to its shores to shed the shadows of a past self. But nothing we give to the water is ever really gone; it all ends up here, where the river deposits its secrets before its final transformation. Kipling's words, which had come sing-songing into my head on the foreshore at New Year's Eve, echoed out again. *For they were young, and the Thames was old, and this is the tale that the River told.* Rivers are a way for us to make sense of our short lives, a living manifestation in the landscape that everything with a beginning must have an end. For Conrad, it promised adventure and success. I have always felt slightly anxious here, a thrill in my blood and a far-off buzzing just reaching my ears. Taking that one final deep, steadying breath before what comes next.

But perhaps this is no end at all. Hilaire Belloc believed that the Thames was just one part of a much greater river that runs on further east into Europe, the sea merely an estuarine interlude in this greater stream. 'Through the flats that bound the North Sea and shelve into it imperceptibly, merging at last with the shallow flood, and re-emerging in distant sandbanks and less conspicuous shoals, run facing each other two waterways far inland, which are funnels and entries, as it were, scoured by the tide,' run the opening lines of his *The River of London*. In his vision, the Scheldt – the river which runs north through France and Belgium and meets the North Sea in the Netherlands about opposite our current position – and the Thames are 'two antagonists facing each other before conflict across a marked arena' and there is no meaningful boundary between the two because they are in fact one. It was a notion that grew in popularity at the end of the nineteenth century, when geological evidence mounted in favour of some kind of prehistoric 'land bridge' between Britain and the Netherlands. H. G. Wells wrote a short story in 1897 that was set in a stone age 'when a broad and sluggish Thames flowed through its marshes to meet its father Rhine' and it was possible to walk to France without getting wet.

The idea of this conjoined river is a seductive one, harking back to prehistory, when Britain was a peninsula of the proto-European continent and the Rhine, Thames and Scheldt rivers drained into the same wide stream that followed the path of today's English Channel. Archaeologists call the drowned land

through which this mega-river once flowed Doggerland, named
for Dogger Bank, the sandbank that lies about sixty miles off
the British coast to the north-east of East Anglia. Before it was
submerged at the end of the last ice age around 6500 BC, it
was a richly fertile plain probably inhabited by humans (a
harpoon and a fragment of a skull have been recovered from
material dredged up from the seabed). Doggerland didn't disappear all at once – there would have been an interim period
when the previously solid continent became an archipelago
of swampy, fen-like islands, probably not that dissimilar to
the Thames estuary as it is today. If I half closed my eyes as
I looked ahead, I could imagine that *Cantilena* was slipping
towards them now, the silver sheen of the horizon disturbed by
muddy islets. But of course, there was nothing there.

I lay back carefully on the deck and looked up at the sky.
The clouds were slowly shifting and building into great billows
of feathery grey. The sail curved like the spiral of a shell above
me, the kind to pick up on a beach and hold to your ear to hear
the roar. I felt unmoored as the boat rocked beneath me, my
gaze on the horizon no longer holding me steady. My blood was
rising and falling with the waves, tuning me to the frequency of
the water beneath. *In my beginning is my end*, T. S. Eliot wrote,
his lines sliding time and place over and through each other.
I could hear the distant murmur of my parents' voices back
in the cockpit and the slapping rush of the water against the
hull. Nothing changes; nothing is the same. The deck lurched
upwards and my stomach swooped. The sail went slack suddenly, the wind momentarily evaporating, as if a great breath
was being drawn in all around me. Then it crackled back into
shape and the boat surged on.

Select Bibliography

Books are listed under the chapter in which they are first referenced, with the exception of works by or about Joseph Conrad, which are all collected under Chapter 2.

Introduction

Adams, Anna (ed.), *Thames: An Anthology of River Poems* (Enitharmon, 1999)

Cohen, Ben, *The Thames, 1580–1980: A General Bibliography* (Oak Knoll Press, 2008)

Chapter 1: Thames Head to Tower Bridge

Ackroyd, Peter, *Thames: Sacred River* (Vintage, 2008)

Arnold, Matthew, *Essays in Criticism* (A. L. Burt, 1865)

Bede, *The Ecclesiastical History of the English People* (Oxford University Press, 2008)

Belloc, Hilaire, *The Historic Thames* (I. B. Tauris, 2008)

Bolland, R., *Victorians on the Thames* (Evans Brothers Ltd, 1974)

Brown, Bryan (ed.), *The England of Henry Taunt* (Routledge & Kegan Paul, 1973)

Canter, David, *The Psychology of Place* (Architectural Press, 1977)

Chesshyre, Tom, *From Source to Sea: Notes from a 215-Mile Walk along the River Thames* (Summersdale, 2017)

Coleridge, Samuel Taylor, *The Major Works* (Oxford University Press, 2008)

Croad, Stephen, *Liquid History: The Thames Through Time* (Batsford, 2003)

Davies, Caitlin, *Downstream: A History and Celebration of Swimming the River Thames* (Aurum, 2015)

Eates, Margot, *Paul Nash: The Master of the Image, 1889–1946* (John Murray, 1973)

Grahame, Kenneth, *The Wind in the Willows* (Penguin, 2005; first published 1908)

James, Henry, *English Hours* (I. B. Tauris, 2011; first published 1905)

Jerome, Jerome K., *Three Men in a Boat* (Penguin, 1974; first published 1889)

Larkin, Philip, *All What Jazz* (Faber & Faber, 1985)

Lewis, C. S., *Spirits in Bondage* (HarperCollins, 2017)

Latham, Robert (ed.), *The Shorter Pepys* (The Folio Society, 1985)

MacDonald, Margaret F., and Patricia de Montfort, *An American in London: Whistler and the Thames* (Dulwich Picture Gallery, 2013)

Morris, William, *News from Nowhere* (Longmans, Green and Co., 1934; first published 1890)

Morris, William, and May Morris (eds.), *Complete Works of William Morris* (Cambridge University Press, 2012)

Nash, Paul, *Outline, an Autobiography* (Lund Humphries Ltd, 2016)

Prince, Alison, *Kenneth Grahame: An Innocent in the Wild Wood* (Faber & Faber, 2009)

Sayers, Dorothy L., *Gaudy Night* (Hodder & Stoughton, 1987)

Taunt, Henry, *A New Map of the River Thames from Oxford to London* (Henry W. Taunt, 1873)

Waller, Philip, *Writers, Readers, and Reputations: Literary Life in Britain 1870–1918* (Oxford University Press, 2006)

Westall, William, and Samuel Owen, *Picturesque Tour of the River Thames* (R. Ackerman, 1828)

Williams, Rosalind, *The Triumph of Human Empire: Verne, Morris and Stevenson at the End of the World* (University of Chicago Press, 2013)

Wilson, D. G., *The Victorian Thames* (Alan Sutton Publishing Ltd, 1993)

Wilton, Andrew, *Turner in His Time* (Thames & Hudson, 2006)

Wyld, James, *The Oarsman's and Angler's Map of the River Thames from Its Source to London Bridge* (James Reynolds, 1881)

See also the following website, which is very useful for maps: https://thames.me.uk/.

Chapter 2: Upper Pool to Cuckold's Point

Achebe, Chinua, *Hopes and Impediments: Selected Essays, 1965–1987* (Heinemann, 1988)

Alford, Stephen, *London's Triumph: Merchant Adventurers and the Tudor City* (Allen Lane, 2017)

Bentley, James, *East of the City, North of the Thames: The London Docklands Story* (Pavilion Books, 1997)

Bloom, Clive, *Violent London: 2000 Years of Riots, Rebels and Revolts* (Palgrave MacMillan, 2003)

Bloom, Harold, *Joseph Conrad's Heart of Darkness* (Infobase, 2009)

Borrow, George, *Lavengro: The Scholar, the Gypsy, the Priest* (Gresham, 1900; first published 1851)

Casement, Roger, *Roger Casement's Diaries: 1910. The Black and the White* (Penguin, 1997)

Coloquhon, Patrick, *A Treatise on the Police of the Metropolis* (Joseph Mawman, 1800)

Conrad, Joseph, *A Personal Record* (Doubleday, 1923; first published 1912)

Conrad, Joseph, *Heart of Darkness and Other Tales* (Oxford University Press, 2008; first published 1899)

Conrad, Joseph, *The Mirror of the Sea* (J. M. Dent, 1950; first published 1906)

Cruickshank, Dan, *The Secret History of Georgian London* (Random House, 2009)

Defoe, Daniel, *A Tour Through the Whole Island of Great Britain* (Penguin, 1978; first published 1724–7)

Foster, Janet, *Docklands: Cultures in Conflict, Worlds in Collision* (UCL Press, 1999)

Grenade, L., *The Singularities of London* (London Topographical Society, 2014)

Harper, W. H., *Shakespeare and the Thames* (T. Williams, 1888)

Heseltine, Michael, *My Life in the Jungle* (Coronet, 1991)

Karl, Frederick R., *Joseph Conrad: The Three Lives* (Faber & Faber, 1979)

Marriott, John, *Beyond the Tower: A History of East London* (Yale University Press, 2012)

Milne, Gustav, *The Port of Medieval London* (Tempus, 2003)

Phillips, Hugh, *The Thames about 1750* (Collins, 1951)

Stone, Peter, *The History of the Port of London* (Pen and Sword History, 2017)

Stow, John, *A Survey of London* (John Windet, 1603)

Taylor, John, *Three weekes, three daies, and three houres: Observations and travel, from London to Hamburgh* (Edward Griffin, 1617)

Wade, Stephen, *Criminal River: The History of the Thames River Police* (Robert Hale, 2012)

Chapter 3: Woolwich Reach to Silvertown

Ackroyd, Peter, *London: The Biography* (Vintage, 2000)

Defoe, Daniel, *The Storm* (Penguin, 2005; first published 1704)

Gilbert, S., and R. Horner, *The Thames Barrier* (Thomas Telford Ltd, 1984)

Grieve, Hilda, *The Great Tide: The Story of the 1953 Flood Disaster in Essex* (Essex Record, 1959)

Herbert, A. P., *The Thames* (Weidenfeld & Nicolson, 1966)

Hibbert, Christopher, *The London Encyclopaedia, Third Edition* (Macmillan, 2010)

Picard, Liza, *Elizabeth's London* (Weidenfeld & Nicolson, 2003)

Porter, Stephen, *Pepys's London: Everyday Life in London 1650–1703* (Amberley, 2011)

Schneer, Jonathan, *The Thames* (Little, Brown, 2005)

Sinclair, Iain, *Downriver* (Penguin, 2004)

Trilling, Daniel, *Bloody Nasty People: The Rise of Britain's Far Right* (Verso, 2012)

Wilson, Ken, *The Story of the Thames Barrier* (New Century, 1989)

Worpole, Ken, *The New English Landscape* (Field Station, 2013)

Chapter 4: Gallions Reach to Frog Island

Ackroyd, Peter, *London Under* (Vintage, 2012)

Ashton, Rosemary, *One Hot Summer: Dickens, Darwin, Disraeli, and the Great Stink of 1858* (Yale University Press, 2017)

Dickens, Charles, *Martin Chuzzlewit* (Penguin, 1999; first published 1844)

Dobraszczyk, Paul, *Into the Belly of the Beast: Exploring London's Victorian Sewers* (Spire, 2009)

Halliday, Stephen, *The Great Stink of London: Sir Joseph Bazalgette and the Cleansing of the Victorian Metropolis* (History Press, 2001)

Jackson, Lee, *Dirty Old London* (Yale University Press, 2014)

Mayhew, Henry, *London Labour and the London Poor* (Penguin, 1985; first published 1851)

Scott, A. De C., *London Water: A Review of the Present Condition and Suggested Improvements of the Metropolitan Water Supply* (Chapman and Hall, 1884)

Thurston, Gavin, *The Great Thames Disaster* (Allen & Unwin, 1965)

Wheeler, Alwyne, *The Tidal Thames: The History of a River and Its Fishes* (Routledge & Kegan, 1979)

Wood, Thomas L., *London Health and London Traffic* (Edward Stanford, 1859)

Chapter 5: Crayford Ness to Coalhouse Point

Barker, Nicola, *Behindlings* (Fourth Estate, 2011)

Gardner, Helen (ed.), *The New Oxford Book of English Verse* (OUP, 1972)

McGarry, John E., *The Cuban Bus Crisis: Tales of CIA Sabotage* (CreateSpace, 2013)

Mckenzie, Lisa, http://blogs.lse.ac.uk/brexit/2018/01/15/
    we-dont-exist-to-them-do-we-why-working-class-
    people-voted-for-brexit/

Miller, Sam, 'Gandhi the Londoner', *Granta 130: India*,
    March 2015

Orwell, George, *Down and Out in Paris and London* (Penguin,
    2001; first published 1933)

Sampson, Fiona, 'The Wilderness in Us', *New Humanist*,
    Spring 2018

Seabrook, Jeremy, *Cut Out: Living without Welfare* (Pluto
    Press, 2016)

Yeandle, Sue, with Lucy Shipton and Lisa Buckner, 'Local
    Challenges in Meeting Demand for Domiciliary Care in
    Thurrock' (Centre for Social Inclusion, Sheffield Hallam
    University, 2006)

Chapter 6: Mucking No. 5 to Lower Hope

Ballantyne, R. M., *The Floating Light of the Goodwin Sands*
    (James Nisbet & Co., 1870)

Clark, A. (ed.), *Excavations at Mucking. Volume 1: The Site Atlas*
    (English Heritage, 1993)

Evans, Christopher, Grahame Appleby and Sam Lucy, *Lives
    in Land: Mucking Excavations by Margaret and Tom Jones,
    1965-1978* (Oxbow Books, 2016)

George, Rose, *Deep Sea and Foreign Going* (Portobello Books,
    2014)

Jones, M. U., 'An Ancient Landscape Palimpsest at Mucking',
    Transactions of the Essex Archaeological Society, Vol. 5,
    1973, pp. 6–12

Lichtenstein, Rachel, *Estuary: Out from London to the Sea*
    (Hamish Hamilton, 2016)

Chapter 7: Cliffe Fleet to the Medway

Bennett, Alfred Rosling, *The First Railway in London* (Conway Maritime Press, 1912)

Dickens, Charles, *Great Expectations* (Penguin, 2004; first published 1861)

Forbes, Urquhart A., and W. H. R. Ashford, *Our Waterways: A History of Inland Navigation Considered as a Branch of Water Conservancy* (John Murray, 1906)

Gottfried, Rudolf (ed.), *Spenser's Prose Works* (Johns Hopkins Press, 1949)

Gray, Adrian, *The London, Chatham and Dover Railway* (Meresborough Books, 1984)

Hamilton, A. C. (ed.), *Spenser: The Faerie Queene* (Routledge, 2006)

Hasted, Edward, *The History and Topographical Survey of the County of Kent* (W. Bristow, 1797)

Hogarth, William, *The Five Days' Peregrination around the Isle of Sheppey of William Hogarth and His Fellow Pilgrims* (Streeter Press, 2011; first published 1732)

McCabe, Richard, *Spenser's Monstrous Regiment* (Oxford University Press, 2002)

Owens, W. H., *The Royal River: The Thames from Source to Sea* (Cassell, 1885)

Rolt, L. T. C., *The Thames from Mouth to Sea* (William Clowes, 1951)

Thomas, R. H. G., *London's First Railway: The London & Greenwich* (Northumberland Press, 1972)

Tomalin, Claire, *Charles Dickens: A Life* (Penguin, 2012)

Vaux, James Hardy, *Memoirs of James Hardy Vaux, written by himself* (John Murray, 1819)

Chapter 8: Deadman's Island to the Nore

Barker, Nicola, *Wide Open* (Faber & Faber, 1999)

Barker, Nicola, *Darkmans* (Fourth Estate, 2011)

Fletcher, Geoffrey, *London's River* (Hutchinson & Co., 1966)

Hill, David, *Turner on the Thames* (Yale University Press, 1993)

Wyllie, W. L. and M. A., *London to the Nore* (A. & C. Black, 1905)

Epilogue

Belloc, Hilaire, *The River of London* (T. N. Foulis, 1912)

Eliot, T. S., *Four Quartets* (Faber & Faber, 2001; first published 1941)

Wells, H.G., *The Complete Short Stories of H.G. Wells* (J.M. Dent, 1998)

Acknowledgements

This book was in my head for many, many years before I started writing. I'm very grateful to those who helped it become real: my agent, Sophie Lambert, for her help in shaping the idea at a crucial early stage and her support throughout, and my editors, Laura Barber and Bella Lacey, who made what I wrote infinitely better and more readable with their wise and perceptive contributions. I am also very much obliged to the whole team at Granta, who produced such a beautiful book and expertly set it on a course out into the world.

Much of my research took place in libraries and archives around the country, and I would like to thank staff at the following institutions for their assistance: Bebington Central Library on the Wirral, the Bodleian Library in Oxford, the British Library in London, Gladstone's Library in Hawarden, the John Harvard Library in Southwark, Liverpool Central Library, the Museum of London and the Museum of London Docklands, the National Railway Museum library in York and the Wellcome Collection in London. A generous grant from the K Blundell Trust and the Society of Authors made some of this work possible.

I am also grateful to the following people for their advice

and encouragement along the way: Stephanie Boland, Anoosh Chakelian, Rachel Cooke, Sarah Ditum, Cal Flyn, Tom Gatti, Rose George, Veronica Horwell, Oskar Cox Jensen, Tracy King, Anna Leszkiewicz, Helen Lewis, Jonny Medland, Elizabeth Minkel, Anya Palmer, Mike Pitts, Dani Quinn, Samira Shackle, Daniel Trilling, Robin Whelan, Emma Whipday and Helen Zaltzman.

My parents, Des and Terry Crampton, have been unfailingly patient and generous as I tried to do their story justice. My sister, Steph, was there for it all, and despite having had to share a cabin with me when we were children still talks to me now.

I owe a great deal to our unfailingly cheerful Clumber spaniel, Morris, without whom I probably would not have gone outside at all during the writing process. Finally, my biggest debt of gratitude is to my husband, Guy. It is only because of his unshakeable belief that I could, in fact, write a book that you are reading this one now.

Permissions

Excerpt from *Cut Out: Living Without Welfare* by Jeremy Seabrook, Copyright © 2016. Reproduced with kind permission of Pluto Books Ltd through PLSclear.

Excerpt from *The New English Landscape* by Ken Worpole, first published by Field Station in 2013. Reproduced by kind permission of the author.

Illustration Credits

The author and publisher have made every effort to trace copyright holders. Please contact the publisher if you are aware of any omissions.

Illustrations with no credit indicated are © the author

Index

Numbers in *italics* refer to illustrations.